Ben Jonson's Comedies on the Modern Stage

Theater and Dramatic Studies, No. 27

Oscar G. Brockett, Series Editor
Leslie Waggener Professor of Fine Arts
and Professor of Drama
The University of Texas at Austin

Bernard Beckerman, Series Editor, 1980-1983
Brander Matthews Professor of Dramatic Literature
Columbia University in the City of New York

Other Titles in This Series

No. 20	*William Poel's Hamlets: The Director as Critic* (Beckerman)	Rinda F. Lundstrom
No. 21	*Gertrude Stein's Theatre of the Absolute* (Beckerman)	Betsy Alayne Ryan
No. 22	*Boulevard Theater and Revolution in Eighteenth-Century Paris* (Beckerman)	Michèle Root-Bernstein
No. 23	*The Theatrical Designs of Charles Ricketts* (Beckerman)	Eric Binnie
No. 24	*Left-Wing Dramatic Theory in the American Theatre* (Beckerman)	Ira A. Levine
No. 25	*Spectators on the Paris Stage in the Seventeenth and Eighteenth Centuries* (Brockett)	Barbara G. Mittman
No. 26	*New York's First Theatrical Center: The Rialto at Union Square* (Brockett)	John W. Frick
No. 28	*George Sand's Theatre Career* (Brockett)	Gay Manifold
No. 29	*Black Performance in South Africa* (Brockett)	Peter F. Larlham

Ben Jonson's Comedies on the Modern Stage

by
Ejner J. Jensen
Professor of English
University of Michigan
Ann Arbor, Michigan

UMI RESEARCH PRESS
Ann Arbor, Michigan

Copyright © 1985
Ejner Jacob Jensen
All rights reserved

Produced and distributed by
UMI Research Press
an imprint of
University Microfilms International
A Xerox Information Resources Company
Ann Arbor, Michigan 48106

Library of Congress Cataloging in Publication Data

Jensen, Ejner J.
 Ben Jonson's comedies on the modern stage.

 (Theater and dramatic studies ; no. 27)
 Bibliography: p.
 Includes index.
 1. Jonson, Ben, 1573?-1637—Stage history—1800-1950.
2. Jonson, Ben, 1573?-1637—Stage history—1950- . 3. Theater—
Great Britain—History—20th century. 4. Theater—United States—
History—20th century. I. Title. II. Series.

PR2642.S72J46 1985   792.9'5   84-28085
ISBN 0-8357-1632-5 (alk. paper)

Contents

Preface *vii*

Introduction *1*

1 Jonson in the Nineteenth Century *7*
2 Jonson on the Twentieth-Century Stage *27*
   Eastward Ho
   Epicoene
   Every Man in His Humour
   Bartholomew Fair
   Volpone
   The Alchemist

3 Jonson Redivivus *111*

Notes *125*

Bibliography *149*

Index *153*

Preface

This study of the stage history of Ben Jonson's comedies documents the appearances of these plays from 1899 to 1972, the four hundredth anniversary of the playwright's birth. In compiling this record, I have tried to bring together all the relevant material, though that effort inevitably falls short of re-creating the moment by moment unfolding of the plays in the theatre. In any event, my aim is to record the stage history of Jonson's comedies and not to reconstruct the staging of any single performance or series of performances.

My work on this project has benefitted from the generosity of archivists and research personnel in a number of theatres and libraries. Among the libraries that afforded me generous help, I include the following: the Birmingham Public Library, the British Library and (especially) the Newspaper Library at Colindale, the Drama League, the Harvard Theatre Collection, the Graduate Library of the University of Michigan, the Manuscripts Division of the University of Minnesota Libraries, the New York Public Library of the Performing Arts at Lincoln Center, the Nuffield Library of the Shakespeare Centre at Stratford-upon-Avon, and the Library of the Shakespeare Institute. The archives to which I enjoyed access include those of the following groups or theatres: the Birmingham Repertory Theatre, the Bristol Old Vic, the Cambridge Playhouse, the Chichester Festival, the Cleveland Playhouse, the Guthrie Theatre, Lincoln Center, the Nottingham Playhouse, the Old Vic, the Oxford Playhouse, the Stratford (Ontario) Festival. Interviews with Jean Gascon, Frank Hauser, Lee Montague, and David William gave me additional insight into the challenges of producing Jonson's comedies.

A grant from the Horace H. Rackham School of Graduate Studies aided me materially in the preparation of this study, especially in the matter of expenditures for travel. I owe a different debt to colleagues both at the University of Michigan and elsewhere who have been major sources of support to me over the years from the time this project was first conceived to its fulfillment. At the risk of omitting some significant names I want to mention especially the following: Hubert English, Charles Forker, Bert Hornback, and David McPherson. I should also mention Sten Jensen, who wondered again and again when "Ben Jonson" was going to be published. I commend to him these words from Virgil, which seem to describe not merely a great many academic enterprises but certain crucial passages in nearly everyone's personal life as well: *forsan et haec olim meminisse juvabit.*

Finally, I want to express my thanks to Russell Fraser for extraordinary personal kindness and professional support at an early stage of this project.

Introduction

Robert Gale Noyes, introducing his detailed study of Jonson's early stage fortunes, cites the need for an analysis of Jonson's reputation which would demonstrate "by what processes the plays of the one-time dramatic idol came to be considered sorry reading." Such an investigation, he thought, would provide "a vital complement to the actual history of Jonson's plays on the London stage, since the history of the plays themselves as acting dramas largely determined what was written about their author."[1] The pages that follow attempt to delineate the sequel of the story told by Noyes: nearly a century's absence from the stage reinforced by a deadening weight of negative criticism or simple dismissal, followed by a steadily growing number of stage presentations and a striking increase in critical and scholarly attention. On one point, however, Noyes seems to have worked with an assumption that is almost wholly inapplicable to the study of Jonson's return to the twentieth-century stage. It is simply not the case during this later period that "the plays themselves as acting dramas largely determined what was written about their author."[2] The great bulk of modern commentary on Jonson is contained in academic criticism of the plays—in scholarly editions, monographs, and articles and essays. Moreover, academic criticism and the actual production of plays seem, especially with respect to Jonson, rather widely separated fields of endeavor. While it is undeniable that this separation is a matter for regret, it would appear that it is also comprehensible. The bulk of Noyes' material comes from theatre reviews and occasional pieces—prologues, epilogues, poems—devoted to the celebration of Jonson's skill as a dramatist. This material is, by definition, close to the stage: it springs from responses to specific productions, and it is directed to those who may themselves enjoy the opportunity of seeing the play performed; or it praises Jonson's craft, and comes from those who will emulate the master's great achievements.

In our own time, critical approaches to Jonson have grown out of the academy. In most cases, the aim of such criticism has not been to record a response but to establish a thesis, or to find a way of understanding the plays in their historical and cultural context, or to demonstrate the playwright's didactic intention. It is not surprising, then, that spectators often visit Jonson revivals with a primarily antiquarian interest in mind or (worse yet) with the thought that they will be the audience at some morality lecture-demonstration.

It is a curious and unfortunate fact that those who study early drama treasure every scrap of antiquarian notice of the plays in which they have an interest but attend in only perfunctory ways to similar observations drawn from the recent past or from contemporary stagings of the works. The losses here are significant. No one would argue that each new stage production of a Jonsonian comedy provides material for a comprehensive or exciting new interpretation. One might argue, however, that the test of performance frequently brings out elements of the play that have been ignored—or misunderstood, or undervalued—in the past. Thus Ronald Bryden's description of the last scene of *Bartholomew Fair* in the 1969 Royal Shakespeare production offers a new insight into an episode that has often seemed difficult or unpleasing or both: he draws a striking picture of

> the final puppet-show, with the cast crowding the stage in the deepening shadow of orange flares, their backs to the audience, to listen to a Dionysius doll argue with [Willoughby] Goddard's fleshy Puritan the case for the theatre as a castigating image of its time.[3]

To Bryden, this episode became one of these transforming moments of which the theatre is sometimes capable, and it made of the relative "shapelessness" of the play "a microcosm . . . of the whole history of comedy as a mirror of human folly through the ages." Bryden's remarks provide a starting point for a new understanding of the total play. In just that single observation he reveals new dimensions of what *Bartholomew Fair* may mean to a twentieth-century spectator. Similarly, when Derick Grigs reports that the 1969 Oxford Playhouse production of *Volpone* succeeded in part because of Frank Hauser's decision to work for a highly stylized performance, it becomes clear that the animal ferocity of that play need not depend on masks or mimicry but emerges most successfully when the actors achieve a proper distance from their material.[4]

Twentieth-century theatre reviews can, on occasion, fix in detailed and precise language both the significance of a particular production and the methods by which it achieves that significance. The instances of such skillful reviewing are all too rare; and it seems clear that many factors in our culture militate against the sort of review that would successfully capture the essence of even a great production. Nevertheless, when such reviews do appear they make up a part of the playwright's history; and in their success they become more than just an entry in the theatrical record: they constitute, in fact, a uniquely valuable sort of criticism. In the records of production for Jonson's comedies I have tried to call attention to those reviews that make some new contribution to our understanding of the play that is being discussed, just as later, in the discussion of twentieth-century Jonson criticism, I point to those aspects of individual studies that most effectively suggest the play's potential strengths as a stage vehicle.

Yet it is important to recognize that in these matters as in most others the shadow cast by Shakespeare makes our perception of Jonson rather imperfect. When theatrical reviewers approach a Shakespearean production, chances are good that they have seen other versions of the play. Moreover, it is likely that their knowledge of past performances and indeed of the entire production history of the play will condition their expectations and focus their attention. And this is to say nothing of their knowledge of the critical heritage. Thus an experienced reviewer who attends a performance of *Much Ado About Nothing* will be especially attentive to key scenes and even to single moments and phrases in the play—to the spying scene (II.3) where Benedick is duped, to the bumbling efforts of Dogberry to inform Leonato of his discovery, to the particular inflections of Beatrice's "Kill Claudio."[5] Nor will the results of such attentiveness go unappreciated, for among his readers such a reviewer may number many who share in his detailed knowledge of the play. Such familiarity cannot be expected by those who assess productions of Jonson's comedies, and in most cases the reviewers themselves do not have the store of detailed knowledge that they would bring to a play by Shakespeare. Thus any account of Jonson's stage fortunes is bound to differ in important ways from the various efforts to record the production history of the plays of Shakespeare. The context for discussion and evaluation in the latter case is, quite simply, infinitely richer.[6]

What these circumstances signify for the reader of this account can be (and probably should be) set out quite directly. The description of particular stagings of the several comedies will vary in length and in degree of specificity. The coherence of the history of each single play's stage fortunes will depend less on a recurrent treatment of specific scenes or dramatic moments than on repeated concern with general problems of staging. Thus one sees no pattern of attention to IV.7. in *The Alchemist,* the great scene where all the plot elements mass together only to explode from the center; but one does discover, again and again, questions about the pace of the play and about how completely an emphasis on its farcical aspects threatens its worth as dramatic satire.

In its design, this study consists of three unequal parts. Chapter 1 records the nineteenth-century rejection of Jonson and tries to clarify the grounds of that rejection. For the most part, the critical attitudes toward the works and the man are of a piece; thus Ben Jonson is condemned both as a playwright who could not create sympathetic characters and as a person whose concern and love for his fellow creatures was almost nonexistent.[7] In allowing the nineteenth-century commentators to speak for themselves, I have not been unaware that their views often lack the historical perspective that we enjoy today. Even Noyes, writing in 1935, lacked the comprehensive understanding of theatrical and critical history which the last forty years of scholarship have provided. *The London Stage* is the outstanding achievement, and its detailed analysis of the theatrical record suggests a variety of possible corrections to Noyes' evaluation of Jonson's importance in the Restoration and after.[8] I have, nevertheless, contented myself with only a few observations about Jonson's reputation before 1800, preferring to concentrate on the strength and virulence of the critical opinion that kept his plays off the stage for nearly an entire century. That such antagonism had a long and deep growth must be readily apparent, and I touch only briefly on its origin and progress.

The center of this study is a record of twentieth-century stage productions of Jonson's plays in both the British Isles and America. I begin with plays that have enjoyed only slight attention and work toward *Volpone* and *The Alchemist,* each of which has enjoyed a remarkable life on the modern stage. In this, the largest section of the work by far, my method is directly opposite that of Noyes, for reasons that are perhaps obvious. His story was of a decline, while this account describes a revival in interest. In preparing the brief production histories of Jonson's comedies I have used all the materials I could locate. This means that for some productions I have enjoyed nearly unlimited resources—press cuttings, costume sketches, photographs, interviews with actors and directors, even videotapes of productions. In the cases of certain recent productions I have been able to see the performances themselves. For other productions I have been dependent on meager reviews in obscure periodicals. The imbalance created by such discrepancies is unavoidable; in some cases it will be readily apparent. I have been aware of the dangers of such an imbalance and have tried to avoid them whenever possible. However, my primary aim has been to record the history of the staging of Jonson's plays, not to reconstruct the stagings themselves in detail.

I should note that I have limited my discussion to professional productions of Jonson's comedies. Thus I exclude performances by the Marlowe Society and such productions as that of *Sejanus* given by the Elizabethan Stage Circle under the direction of William Poel in 1928. In a very few cases I have provided some basic information about amateur performances simply to indicate that a play has had more public exposure than its professional record would indicate. *Bartholomew Fair* is the important instance here, since its very large cast makes frequent stagings unlikely. I have also made a distinction between public and professional stagings from time to time, although the terms are not wholly satisfactory. I am thinking primarily, however, of Poel's productions or those of the Phoenix Society as opposed to those productions designed for longer runs or as part of a repertory season and expected to pay their own way.

There are two exceptions to the design described in the preceding paragraph. I have not set out any details concerning Poel's version of *Poetaster*, first presented in 1916, since that play seems to have been revived exclusively on the grounds of its historical interest. In the second instance, I have been unable to discover any records of a 1903 production of *The New Inn* by members of the Old Vic Company.[9] The year 1972 marks the closing date for the record of twentieth-century productions of the plays.

In the final chapter I offer an explanation for the revival of interest in Jonson in our time. Again, I seek for causes in both the *Zeitgeist* and in the particulars of literary and theatre history. Jonson's return has been made possible in part because ours has been an age of satire. But he has also been made more accessible to us by the growth of academic criticism and by the increasing interest, since the time of Poel, in the Elizabethan theatre.

1

Jonson in the Nineteenth Century

In his review of William Gifford's 1816 edition of Jonson, John Genest acknowledged that "The Public is greatly indebted to Gifford for what he has done"; but he went on to say that, despite the editor's attention, "all his labours will hardly revive a taste for Ben Jonson."[1] The tide of critical opinion had, in fact, been running against Jonson for a long time. Bishop Hurd's warnings against literary borrowing and his specific condemnation of Jonson as a "servile imitator" had been echoed in Edward Young's *Conjectures on Original Composition* (1759).[2] There, Young argued that "*Imitators* only give us a sort of Duplicates of what we had, possibly much better, before; increasing the mere Drug of books, while all that makes them valuable, *Knowlege* and *Genius,* are at a stand"; and he went on to apply this dictum to the case of Jonson, taking the opportunity at the same time to make the by now inevitable (and increasingly damaging) comparison with Shakespeare:

> *Johnson,* in the serious drama, is as much an Imitator, as *Shakespeare* is an Original. He was very learned, as *Sampson* was very strong, to his own hurt: Blind to the nature of Tragedy, he pulled down all antiquity on his head, and buried himself under it; we see nothing of *Johnson,* nor indeed, of his admired (but also murdered) antients; for what shone in the Historian is a cloud on the Poet; and *Cataline* [sic] might have been a good play, if Salust [sic] had never writ.[3]

By 1800, the movement foreshadowed by Hurd and Young in mid-century had triumphed completely. Romanticism, with its stress on the creative imagination and its celebration of the values of spontaneity and naturalness, presented a hostile intellectual climate for the carefully designed, self-consciously correct products of Jonson's dramatic craftsmanship. Without the support of neoclassical critical doctrine, Jonson could no longer stand as a major literary force. One measure of his decline appears in the nearly reflexive use of the comparison with Shakespeare, which had by this time become a mere critical formula. Another reveals itself in the infrequency of appearances of Jonson's name in the correspondence of the leading men of letters in the nineteenth century. Again, Shakespeare figures prominently in the poetry of the eighteenth and early nineteenth centuries—in poems by Collins, Gray, Wordsworth, Keats, and others. Jonson receives almost no attention of this kind; and when one looks at the sorts of values celebrated in the poems that refer to Shakespeare, it is easy enough to see that Jonson had no place in the critical scheme of which they are a significant expression.

William Collins, in his "Verses Humbly address'd to Sir Thomas Hanmer on his edition of Shakspear's Works" (1743), makes explicit the contrast between the two playwrights. Shakespeare is the apotheosis of art's perfection:

> The beauteous Union must appear at length,
> Of *Tuscan* Fancy, and *Athenian* Strength,
> One greater Muse *Eliza's* Reign adorn,
> And ev'n a *Shakespear* to her Fame be born!

Jonson, on the other hand, shares nothing of that glorious unity:

> No second Growth the Western Isle could bear,
> At once exhausted with too rich a Year.
> Too nicely *Johnson* knew the Critic's Part,
> Nature in him was almost lost in Art.[4]

Gray's "Progress of Poesy" presents a Shakespeare who receives from Nature herself a pencil with which to paint "the vernal year," and golden keys to "unlock the gates of Joy; / Of Horrour . . . and thrilling Fears, / Or ope the sacred source of sympathetic Tears."[5]

The romantic poets certainly read Jonson, but he seems to have made no deep impression. His name appears but twice in Keats' letters, once in Shelley's; yet seventeen of his plays are mentioned in Shelley's *Journal*, and Keats complains of a leaking pen "which has made a little mark on one of the Pages of Brown's Ben Jonson, the very best book he has."[6] The influence of Shakespeare, however, is everywhere apparent. Shelley ranks him with Dante and Milton as "philosophers of the very loftiest power."[7] Wordsworth, in *The Prelude*, describes him as a force that prompted the imaginative power "beyond the suburbs of the mind"—

> . . . when realities of act and mien,
> The incarnation of the spirits that move
> In harmony amid the Poet's world,
> Rose to ideal grandeur, or, called forth
> By power of contrast, made me recognize,
> As at a glance, the things which I had shaped,
> And yet not shaped, had seen and scarcely seen,
> When, having closed the mighty Shakespeare's page,
> I mused, and thought, and felt, in solitude.[8]

André Maurois writes of a period in Byron's life as follows: "*King Lear, Hamlet, Macbeth*—his evenings were passed in seeing Shakespeare. He knew Shakespeare by heart. He lived Shakespeare. . . . And in that winter of 1814 life itself was Shakespearean," a view that G. Wilson Knight corrects only because it makes too limited a claim: "It was not only in 1814 that Byron lived Shakespeare. He was always doing it."[9] How far Keats felt the power of Shakespeare appears in a variety of ways in the letters—in his asking others to write of their responses to the plays, in his describing "Things real—such as existences of Sun, Moon, & Stars and passages of Shakespeare," or in his concluding a letter to Haydon with, "So now in the name of Shakespeare, Raphael, and all our Saints, I commend you to the care of heaven."[10] But the particular importance of the great dramatist for Keats, who regarded Shakespeare as something like his presiding genius, appears most strikingly in one of the greatest passages in the letters. After asserting that "if Poetry comes not as naturally as the leaves to a tree it had better not come at all," Keats goes on in a more personal vein: "However it may be with me I cannot help looking into new countries with 'O for a Muse of fire to ascend.' If Endymion serves me as a Pioneer perhaps I ought to be content. I have great reason to be content, for thank God I can read and perhaps understand Shakespeare to his depths."[11] This sort of enthusiasm for Shakespeare springs from a commitment to literary values directly opposed to those that had formerly insured Jonson his high critical standing. While the criterion of negative capability provided solid ground for praise of a poet who could delight equally in the creation of an Iago or an Imogen, it could lead only to rejection of one who, like Jonson, exercised the most judgmental role in his creation of figures for the stage. One useful measure of Jonson's remoteness from popular appeal may be discovered by looking at the one writer from this period from whom he attracted considerable attention. In Robert Southey's *Common-Place Book*, that staggering accumulation of reading notes, Jonson has a prominent place.[12] He earns it, however, not on the grounds of literary merit, but on the grounds of his usefulness as a recorder of a transient social scene. Jonson becomes here a mine for antiquarians, but his art is remote as can be from the world of poetry encompassed by romantic theory. That world is dominated by Shakespeare. His praises are everywhere, familiar and unanimously granted. In 1815, Wordsworth declared that "Of the human and dramatic Imagination the works of Shakespeare are an inexhaustible source."[13] Just over twenty years later, he wrote that, "modesty, and a deep feeling how superfluous a thing it is to praise Shakespeare, have kept me often, and almost habitually, silent upon that subject. Who thinks it necessary to praise the sun?"[14]

Thus the changes in critical sensibility which had been growing throughout the eighteenth century, while they meant new freedom for some writers, were not effected without certain disruptions and without taking their toll of certain literary reputations. Jonson's stock as a literary figure all but submarined (declined is far too gentle a word); but his worth as a dramatist, whose plays might claim some attention on the stage, experienced an even sharper devaluation. Noyes' view that the departure from the stage of "the brilliant school of actors" trained by Garrick spelled doom for Jonson's plays is supported by Allardyce Nicoll in *The History of Early Nineteenth Century Drama: 1800–1850*.[15] For one can see, according to Nicoll, that "In acting, in dramatic workmanship, and in management Garrick and his companions joined hands with Alleyn and Shakespeare. About the year 1800 the new age was born, and . . . the theatre and all connected with the theatre broke the bonds of the past."[16]

But just as with critical taste, so with theatrical fashions, these changes were not without their foundation in developments of the past century. The theatrical record as documented in *The London Stage* makes it clear that Jonson's place in the London theatre after the Restoration was less secure than it had seemed to earlier writers. Moreover, Leo Hughes, in a study designed to illustrate both the power and the inclinations of the theatre public from the time of Dryden to that of Sheridan, has argued persuasively for a view of that period which sees a steady and increasing movement away from the dramatic values one may discern in the plays of Ben Jonson.[17] "From the universal chorus of adulation for the work of this Elizabethan dramatist that extends throughout the period and from the repeated references to scenes in his plays," Emmett Avery and Arthur Scouten clearly imagined that Jonson's dramas would have greater prominence in the repertory than their evidence allowed them to describe. The "Calendar of Performances," however, "shows no increase in the known productions of Jonson's plays." Noyes, evaluating the same evidence— "fifteen titles distributed between the King's Company and the Duke's Company," with "performances . . . recorded for . . . seven of these"— could see Jonson as a "dramatic idol."[18]

Such discrepant estimates of Jonson's reputation can hardly be reconciled, though perhaps they may be explained. The first thing to say about them is that they emerge from quite different approaches. One method seeks to amass a comprehensive set of data that will serve as a resource for exploration of many questions about the theatre and its operations, the prominence of certain writers and works, and the skill and popularity of individual actors. The other begins with a thesis about a particular writer and searches the available data for evidence relating to his reputation and the presentation and public reception of his plays. Today, nearly fifty years after the publication of Noyes' book, it would be churlish to remark its deficiencies in a detailed fashion. What does need to be said, however, is that the method Noyes employed in assessing Jonson's reputation from the Restoration through the Garrick years is especially open to question on the matter of his handling of allusions. While there exists an immensely impressive volume of such references, there is yet no certain way of determining the relation of a particular reference to the writer's experience. Like some of the allusions to Shakespeare one may hear today, some of the allusions to Jonson may constitute a reflexive deference to custom rather than a reasoned aesthetic evaluation.[19]

Restoration praise of Jonson, including the tributes of Dryden and Sir Robert Howard and the more fervid encomiums of Shadwell, was surely founded on a thorough knowledge of Jonson's plays, a knowledge that came from the theatre as well as the study. But even before 1700, the theatrical world was changing; and after the turn of the century, any comments that cite Jonson's plays as paradigms of comic excellence or rank him as the model dramatic craftsman must be judged in the light of our knowledge that the process of change was becoming swifter and more radical. Scenes and machines, song and dance—all put into the service of a varied and lively effort at entertainment—soon constituted the staple theatrical fare. Thomas Brown, writing in 1699, thought that the playhouses had become little more than substitutes for such grab-bag entertainments as Bartholomew Fair itself: "Poetry is so little regarded there, and the audience is so taken up with show and sight, that an author will not much trouble himself about his thoughts and language, so he is but in fee with the dancing-masters, and has a few luscious songs to lard his dry composition."[20]

Brown's complaint did not, however, express the prevailing view. The taste of the audience largely determined the nature of theatrical fare, and what the public wanted was "*entr'acte* entertainment, lavish scenes, intricate machinery, expensive habits, and song and dance."[21] In his reading of the evidence, Leo Hughes finds "that the mid-seventeen-twenties . . . represent a kind of watershed in taste. Two changes were rapidly taking place: first, a further flight from head to ears and eyes, the shift to eyes requiring only a year or two; second, a sharp increase in the number of theatre-goers."[22] These factors, involving as they did the creation of new forms of popular entertainment and a diversity of demands from the potential audience, became even more significant after the opening of Lincoln's Inn Fields in 1714-15. In response, the theatre managers hit on the expedient of "a three-hour program of varied entertainments" and thus "became concerned with afterpieces, prologues, epilogues, skits, songs, dances, imitation, burlesques, processions, instrumental music, even animal acts."[23] The result of such searching after novelty was, inevitably, a diminution of the value attaching to legitimate drama. Protests continued, but to little effect. In *The Universal Spectator* for 10 April 1731, a writer commented that

> In the present Condition of Theatrical Entertainments, the true *End* of the Stage is almost wholly lost; we go not thither to see Folly exposed, but to see it acted; whence the Paradox is solved, that the most applauded Pieces for some Years past in our Theatres, have not been the *Composition* of *Poets,* but of *Dancing-Masters.*[24]

In 1758, a poet deplored the theatrical taste of an age in which

> JONSON, OTWAY, all our Nation's Pride,
> For Noise, and Nonsense, are thrown quite aside.[25]

Similar complaints echo throughout the entire eighteenth century. Although the early 1800s do witness a search for novelty that produced an enormous number of new plays, a turning to adaptations from French and German dramas as a means of satisfying the public appetite for fresh entertainments, and a proliferation of melodrama, spectacle, and pantomime, all of these developments were at least implicit in the stage history of the preceding one hundred years. What takes place in the nineteenth-century theatre is an acceleration of change and a hardening of attitudes which in each case turn out to be inimical to the stage fortunes of Jonson's comedies.

In two additional and closely related areas one can see still further evidence in the eighteenth-century theatre of developments that would make the stage increasingly inhospitable to Jonson. The first of these is the development of new dramatic forms—most particularly, sentimental comedy. The second is the growing emphasis on character in the drama and the related interest in the portrayal of a character's passions. As mid-century approached,

> the reading public for whom Swift and Pope wrote and the theatre-goers who applauded the plays of Congreve and Gay were yielding to a new audience affected by a recrudescence of English Puritanism. Outside the theatre, Richardson's *Pamela* and Young's *Night Thoughts* were being provided for this new middle class audience; within, the "weeping comedies" and the *drame* from France were supplanting the comedy of manners.[26]

The major forms, then, were being altered to cater to the taste of a changing audience. This is part of what F. W. Bateson describes when he writes that " 'Sentimentalism' meant the return of what we may call sympathy to the theatre."[27] In judging the presentation of the new kinds of drama, appropriate criteria were being adduced, criteria that stressed character over plot and the convincing presentation of passion as the central element of character. Charles Harold Gray remarks this shift in critical practice: "From the middle of the century we shall meet frequent demands for the powerful exhibition of passion, and critics will even give up all the 'rules' if this exhibition—added to the creation of true characters—be afforded."[28] Thus Arthur Murphy, in 1753, could declare that "Fable is but a secondary Beauty; the exhibition of Character, and the Excitement of the Passions, justly claiming the Precedence in dramatic Poetry." This emphasis on character leads directly to the romantic fascination with passionate heroes and, in the theatre, to the importance of strong and affecting central figures.[29] Again, these qualities are almost directly opposed to the chief features of Jonsonian comedy.

The tendencies I have just described—an emphasis on spectacle and show rather than legitimate drama, the rise of sentimental comedy, a concern for character and the exhibition of passions in the portrayal of character—all become more pronounced as the nineteenth century unfolds. The objections to Jonson and his dramatic works which had been given persistent but not vociferous expression in the eighteenth century now begin to rise in a chorus of denunciation. In the face of such hostility, it is no surprise that the plays become, for nearly one hundred years, exiles from the popular stage.

But before proceeding to document that hostility further, it may be helpful to ask if there were any countervailing forces, any critics who could defend Jonson and assert the merits of his plays. Two efforts come to mind, radically different in kind and even more dissimilar in temper. The first of these is Charles Lamb's *Specimens of English Dramatic Poets Who Lived about the Time of Shakespeare* (1808); the second is William Gifford's edition of *The Works of Ben Jonson* (1816). Lamb's collection had as its avowed aim "to illustrate what may be called the moral sense of our ancestors"; but he also intended, by revealing some unremarked beauties in the works of "old Marlowe, Heywood, Tourneur, Webster, Ford, and others: to show what we have slighted, while beyond all proportion we have cried up one or two favourite names."[30] The traditional view of Lamb's activity and its influence has accorded him the highest praise for his work in bringing before the public evidence of the greatness of England's dramatic past. His influence touched both Coleridge and Wordsworth, helped give shape to a series of "Analytical Essays on the Old English Drama" in *Blackwood's,* and provided the impetus for William Hazlitt's *Lectures on the Dramatic Literature of the Age of Elizabeth,* delivered at the Surrey Institution in 1821 and published in that same year.[31] Swinburne's ecstatic enthusiasm charted an even larger claim for Lamb's importance in restoring the earlier dramatists to public knowledge and favor:

To him and to him alone it is that we owe the revelation and the resurrection of our greatest dramatic poets after Shakespeare. All those who have done hard and good work in the same field, from the date of Mr. Collier's supplementary volume to Dodsley down to the present date of Mr. Bullen's no less thankworthy collection of costly waifs and strays redeemed at last from mouldering manuscript or scarce less inaccessible print—all to whom we owe anything of good service in this line owe to Lamb the first example of such toil, the first indication of such treasure. He alone opened the golden vein alike for students and for sciolists: he set the fashion of real or affected interest in our great forgotten poets. Behind him and beneath we see the whole line of conscientious scholars and of imitative rhetoricians: the Hazlitts prattling at his heel, the Dyces labouring in his wake. If the occasional harvest of these desultory researches were his one and only claim on the regard of Englishmen, this alone would suffice to ensure him their everlasting respect and their unalterable gratitude.[32]

This impressive assertion takes yet another form in Swinburne's sonnet "On Lamb's Specimens of the Dramatic Poets," which begins with a Marlovian echo nicely turned to harmonies suitable to the "gentlest name" of the Romantic critic-poet:

> If all the flowers of all the fields on earth
>   By wonder-working summer were made one,
>   Its fragrance were not sweeter in the sun,
>   Its treasure-house of leaves were not more worth
> Than those wherefrom thy light of musing mirth
>   Shone, till each leaf whereon thy pen would run
>   Breathed life, and all its life was benison.[33]

But Lamb's influence was, in fact, rather more limited than Swinburne's high-sounding phrases would lead one to believe. Lamb, as James Russell Lowell put it, "came to the old English dramatists with the feeling of a discoverer"; and yet for all that such a figure implies in the way of enthusiasm and critical energy, it suggests something of single-mindedness as well. What Lamb saw was conditioned in large measure by his own artistic talents and predispositions. Thus, says Lowell, "Himself a fragmentary writer, he had more sympathy with imagination where it gathers into the intense focus of a passionate phrase than with that higher form of it, where it is the faculty that shapes, gives unity of design, and balanced gravitation of parts."[34] The proof of Lowell's assertion is to be found scattered throughout the *Specimens*—in Lamb's appreciation of Webster, for example, and in his hyperbolic admiration of Ford, or in the critical myopia that would represent Marston by, among other similar "poetic" excerpts, the Prologue to *Antonio's Revenge*, described as follows:

This prologue, for its passionate earnestness, and for the tragic note of preparation which it sounds, might have preceded one of those old tales of Thebes, or Pelops' line, which Milton has so highly recommended, as free from the common error of the poets in his days, "of intermixing comic stuff with tragic sadness and gravity, brought in without discretion corruptly to gratify the people."—It is as solemn a preparative as the "warning voice which he who saw the Apocalypse, heard cry."[35]

Certainly the very nature of his project led Lamb to look for anthology pieces, speeches and scenes that would create, without the benefit of any dramatic context, an effective impression. Dramatic values of the sort Lowell describes Lamb largely ignores; and he rarely speaks of the effects a scene will create, nor does he mention the increased power that might result from staging the works represented by his *Specimens*. This is not to say that Lamb's achievement was negligible, for his work had a considerable importance in reminding the public and even his fellow writers and critics of the wealth of fine dramatic literature created by Shakespeare's contemporaries. But he wrote of *Dramatic Poets,* not *Dramatists;* and thus he failed to assert the need for these earlier playwrights to have a hearing in the only court where a valid verdict on them might be returned—on the stage itself. For some dramatists this was a matter of less importance than for others. For Webster or Ford, Lamb's brief suggestion of the main narrative line reinforced by judicious excerpts from the most striking scenes could give an adequate sense of poetic imagination and power. But such a method served other playwrights less well. Moreover, Lamb's avowed aims led him to cast a rather selective net:

The kind of extracts which I have sought after have been, not so much passages of wit and humour, though the old plays are rich in such, as scenes of passion, sometimes of the deepest quality, interesting situations, serious descriptions, that which is more nearly allied to poetry than to wit, and to tragic rather than to comic poetry.[36]

Now in all this it should be clear that Jonson stood to profit only slightly from Lamb's advocacy. A look at the actual *Specimens* set out in the playwright's behalf may make this even clearer. Eight plays represent Jonson's achievement in the drama: *The Case Is Altered, Poetaster, The Sad Shepherd, Sejanus, Catiline, The New Inn, The Alchemist,* and *Volpone.* Striking omissions from this selection include both of the humor plays, *Epicoene,* and *Bartholomew Fair.* Of the passages quoted, the greatest number are relatively serious and are set down with little concern to establish their concordance with the tone of the work from which they are taken. Three passages from *The Case Is Altered* stand as examples of a kind of decorum, as though Jonson had in each instance struck the essential note for communicating that idea. The first gives, under the rubric "*The present Humour to be followed,*" "AURELIA, PHOENIX-ELLA, *Sisters; their Mother being lately dead*"; the second illustrates "*Presentiment of Treachery, vanishing at the sight of the person suspected*"; and in the third "*Jacques (a Miser) worships his Gold.*"[37] Two long passages from *Poetaster* take up over eight of the thirty-six pages Lamb allots to Jonson. His comments on this contribution to the *Poetomachia* seem peculiarly out of touch with the play, but they tell a great deal about the sorts of impressions he was open to:

> This Roman Play seems written to confute those enemies of Ben. Jonson in his own days and ours, who have said that he made a pedantical use of his learning. He has here revived the whole court of Augustus, by a learned spell. We are admitted to the society of the illustrious dead. Virgil, Horace, Ovid, Tibullus, converse in our tongue more finely and poetically than they expressed themselves in their native Latin.— Nothing can be imaginged more elegant, refined, and court-like than the scenes between this Lewis the Fourteenth of Antiquity and his Literati.[38]

After a number of passages designed "to show the poetical fancy and elegance of mind of the supposed rugged old Bard," Lamb turns to Mammon's banquet speech in *The Alchemist* to provide "a specimen of that talent for comic humour, and the assemblage of ludicrous images, on which his reputation chiefly rests. It may serve after so many serious extracts." Here, Lamb says,

> The judgment is perfectly overwhelmed by the torrent of images, words, and book-knowledge with which Mammon confounds and stuns his incredulous hearer. They come pouring out like the successive strokes of Nilus. . . . If there be no one image which rises to the height of the sublime, yet the confluence and assemblage of them all produces an effect equal to the greatest poetry. . . . Epicure Mammon is the most determined offspring of the author. . . . It is just such a swaggerer as contemporaries have described old Ben to be.[39]

Leaving aside the identification of Mammon with Jonson himself, Lamb conveys a fine appreciation of one important aspect of the play's greatness. But clearly, "comic humours and the assemblage of ludicrous images" were not dramatic achievements Lamb prized. He placed the highest value on literature's affective power, on the ability of the artist to invoke sympathy. Citing the character of Aspatia in *The Maid's Tragedy,* he remarks that "it is artfully contrived, that while we pity her, we respect her, and she descends without degradation. So much true poetry and passion can do to confer dignity upon subjects which do not seem capable of it."[40]

Jonson possessed the ability as a poet to confer dignity on the subjects he chose, but as a playwright it was rarely his concern to elevate or enlarge. His satiric vision focused through the lenses of an intense realism. When he created larger-than-life characters, he did so not to stress their magnificence or build up their emotional grandeur but to contrast their vaunting self-celebration with the pettiness of their aspirations. Jonson saw drama as an instrument for clarifying the audience's moral perception; Lamb saw it as a means of ennobling man. Jonson's plays demand objectivity and a certain tough-mindedness; Lamb's view of drama grows out of subjectivity and a willingness to offer a sympathetic response. Jonson's plays could not, then, earn a very high place of honor among Lamb's *Specimens*. He gained a position there among the other dramatists of his time, but with passages that conform to standards of excellence other than his own. His greatest achievements—as he judged them, and as we would regard them today—were short-weighted in the scale of values administered by Lamb.[41]

The second critical event that might have provided a countervailing force against contemporary literary values and theatrical fashion was the publication in 1816 of William Gifford's edition of Jonson's works. Gifford, the editor of the *Quarterly Review,* seemed eminently suited by the massiveness of his intellectual powers and his wide-ranging knowledge of the ancients to take on such a formidable task. His edition of Massinger had gone some way toward gaining that playwright new critical favor, and he no doubt hoped that he could do as much for Jonson. Unfortunately, there was one respect in which Gifford was, if anything, too much like the subject of his labors. Gifford too had been a poor child who had come to prominence through the exercise of a forceful intelligence, and in his language one detects a certain sensitivity about this background. Moreover, he was impatient of ignorance and quick to assert his own views. But while in Jonson these traits combined with a geniality that buffered their abrasiveness, in Gifford they were exacerbated by a pious certitude that made their offensiveness even more grating.

These unfortunate traits of character appear nowhere more prominently than in the editorial matter of Gifford's edition of Jonson. While it is probably not entirely true that "a feeling that there was a concerted attempt to blacken Ben Jonson furnished him with the stimulus to undertake the enormous labor of editing this author,"[42] it is certainly the case that much of the space and a great share of the energy in Gifford's *Jonson* is devoted to attacks on the calumniators of Ben, particularly those who find him sneering from time to time at his great contemporary, Shakespeare. Thus all the commentators on Shakespeare, Drummond, the eighteenth-century editors of Jonson—all who in the course of their literary studies found Ben patronizing the older playwright or criticizing him, or remarking his habits of composition—are found to be allied in a grand conspiracy against Gifford's playwright.[43] The exposure of this conspiracy and its eventual overthrow is the aim that guides and sustains

Gifford in the "Memoirs" of Jonson that take up most of Volume I and in the notes to the plays that follow. It is as though personal animosity were the only impetus to scholarly discussion. Moreover, Gifford's vindictiveness knew no bounds. He could write of Drummond of Hawthornden or of Alexander Gill, the author of the verses on Jonson's *Magnetic Lady*, as though they were enemies who were crouching at the very moment, venomed quills in hand, to release yet more noxious ink into the flood of vituperation that ran through the history of Jonson criticism. Drummond is a "bird of prey," who delivered Jonson's remarks to the world in "rude and naked deformity"; Gill, "Splenetic, turbulent, and ferocious," "was a bad poet and a worse man; and calumny and falsehood were the elements in which he loved to move."[44] Similarly, Aubrey, who claimed that Jonson " 'killed Mr. Marlow the poet, on Bunhill, coming from the Green Curtain playhouse,' " is described as "this 'maggoty-pated' man" who "thought little, believed much, and confused everything."[45]

But the tendency of his argument and even its unremittingly abusive tone should come as no surprise, for Gifford announces his purpose early in the work:

> The reader ... who has the courage to follow me through these pages, must be prepared to see many of his prejudices overthrown, to hear that he has been imposed upon by the grossest fabrications, and (however mortifying the discovery may prove), that many of those who have practised upon his integrity and surprised his judgment, are weak at once and worthless, with few pretensions to talents, and none to honesty.[46]

And later, after a particularly long note on a passage in *Epicoene* "which has furnished the commentators with such abundant materials for convicting Jonson of 'the most inveterate malignity to Shakespeare,' " Gifford pledges that "if I cannot disencumber the pages of Shakespeare from the scurrility, and falsehood, with which they are disgraced, I will, at all events, show that nothing but the grossest stupidity can, in future, attend to them with decency or credit."[47] In pursuit of this aim, Gifford spares no one who bears even the slightest responsibility for perpetuating the falsehood of Jonson's envy of and malice toward Shakespeare. Malone and Steevens are his chief targets, but even relatively minor figures take verbal lashings of considerable violence. Chalmers, "the Lepidus of the grand triumvirate of Jonson's enemies," gets more than his share of abuse; Steven Jones is described as one who "could grovel in falsehood for the gratification of his senseless enmity to Jonson"; and even Sympson and Seward, who merely assisted Whalley in preparing his edition of Jonson, come under proscription: they "led him astray, and where he would have been simply wrong, if left to himself, rendered him absurd."[48]

This strain of hyperbolic language dominates and finally defaces the whole of Gifford's edition. For in defending Jonson against an imaginary conspiracy, Gifford was led not merely into voicing malicious and bitter denunciations of earlier critics but into making claims for Jonson that were both ill-founded and excessive. One may grant *Volpone* "a station among the noblest exertions of human wit" and even, allowing for an editor's enthusiasm, admit that *The Alchemist* may be called a "prodigy of human intellect." But one may well take exception to the idea that *The Staple of News* displays "language . . . forcible, and in some places highly poetical" or that it contains "satire . . . powerful and well directed."[49] Gifford's excessive partisanship, which sometimes verges on a kind of paranoia, might have caused some readers to smile as they remembered "the vehement language into which his zeal . . . has occasionally betrayed him."[50] Other readers, less sympathetic to Gifford's Tory affiliations and less willing to excuse his harshness, might have found this edition of Jonson a barrier rather than a path to the playwright himself. In any event, Gifford's edition did little to restore Jonson's claim to a high rank among English playwrights. For that claim, as the reviewer in *The British Critic* pointed out, could only be established by a demonstration of the viability of Jonson's plays on the stage. And here, the great Elizabethan dramatist was clearly not even in contention:

> Of the sixteen plays which are remaining to us from the pen of Jonson, it is a singular fact, that not one retains possession of the modern stage. The Alchymist [sic], indeed, was indebted to a perversion of Garrick's wonderful and versatile talents for a temporary revival; but it was the actor, not the play, which caught the public taste.[51]

From this observation it was but a short step to the judgment that Jonson must henceforward be subjected to another sort of test: "We must . . . treat him, in the present day, as the dramatist of the closet only."[52]

Yet even as a closet dramatist Jonson suffered from defects that by the measure of nineteenth-century critical standards severely restricted his value. He was too analytical a writer, and he lacked the fancy that might have given his abstract notions a fictional life. His characters—types rather than individuals—seemed devoid of any power over the reader's interest or concern. Jonson's abiding attention to the particulars of his own society made him appear too narrowly interested in manners and not sufficiently aware of the poet's need to deal with large and significant general truths. Other obstacles to his appreciation were his bawdiness and his pedantry; on the one hand he was too often merely vulgar, while on the other his works stood remote from popular understanding. Together, these deficiencies made Jonson, for the nineteenth century, not simply a closet dramatist, but a playwright of the back shelf, a writer whose work for the theater was judged to be undesirable. Tennyson's inability to read Shakespeare's greatest contemporary—he is reported to have said "I can't read Ben Jonson, especially his comedies. To me he appears to move in a wide sea of glue"[53]—is no eccentric judgment, not one of those inexplicable blind spots writers and critics have, like Matthew Arnold's dislike of Chaucer. It is a view of Jonson perfectly consonant with the majority opinion of Tennyson's century. In an age of romanticism—an age which placed such high value on the individual, an age which worshipped beauty and mystery and questing—in such an age Jonson's stolid classicism and the clarity of his satiric vision must necessarily have suffered neglect and even abuse.

The charge that Jonson was devoid of fancy grew in part out of the contrast with Shakespeare which most students recall from Milton's juxtaposition of the Stratford playwright's "native woodnotes wild" over against the "learned sock" of Camden's pupil. By the beginning of the nineteenth century, not only was the contrast firmly established and (as I have suggested above) nearly inevitable, but the values represented by Shakespeare were being more rigorously defined as romantic critical theory prepared places of highest honor for fancy and the imagination. Thus Coleridge notes that Jonson's plays exhibit a mind at work but reveal nothing of that organic development that romantic theory required of the greatest literature and that Keats thought of as coming "as naturally as the leaves to a tree": "In all his works, in verse or prose, there is an extraordinary opulence of thought; but it is the produce of an amassing power in the author, and not of a growth from within."[54] Hazlitt takes up the same theme in Lecture II, "On Shakspeare and Ben Jonson," of *The English Comic Writers*. Here the contrast between a Shakespeare who is inventive and wide-ranging, a poet of the freest imagination, and a Jonson who is a conscientious but mechanical craftsman, is elaborated in great detail and with a variety of figures. "The one," writes Hazlitt, "gives fair-play to nature and his own genius, while the other trusts almost entirely to imitation and custom." Moreover, Jonson's "genius . . . resembles the grub more than the butterfly, plods and grovels on, wants wings to wanton in the idle summer's air, and catch the golden light of poetry." Everywhere Jonson is deficient, and not merely deficient but at the opposite pole from what constitutes valid literary achievement: "His style is as dry, as literal, and meagre, as Shakspeare's is exuberant, liberal, and unrestrained"; and while "Shakspeare's characters are men; Ben Jonson's are more like machines." Finally, Shakespeare's "humour . . . bubbles, sparkles, and finds its way in all directions, like a natural spring. In Ben Jonson it is, as it were, confined in a leaden cistern, where it stagnates and corrupts;

or directed only through certain artificial pipes and conduits, to answer a given purpose."⁵⁵ Such a telling difference, in Leigh Hunt's view, may even had had its origin in a conscious choice made by the lesser playwright: "Upon comparison of his learning with his fancy, it seems likely that nothing but a perversion of his love of originality, and perhaps a consciousness that he could never meet Shakespeare on equal terms in the walk of humanity, determined him on being a local humorist in the cloak of a scholar. What he wanted, besides the generalizing power, was sentiment."⁵⁶ The contrast between Jonson and Shakespeare was unequivocal: on the one hand, the genius-artist; on the other, the scholar-craftsman; and even when Shakespeare was not brought into the question, the judgment on Jonson remained the same. Thus the reviewer in *The British Critic* could say of him: "Jonson was a man of extraordinary talents and acquirements, rather than eminent genius; a profound thinker, rather than a great poet. He possessed force, cleverness, energy, and precision; he wanted imagination, fire, melody, tenderness."⁵⁷ John Addington Symonds, ordering the Elizabethan deities, argued that Jonson's "throne is not with the Olympians but with the Titans; not with those who share the divine gifts of creative imagination and inevitable instinct, but with those who compel our admiration by their untiring energy and giant strength of intellectual muscle."⁵⁸ A similar ranking is found in Swinburne's *Study of Ben Jonson,* where he distinguishes two classes of writers—"the gods of harmony and creation," who include Shakespeare, Milton, and Shelley; and "the giants of energy and invention," who have among their number Jonson, Dryden, and Bryon.⁵⁹

Related to Jonson's lack of imagination or fancy is his failure to create characters who interest an audience. Dealing in types rather than individual creations, he seemed to the nineteenth century incapable of creating characters who could excite a response. Even Gifford, never less than a partisan, found that Jonson fell short in this regard. In search of an explanation for Jonson's relative unpopularity, he finds it in part in the difference between the humors and the passions. The latter, he says, have "a natural loftiness and swelling . . . which fills the mind, and, when tempered with the gentler feelings, interests while it agitates."⁶⁰ These effects Jonson, using other methods, could not achieve. Coleridge, while noting Jonson's real achievements in character drawing, outlined at the same time the limitation of his method:

> The characters in his plays are, in the strictest sense of the word, abstractions. Some very prominent feature is taken from the whole man, and that single feature or humour is made the basis upon which the entire character is built up. Ben Jonson's *dramatis personae* are almost as fixed as the masks of the ancient actors; you know from the

first scene—sometimes from the list of names—exactly what every one of them is to be. He was a very accurately observing man; but he cared only to observe what was external or open to, and likely to impress, the senses."[61]

A writer in *The Yale Literary Magazine* in 1843, clearly a young man whose judgments reflect those of his age, comes to a similar conclusion, writing of *Every Man in His Humour* that the play "is not a naked statue revealing every portion of the frame, the fine muscles and the well-turned limbs, but a clothed and masked figure, disclosing nought of what is within, though every fold of the doublet, every wrinkle of the coat, be chiseled to the life."[62] George Daniels, commenting on *Every Man in His Humour* in 1850, says much the same thing. While Shakespeare's comic characters seem to invite us in and to ask us to share with them, "there is nothing in Jonson's most humorous characters that invites us to a near approach."[63] Symonds saw this as a major failing in Jonson. Unlike Shakespeare—or Marlowe even—Ben was unable to achieve characters of real complexity; and "though we retire from his theatre, overwhelmed by the man's prodigious inventive and delineative force, we feel that we have been, after all, at a marionette show, where the puppets are moved by wires."[64]

But it was not merely their lack of depth that made Jonson's characters appear so remote from the reader's concern, it was their failure as well to extend any claim to his moral interest. Coleridge, speaking of *Volpone*, makes just such a point in a way that suggests how great a loss he considers this to be:

> This admirable, indeed, but yet more wonderful than admirable, play is from the fertility and vigor of invention, character, language, and sentiment the strongest proof how impossible it is to keep up any pleasurable interest in a tale in which there is no goodness of heart in any of the prominent characters. After the third act, the play becomes not a dead, but a painful, weight on the feelings.[65]

Symonds puts the same case even more strongly:

> We rise from the study of *Volpone*, as we do from that of some of Balzac's masterpieces, with the sense that all these human reptiles, true enough in their main points to life, yet over-fattened in the vast slime of the poet's brain, represent actual humanity less than they represent ideals, which the potent intellect, brooding upon one vice of man's frail being, has diversified into a scene of splendidly imagined specimens.[66]

Both these critics point to what Swinburne later would call Jonson's leading fault, his "want of sympathy."[67] Jonson, in this view, was an artist who "took so much interest in the creations, that he had none left for the creatures of his intellect or art."[68] Jonson's characters did not call forth the sort of involvement and sympathy that the nineteenth century demanded of the persons of the drama. Type figures, moral abstractions animated by artificial means to serve their puppet functions in the play's intellectual scheme, they had no independent existence and thus made no successful appeal to the reader's emotional interest.

In view of these reservations about Jonson's ability to create sympathetic dramatic characters, the interest that Charles Dickens took in the dramatist seems at first wholly anomalous. Dickens and his friends produced *Every Man in His Humour* first in 1845 and then again in both 1847 and 1848. He took the part of Bobadill. In 1848 he planned a production of *The Alchemist* with himself as Mammon, but this project was abandoned after two or three rehearsals. There are, I think, two primary explanations for Dickens' fascination with Jonson. The first concerns the technique of character drawing: Dickens, the master of gestural language ("May I?, May I?"), the creator of Pumblechook and Uriah Heep, surely responded to Jonson's great achievements in this kind—to the tag-along earnestness of Stephen and the labored spontaneity of Bobadill's oaths. Secondly, it seems clear that Dickens adapted Jonson to his own purposes; and it was this, I believe, that "enabled him to present in Bobadill, after a richly coloured picture of bombastical extravagance and comic exaltation in the earlier scenes, a contrast in the later of tragical humility and abasement, that had a wonderful effect."[69] But the perception that Dickens had of Ben Jonson was, after all, derived primarily from the play most amenable to the nineteenth century and it was, besides, a perception that was not widely shared. With respect to the major comedies especially, the standard nineteenth-century view remained constant. Jonson's toughminded assessment of the figures in his satiric plays had little appeal.

Jonson's lack of true imaginative fire and his failure to create characters who could enlist sympathy were weaknesses over which he had no control. His insistent focus on the contemporary scene and his limiting interest in "manners" constituted another matter altogether. Here, Coleridge thought, Jonson had taken the wrong direction, and that was simply too bad for him: "the poet who chooses transitory manners, ought to content himself with transitory praise. If his object be reputation, he ought not to expect fame. The utmost he can look forward to, is to be quoted by, and to enliven the writings of, an antiquarian."[70] Barry Cornwall (Bryan Waller Procter) agreed with this position, asserting that he could not join those who united in praise of the playwright's judgment since he found him in several areas markedly injudicious, most particularly in his choosing "subjects of contemporary fashion and interest as the groundworks for the display of his humours."[71] Dibdin, at the very beginning of the century, said of *The Alchemist* that it "will probably

2

Jonson on the Twentieth-Century Stage

In assembling the accounts of individual twentieth-century productions of Jonson's comedies that comprise this chapter, I have tried, given the available resources, to create the most accurate and comprehensive possible view of what actually happened on stage. What unity the accounts possess as a group comes from the responses they offer to large questions about Jonson and his drama. Two issues are dominant. The first of these encompasses a great many subsidiary matters, and it is simply the question of how time-bound and narrowly focused the plays of Jonson are. Can these plays—even the greatest of them—be more than museum pieces? Are the affectations of a Bobadill or the blatant hypocrisy of a Zeal-of-the-Land Busy ludicrous or despicable to a contemporary audience, or are they merely bizarre manifestations of Jonson's bold character drawing that exist without reference to a credible psychology or to a scheme of moral values that excites one's interest? The second issue is narrower and relates to the mode of presentation of these plays. If Jonson is not well served by productions that emphasize rapid pace, zany behavior, and slapstick action, how does the other side of his comedies—the sinister cruelty of *Volpone* and the calculated meanness of *The Alchemist*—receive adequate attention in theatrical presentation?

Responses to the first issue have taken a variety of forms. One way of answering the charge of antiquarianism is to transport the play—setting, dress, language, and all—to another era. This was the way Tyrone Guthrie took with *The Alchemist* in 1962; and, in a modified fashion, this was the way of Terry Hands in the 1969 Royal Shakespeare production of *Bartholomew Fair*. Another means of avoiding the antiquarian label is to shape the production in such a way as to avoid specific references to any time or place—to bring out, in other words, only the most abstract and generalizable features of its meaning. This approach has been tried with nearly all the plays, perhaps most successfully in those productions of *Volpone* that focus on its animal imagery.

The second issue has remained unresolved throughout the twentieth century, at least so far as stage productions are concerned. Although some productions have found more or less satisfactory ad hoc answers to the issue of what style might serve the needs of a particular play, no one of the plays has called forth for itself what might be described as a traditional style; and certainly nothing like a Jonsonian style exists that might be used for any of the plays in the modern repertory. Nevertheless, there has been general agreement on one view, which is that the farcical way with Jonson is wholly unsatisfactory. Particularly in the accounts of *The Alchemist* on stage, but scattered too in reviews of productions of the other plays, theatre critics have consistently damned those efforts that have sacrificed Jonson's moral vision and his satiric toughness in pursuing cheap laughs by means of broad, physical comedy. Here, of course, the reviewers and the academic critics are wholly in agreement. Implicit in that consensus is the view that the dark side of Jonson's comedies must gain adequate expression on the stage if the plays are to achieve full success, but there has been no agreement on how that side should be presented. In this respect, Jonson's return to the stage has been less than wholly triumphant. It has been marked at times by doubt and timidity, represented by abbreviated texts and intellectual shallowness. But at other times it has been full-blooded and celebratory, vital and biting at once in the manner of true satire, a mirror of our customs as well as those of Jonson's London. The pages that follow present the record of that return through 1972, the year of Jonson's quatercentenary.

Eastward Ho

Eastward Ho, the joint production of Jonson, Chapman, and Marston, has steadfastly resisted all critical attempts to analyze its parts and distribute them among the authors. Although many scholars have advanced theories about the play's composition, no one has provided the sort of evidence that might command general assent. Perhaps it is this uncertainty about its authorship that has kept the play from receiving the critical attention it deserves. Although it stands as one of the finest examples of Jacobean city comedy, it has remained in the shadow of other plays that contain far less comic inventiveness and nothing like its detailed portrait of the social milieu of seventeenth-century London. Critical neglect of *Eastward Ho* has been mirrored in the lack of favor the play has experienced from theatre people. Herford and Simpson record no production after 1751; it was not seen in the nineteenth century; and it was not until 1953 that the play finally reached the stage in modern times. Then it was produced at the Mermaid Theatre at the Royal Exchange, with a company headed by Bernard Miles (who took the minor role of Slitgut) under the direction of Joan Swinstead.

The reviewer for *The Stage* advised that "no collector of theatrical curiosities should miss it. Nor should anyone who likes robust fun robustly presented."[1] Again, as so often with Jonson's more familiar plays, particularly *Volpone* and *The Alchemist,* critics remarked the contemporary relevance of Jonson's characters and his comic resources. One reviewer found in the play "Cockney humour, unchanged for nearly 400 years,"[2] while another suggested that "The impoverished bogus and rather precious knight, Sir Petronel Flash, can be seen any day about five in certain Mayfair haunts."[3] Gerard Fay, writing in *The Spectator,* complained that Bernard Miles had turned the job of directing over to Miss Swinstead, "especially when his company is one that needs leadership." Fay did not respond with much warmth to this revival of a long-forgotten comedy, but he did admit that all around him people were laughing heartily at the proceedings. His only praise for the production, and that rather grudgingly offered, he directed at the use of the new Mermaid stage, which "comes well out of this difficult piece of production, especially when all three levels of it are used at the same time."[4]

Fulton Mackay as Quicksilver received praise from nearly all the reviewers, while the critic in *Punch* recalled two memorable scenes: Sir Petronel Flash crawling on shore, convinced that he has landed in France—"I know't by th' *elevation* of the *Pole*; and by the *altitude* and *latitude* of the *climate*" (IV.i.151-152)—and Bernard Miles, "when he stumps up and down the Mermaid's balcony in an ecstasy of ghoulish glee as he reports the varying fortunes of the other roisterers battling in the tide."[5] But the reviews concentrated primarily on the play's total impact rather than on characters or individual scenes, a natural enough choice given the play's unfamiliarity; and their assessments were favorable without ever becoming enthusiastic. If *Eastward Ho* was not a very good play, it was nevertheless "unquenchably gay"; and its bustling, flowing action reminded one "how thoroughly the theatre learned the benefits of continuity, long before the cinema."[6] Ivor Brown considered it a comedy

> which has no high merit of language or character, but is full of London laughter and the knavery and uproar of riverside streets and taverns. Nothing is subtle, nothing is protracted, all is brisk. The eternal types of comedy, grave merchant with marriageable daughters, foppish niffle, pert apprentice, and so on are put through their usual motions of intrigue and calamity with speed and gusto.[7]

This single revival of *Eastward Ho* did little to advance the play's claims to attention from the theatregoing public, and it had no conspicuous effect on its critical reputation. As a theatrical event it was "interesting but not significant," to quote a damning judgment that a professor of my acquaintance often used on papers that led to no meaningful point.

After three hundred and fifty years, *Eastward Ho* emerged briefly only to disappear once again. It constituted a minor but transient sign of prosperity in the revival of Jonson's theatrical fortunes in this century.

Epicoene

While *Eastward Ho* has consistently occupied an ambiguous and rather neglected position in the Jonson canon, the reputation of *Epicoene* has varied considerably. Cited in the *Essay of Dramatic Poesy* as "the pattern of a perfect play," it has enjoyed no such advocacy since Dryden's time. After a final production in 1784, the play suffered, with most of Jonson's other dramatic works, total neglect for well over a hundred years. In the first three quarters of this century it has been presented on the professional stage six times.[1] It ran for seven performances from 8 May to 13 May 1905, in a production by the Mermaid Repertory Company at the Great Queen Street Theatre.[2] Philip Carr directed, Cyril Cattley played Epicoene, and Milton Rosmer took the role of Sir Dauphine Eugenie. The Phoenix Society presented *Epicoene* at the Regent Theatre on 16 and 18 November 1924. Cedric Hardwicke was Morose and Raymond Massey, Sir Dauphine Eugenie; the director was Allan Wade.[3] The Phoenix production marks the last appearance of *Epicoene* in London in this century. Since 1924 the play has been presented at Birmingham, at Bristol, and by two different companies at Oxford. The Birmingham Repertory Company production of 1947, with a young company directed by Willard Stoker, excited some rather surprising comment. The Bristol Old Vic version of Jonson's play ran for two weeks, from 10 November to 28 November 1959. Directed by John Hale and designed by Patrick Robertson, this treatment of the play was shaped by the conviction that in *Epicoene* Jonson put aside his "high and moral purpose" and "set out with the sole object of making his audience laugh."[4]

In 1964, the Margate Stage Company brought *Epicoene* to Oxford for three days, 10 September to 12 September. Directed by Gerald Frow, who also played Cutbeard, this version of the play was updated and set in "the pseudo section of London (or any other city) in the present day—when such things and such people (alas!) still happen."[5] It received little favorable notice. Four years later the Oxford Playhouse Company presented the play. Frank Hauser, who had directed it for the Oxford University Dramatic Society (OUDS) while a student at Oxford in 1948, here created a production marked by fidelity to Jonson's text and to his style.[6] In a program note that quoted Jonson lovers as distant in time from one another as Samuel Pepys and Ray Heffner, Hauser concluded by quoting from Dryden, whose "Examen" of *The Silent Woman,* written in 1668, three hundred years earlier, was in a sense being tested by this production: "As for Jonson, . . . something of art was wanting to drama, before he came."

The Mermaid company featured revivals of plays from the earlier periods of English drama. Their program for *Epicoene* announces that the company will present *The Knight of the Burning Pestle, The Duchess of Malfi,* and (by special request) Vanbrugh's *Confederacy.* Their production of *Epicoene* encountered the same sort of criticism that greeted most of the stagings of Jonson early in this century. The play, one critic wrote, was typical of its author's work, too concerned with capturing the humors of his age "and in setting down a record of its passing manners to reach the essential and the truly human in character, to avoid the ephemeral and eccentric in drama." In this view, Jonson wrote according to a simple and finally tedious formula; the plays consist of "a group of grotesque Hogarthian figures collected around a central character that is itself the incarnation of a particular humour."[7] The business of Morose's humor, wrote another reviewer, "although turned to ingenious and diverting account, is made the basis of a very different order of fun from what one would look for in a play of the present date."[8] Jonson, the critics seemed to agree, was distinctly for an age; or at least he was not for their age, which in its main critical assumptions was still the nineteenth century. And this presentation of *Epicoene*, "rather lame and halting," without the speed required by its ever-heightening development of farcical business, convinced no one that the playwright had been the victim of undeserved neglect.[9]

At the hands of the Phoenix Society, *Epicoene* fared somewhat better. There was a good performance by Alfred Clark as Captain Otter, and "the richest comedy" in the scene in which "the sad old valetudinarian consults the doctors on divorce." Cedric Hardwicke's Morose was "monotonous in action," and the collegiate ladies a bit too old, "though they seemed to set off Mr. Godfrey Winn's Epicoene very effectively."[10] The harshest verdict was that of the *Sunday Times,* whose reviewer complained that Jonson, "like some fanatic of the microscope, attributed value according as the object had escaped the notice of others." Though willing to admit that "the parody of pedantry at the end is magnificent," the *Times* critic insisted that "this and some animadversions upon the use of lipstick applicable to our own day are nearly all that can be said for this very dull play."[11]

Beyond these comments, there is very little to tell us how the play was treated or what aspects of its action and theme received the strongest emphasis. But a promising sign appeared in the *Observer* account of this production. The critic took a fresh look at Jonson and at this play, and while his observations are hardly startling or very new even in 1924, they suggest that Jonson was at last being freed from the bonds fashioned in the nineteenth century and that he might be able to assert a distinctive claim to attention in the twentieth-century theatre:

> Ben is a rare but not an insinuating writer. He stuns rather than charms. His pen is both a rapier and a bludgeon, and when he feels a personal antipathy or notes a ridiculous whimsey, he is apt to run amok. Here he combines a schoolboy love of practical joking with a wit that cuts like steel and a diction that is a sort of literary Niagara in spate.[12]

Unfortunately, the twentieth century did not arrive at the same time for everyone. When the Birmingham Repertory Company staged *Epicoene* in 1947, M. F. K. Fraser assaulted their enterprise with all the weapons in the armories of righteous indignation and outraged morality. *Epicoene*, the reviewer warned, is "a dirty play by our lights," and he offered this caution "so that parents shall not subject their children to offensive experience with less than full knowledge of what they shall hear." What are the grave faults of Jonson's comedy? Plainly and simply, they are as follows: "This play presents, as matters for farcical merriment, such topics as contraceptive practice, the impotence of a husband, a woman's purity, and a bride's prenuptial infidelities." In the face of such blatant corruption, the reviewer's job is clear. He must raise his voice in protest, for these are "unfit subjects for this sort of treatment in any theatre which offers its seats unreservedly for public sale, whoever the author, whatever his period."[13]

This confused and alarmingly ignorant account ought not to be taken too seriously, of course, for it is clearly the product of someone who has problems with the basic distinction between art and life. It is, after all, more than a bit absurd to express moral revulsion at the treatment of "a bride's prenuptial infidelities" when both the bride and her infidelities are mere imaginary instruments in a plot against Morose. Nevertheless, the "lights" which could reveal *Epicoene* as a dirty play represent real and persistent attitudes toward Jonson which have continued, even in this century, to hinder appreciation of the theatrical merits of his plays. One of the great values of companies like the Birmingham Repertory is that they are committed in principle to breaking down such built-in resistance. Thus even a lukewarm admirer of Jonson, reviewing this production, could say that the company was doing its job, "which is to show us every man in his humour even if it isn't ours."[14]

Among the reactions to this production of *Epicoene*, T. C. Kemp's was the most favorable. Here, he thought, even "the youth of the present company, not always an asset, is . . . an advantage, as Jonson wrote his women's parts for boys, and the light-weight actresses last night came into their own." But the best thing about the production was simply that it worked—not as a collector's piece but as theatre. Willard Stoker, the director, "has so underlined the comedy and pointed the satire that the play slips its centuries and takes the stage with surprising vigour and freshness."[15]

The Bristol Old Vic production of *Epicoene* in 1959 did little to advance the play's critical reputation, but forestalled arguments about its dramatic worth by approaching it not as a classic but as an eminently stageable farce. John Hale, who had "handled pantomimes and seaside shows," served up "elements of both in a play which critical assessors have been apt to flatter in the past."[16] Hale emphasized visual humor in the play, including mechanically operated earmuffs on Morose and "the kind of joke with a cork that one would expect to find in a Crazy Gang show." This was a production with moments of "sporadic hilarity" in which the pantomime elements threatened more than once to overwhelm Jonson's play.[17] It was, perhaps, too fast and too loud; but it brought *Epicoene* to the stage without apology or special pleading. By 1959, the production of a play by Ben Jonson was no longer a sign of misguided antiquarianism.

Still, the freedom to produce Jonson proved no guarantee that the plays would be presented adequately. The next production of *Epicoene*, by the Margate Stage Company, demonstrated this all too clearly. This "tasteless farrago," a kind of "pop version of Ben Jonson's satirical comedy," was aggressively modern, taking its emphasis from the notion that "ours is the first age since Jonson's to encourage the open exhibition of epicoene attitudes."[18] With that dubious historical proposition as his guide, Gerald Frow attempted a Guthrie-like updating of *Epicoene*, using "jukeboxes, bottle parties, and revving motor-scooters" as the means of tormenting poor Morose. But the modernization seemed intrusive or inconsistent or both—"the leather jacket boys . . . give the thumbs up sign but kiss the ladies' hands"—and this attempt to make Jonson's play a vehicle for contemporary meaning ended up looking "not so much like bold and pointful juxtaposition of old and new as unconfident scissors-and-pastework."[19] A contradiction of another sort appeared in the casting; Epicoene, played by Penny Jones, was Miss Epicoene. The use of a woman in the role was not without precedent. In 1776, Mrs. Siddons had taken the part of Epicoene in a version of the play prepared by George Colman the Elder. But there had been strong objections then to such an innovation, and she had been replaced by a male actor after three performances.[20] Thus, as Ian Donaldson pointed out, her example did not seem to provide a warrant for Mr. Frow's casting decision. This was especially so since, precedent or no, "to have a nicely-rounded girl with shoulder-length hair is to defeat the point that the whole production is apparently striving to exploit: the present day difficulty of telling the boys from the girls."[21] The Margate Stage Company, unwilling to trust Jonson's play, overloaded it with gimmicks designed to establish its contemporary relevance. In the process, they created a stage performance which lacked both "pace and purpose" and which, even more to be regretted, obscured *Epicoene*'s real merits.

Four years later, when Frank Hauser directed the Oxford Playhouse company in *Epicoene,* memories of the Margate production were still fresh, and they provided an effective contrast to Hauser's restrained handling of the play. His version, "admirably straight and true to the text," was set "firmly in the London of 1609."[22] A local reviewer saw this play as adding considerably to Hauser's reputation as an interpreter of Jonson, and he considered it "one of the Playhouse company's most distinguished and memorable achievements of recent years."[23]

Some reviewers thought that this realistic treatment of *Epicoene* was too straightforward. Ian Donaldson, for instance, argued that "the Collegiate Ladies are not appalling enough by half."[24] Yet there was general agreement that this was a successful version of the play, and Irving Wardle welcomed it as "a joyous event that does full justice to some of the best comic tirades Jonson ever wrote."[25] Lewis Fiander as Truewit—"a prancing nutcracker with a sad, beautiful smile"—and Philip Voss as Clerimont led a youthful cast in a production that, more than any other in this century, justified Dryden's praise of *Epicoene*.[26]

One additional production of *Epicoene* should be mentioned before this account of the play's fortunes comes to an end. In 1909, the Marlowe Society at Cambridge University presented this comedy of sexual confusion with an all-male cast. Although the occasion made no great public stir, it did provide the opportunity for a review by William Poel in which he both discussed the performance and used it as a convenient excuse for offering some of his favorite theories. Chief among these in this instance was the notion that *Epicoene,* written for child actors, was irrecoverable in the modern professional theatre. The Marlowe Society approach, feasible enough for an amateur group, could hardly be attempted even in a National Theatre, which, after all, "is not likely to include a group of trained youths."[27] Thus "we must make up our minds," wrote Poel, "to have seen *Epicoene* once and for all." The entire discussion reveals Poel's fondness for the play. As a review, it is frustratingly devoid of specifics. As criticism, it documents Poel's understanding of Jonson and his delight in the comedy's movement. After describing the gallery of plotters and fools and pretenders who make up the cast, he dwells on Jonson's skillful use of them:

> all these people are let loose on old Morose, in a steady crescendo rising through four acts from Truewit's post-horn to a horrible din of quarreling, drinking, fighting, laughter, tears, music, laughter, music, disputing lawyers, and shrieking women, until Sir Dauphine makes his terms, and snatching off Epicoene's wig reveals that the newly married bride is a raw and grinning boy. And meanwhile each of these characters has had its own fortunes developed, and its own justice meted out, in inseverable connection with the main story. As a piece of construction the play is amazing; as a comedy of "humors" and manners it is full of truth; and as a farce it is—or should be—a cause of continuous and ever growing laughter.

This is appreciative criticism at its best; and it suggests, in spite of Poel's main contention, that *Epicoene* ought to be revived again and often.

Every Man in His Humour

Every Man in His Humour has always attracted more interest than its dramatic merits, considered alone, would seem to justify. For a long time it was considered the vehicle that brought Jonson and Shakespeare together, the story being that Shakespeare recommended the play for production by his company after Jonson's earlier dramatic efforts had failed to win acceptance. Shakespeare, whose name appears in the cast list of the folio, is popularly supposed to have taken the role of the elder Kno'well. And of course this play, featuring "deeds and language such as men do use," stands as the paradigmatic manifestation of Jonson's theory of comedy. It was the only play by Jonson to hold the stage with any success into the nineteenth century, and it attracted the interest and admiration of Dickens, who, with his band of amateur players, produced it in 1845. On 5 June 1816, Kean appeared for the first time as Kitely in a benefit performance for himself at the Theatre Royal, Drury Lane. These were not auspicious times for the presentation of Jonson's comedy, as may be gathered from an advertisement in *The Times* the following day:

> MR. JONES'S BENEFIT—— THEATRE-ROYAL, COVENT-GARDEN. TO-MORROW, June 7, will be presented the comic opera of the LORD of the MANOR. After which, for the first time, an entirely new magnificent and festive Entertainment, called VENETIAN VAGARIES; or, Pageantry on Land and Water: the scenery of which will include the Rialto and St. Mark's place, as they appear crowded with a multitude of splendid and grotesque characters, during the time of the grand Venetian Carnival. In the course of the entertainments will be exhibited, the ceremony of the espousals of the Doge of Venice with the Adriatic Sea. The entertainment will conclude with a SHOWER OF BON-BONS, which will pervade the theatre, and convey to the spectators a game at mottos of question and answer.[1]

Hazlitt's review of the Kean *Every Man In* stressed Jonson's stage craftsmanship. Time and again he returned to the idea that characters who seemed dull and spiritless as mere literary creations come to life in the theatre. Thus only Bobadill seems a vital figure when one reads the play, but in a production the other characters take on new dimensions, and "we believe in their existence when we see them." Similarly, Hazlitt comments on the scene in which Brainworm praises Stephen's leg: "The folly here is insipid from its seeming carried to an excess—till we see it; and then we laugh the more at it, the more incredible we thought it before." And Kean's performance, in which he revealed that he was "not only a good actor in himself, but . . . the cause of good acting in others," gave still further evidence of Jonson's mastery as a writer for the theatre. Kean, at the point of confiding his jealousy to Thomas,

> was exceedingly happy in the working himself up to the execution of his design, and in the repeated failure of his resolution. The reconciliation scene with his wife had great spirit, where he tells her, to shew his confidence, that she may sing, may go to balls, may dance; and the interruption of this sudden tide of concession with the restriction—"though I had rather you did not do all this"—was a master-stroke. It was perhaps the first time a parenthesis was spoken on the stage as it ought to be.[2]

After Kean's appearance as Kitely, *Every Man In* was played again at Covent Garden in 1825, on a bill which also offered "a new piece, called *LOFTY PROJECTS*; or, Arts in an Attic" and which concluded with "The PADLOCK." Thereafter, with the exception of the Dickens performance, the play disappeared from the stage for over seventy-five years.[3] Twentieth-century productions of *Every Man in His Humour* have been infrequent and not wholly successful. The play has been staged at Stratford-upon-Avon twice: first by F. R. Benson and his troupe in 1903; later, in 1937, by the Stratford company under the direction of B. Iden Payne. This second production, featuring Donald Wolfit as Bobadill, marked the tercentenary of Jonson's death. Nearly twenty years earlier, in 1909, Payne had directed the play at the Gaiety Theatre, Manchester, with Miss Horniman's Company. The humor comedy was presented by the Theatre Workshop group, directed by Joan Littlewood, in 1960.

On 20 April 1903, for two weeks, F. R. Benson presented Jonson's play at Stratford-upon-Avon. The shrine of his greater contemporary was hardly home ground for Jonson or for his great London comedy, yet one reviewer thought that "even the bigot pilgrim must have been impressed by the masterly characterization of Ben Jonson as displayed in those whimsical personages, Bobadill, Brainworm, Justice Clement, and Master Stephen."[4] The *Times* critic, who regarded the play as "a small thing done well," declared that *Every Man In* was "not a play for the library. It is the work of one who was dramatist first and poet second."[5] Benson, who took the part of Bobadill, "just fails of effect," according to one critic; though "after his thrashing at the hands of Downright," when Bobadill laments, "He hath assaulted me in the way of my peace; despoiled me of mine honour; disarmed me of my weapons; and rudely, laid me along, in the open streets," the same writer found "a wealth of comic pathos in Mr. Benson's rendering of these lines."[6]

A curious mixture of styles disturbed the balance of this production. Justice Clement, "a finished sketch of the humour of his type in the age in which he lived," was "cast in the truest spirit of Elizabethan comedy," while Kitely was "curiously, almost ludicrously modern."[7] On the whole, the Benson company's treatment of Jonson seems to have been more kindly than inspired, and *Every Man In* failed to gain a place among the company's usual repertory offerings. J. C. Trewin, in *Benson and the Bensonians*, mentions the play only once and then merely to say that Frank Benson, in the 1903 production at Stratford, "lunged at the lanthorn-jawed Bobadill, bravo of Paul's."[8]

Every Man in His Humour returned to the English stage six years later, again in the provinces. This time, "Miss Horniman's Company" presented Jonson's comedy at the Gaiety Theatre, Manchester. Directed by B. Iden Payne, the production was an example of his "power to give 'go' and verve to a play which stands in need of those qualities."[9] Indeed, according to one account, "the Gaiety company did their utmost to make the piece 'go,' and if noise would have done it a tremendous success would be chronicled."[10] But noise was not enough, even though the play "went along merrily . . . and there were times when the audience were in high glee."[11] The clearest testimony to this production's failure comes from reviewers' comments on two issues: the play's power in production and its contemporary applicability. On the first issue, critics as distant from one another in time as Hazlitt and Eliot have commented on the way stage productions reveal Jonson's skill as a theatrical artificer. But the Gaiety production had quite a different meaning for the reviewer who argued that "the plot is the usual medley which irritates rather than attracts people of today; the situations are wholly artificial; and the humour which appeals so forcibly to the reader of the play evaporates in the acting."[12] Such criticism reflects on the play's design and its presentation, while a second line of attack suggested that Jonson's play simply had no value for a modern audience. In this vein, one critic wrote of "a certain old-world flavour and ponderosity" in the work "which rather militated against its being a present-day success"; and he went on to assert that "its appeal will be . . . to the antiquarian."[13] A more forceful statement of the same position appeared under the initials G.H.M. in *The Manchester Guardian*. The "deeds and language" of Jonson, this critic argued,

> are not our deeds and our language. Italian fashions no longer corrupt our living; roystering cut-throat cowards are not now commonly to be met with in the aisles of our Metropolitan Cathedral; the shaft which urbanity aims at rusticity has shifted its mark, and we make other sport than Jonson's with our country cousins; jealous husbands furnish us with dramatic material of a different kind. All of which is to say that the comedy which aims at satirizing contemporary affectations is not apt to be the most lasting.[14]

Taking the argument even further, he contrasted what he called true comedy of manners, like Molière's, with Jonson's sort of comedy, which he labeled "comedy of mannerism." This latter kind can remain vital only when supported by wit and poetry, but *Every Man In* has "little wit and no poetry." A plot would help, but here "Jonson's wonderful faculty of marshalling his action relentlessly toward its conclusion . . . finds no better expression than an intrigue the vacuousness and triviality of which make it almost impossible to keep in mind." Yet another saving possibility might have been realized if only Jonson could have laughed with his characters rather than at them; but "the gentleness which drew Dogberry and Verges had no hand in the making of Brainworm and Cob, and Ben Jonson had very little tolerance or sympathy to temper the keenness of his mind." All these charges recall the nineteenth-century rejection of Jonson, and they are repeated in other reviews of this production as well.

The Gaiety *Every Man In* was not, for all these strictures, wholly without value. Even its harshest detractors admitted that there was good fun to be had with the gulls and the tobacco takers; and though the audience allowed "much of the rare wit of Jonson" to pass unnoticed, "certainly they enjoyed the thrashing of knaves and the unmasking of swaggerers."[15] Moreover, at least one reviewer found "two conspicuous successes" among the players. Charles Bibby's Cob was "humorously conceived and delightfully acted," and Esmé Percy's Justice Clement "was made the very type of ceremonious amiability and grandiloquence."[16] But these are isolated comments that fail to suggest any agreement on the merits of this production. The following description gives a better idea of the perspective in which Jonson's play was seen:

> The ladies, Misses King, Goodall, and Potter have but little acting opportunity, but used it to best advantage, and many a merited laugh was won by the accentuating of their speeches or gestures by the bobbing of their farthingales bravely worn.[17]

Inevitably, perhaps, the verdict on Jonson's play was unfavorable. Vestiges of nineteenth-century attitudes toward his kind of comedy, directed at a production of no great strength, led to the judgment that *Every Man In* was a mere curiosity of the stage, something for the antiquarian: "Purely as an experiment the revival of the comedy was interesting, but it is not an experiment to be repeated."[18]

Yet the experiment was repeated, and even supervised by the same man who directed the Manchester production, B. Iden Payne. Director of the Shakespeare Memorial Theatre since 1935, he chose Jonson's humor comedy as the play to be presented in 1937 to mark the tercentenary of the poet's death. The promptbook of this production, located now in the Nuffield Library of the Shakespeare Centre, provides valuable evidence concerning Iden Payne's handling of Jonson's comedy. An addition to the prologue establishes the author's character in a sharp contrast to the gentle Shakespeare whose prayers for indulgence and approbation are so familiar at Stratford. After "like men," the prologue continues,

> I'll only speak what I've heard th'Author say
> By God, 'tis good, and if you lik't, you may.

The promptbook suggests that this was an active, busy production of *Every Man*; and it must have been performed at a rapid pace. Over six hundred lines are cut from the play, among them a surprising number of references to cuckoldry and jokes about horns, until one wonders whether the audience could have been certain of the reasons for Kitely's absurd behavior. Most of the topical allusions are cut, to the considerable detriment of the texture of the play, which Jonson designs so carefully through references to solid and particular details. Brainworm's role is diminished, and the undertones of the discussion of poetry that run throughout the play nearly all disappear.

Despite such major alterations, the production gained considerable critical praise. Ivor Brown, for one, thought that Payne's trimming was both appropriate and successful, "reducing what might be a heavy and slow-moving text to a light and nimble masquerade of cozeners, gulls, and pretenders."[19] The *Manchester Guardian* reviewer agreed, claiming that the extensive cuts only demonstrated how little the plot mattered, since in Jonson character is everything.[20] It was, claimed still another critic, a production which "makes every incident lucid, and brings out many diversions half hidden in the text."[21] Best of all, the characters came to life on the stage, and the actors succeeded in establishing connections between Jonson's humor figures and some recognizable reality. Godfrey Kenton even contrived to make Kitely's "insane suspicions both credible and reasonable, both dramatic and amusing."[22] No mere experiment in antiquarianism, this production of *Every Man In* brought the play's satire out with persuasive clarity so that one could recognize that the playwright's "gang of young men about town . . . have their modern prototypes—you would probably find them at the Drones' Club."[23] Thus the Stratford company presented a version of *Every Man In* that established in some ways Jonson's claim to a place on the modern stage. The next production of this play would make even larger claims, displaying a Jonson who was himself a modern.

Such claims, however, require both a convincing directorial vision and a talented company to confirm its validity on the stage. Joan Littlewood's 1960 Theatre Workshop version of *Every Man In* had neither of these. Her actors, generally young and inexperienced, were unable to fulfill the demands made on them; and they seemed particularly lost in a play which demanded some sense of style. For style, Milton Shulman complained, "is exactly what is missing," and one could see in this production examples of "acting styles ranging from the Method to Restoration Comedy."[24] Despite the addition of "local jokes, interjections, backchat," which produced a kind of Americanization of cockney humor and transformed the play into something more like *Guys and Dolls* than like a Jonsonian comedy, *Every Man In* still seemed to many reviewers to be a hopelessly inferior play.[25] Only Alan Brien, who spent some time exploring the whole question of revising and updating as aspects of an attitude toward the past, seemed wholly in favor of the Workshop production.[26] Julian Holland was perhaps the most vociferous of the critics who rejected the play.[27] To his own leading question—"What other than misplaced academic interest has this pedantic Elizabethan essay in playmaking got to offer theatre-goers today?"—he returned an emphatic reply: "Not much." Another question followed: how, he asked, has Jonson survived? "Hazlitt inserted the pick; Byron placed the banderillas; and Bernard Shaw, that matador of dramatic critics, plunged in the sword. And that over 60 years ago."[28] Given only the evidence of the fortunes of *Every Man in His Humour* on the twentieth-century stage, Holland's wonder at the playwright's staying power seems understandable. But other plays, notably *Volpone* and *The Alchemist*, kept Jonson in the ring, his fierce energy serving him well.

Bartholomew Fair

Bartholomew Fair, the most sprawling and unmanageable of Jonson's great comedies, reached the modern stage in 1921, when the Phoenix Society presented it at the New Oxford Theatre. In 1950, the Old Vic company revived it for the Edinburgh Festival and brought it, later that year, to the reopened Old Vic Theatre. Since that time the play has been produced several times. In 1953, at the time of the Festival of Britain, the

City of London Festival Players brought it to Guildhall. Two years later it was presented at the A.D.C. Theatre, Cambridge; and in 1959 the Oxford University Experimental Theatre presented the play in an outdoor setting at Stratford-upon-Avon. The Dublin University Players, in 1963, produced the play at the Gate Theatre. Yet another professional production was that given by the Bristol Old Vic in 1966. In that same year the National Youth Theatre mounted a production of *Bartholomew Fair* at the Royal Court Theatre. In 1969, the play was presented by the Royal Shakespeare Company at the Aldwych Theatre.

As previous discussions make clear, most of the early productions of Jonson in this century received a mixed critical response. On the one hand, they had to contend with the playwright's public reputation, which was generally unfavorable, and with an audience wholly unfamiliar with the works in the theatre. On the other hand, the plays enjoyed the support of both their theatrical producers and of critics anxious to see a master of the stage restored to his deserved position. A striking instance of this conflict appears in the *Times* account of the 1921 Phoenix Society presentation of *Bartholomew Fair*. Montague Summers had written a program note for the production, and the *Times* reviewer seized on Summers' claims for Jonson as a rhetorical means by which he was able to give shape and direction to his own negative reaction to the play:

> Ben Jonson's personages in this comedy, who illustrate his "brilliant realism," hardly seem to us to be human beings at all, merely personified eccentricities, and they behave so irrationally that we do not care what becomes of any of them. A madman perlustrates the stage, only a little more mad than the others, and, if possible, a little more tedious.

"The fun of the fair," he complained,

> is always noisy and sometimes nauseous, and the "richest humour" of Mr. Roy Byford as the pig-woman is too rich for our stomach. We were very glad, exceeding glad, very exceeding glad, when the play was over. We speak of it, of course, as an entertainment. As a "document" *Bartholomew Fair* is full of interest—but that is another matter.[1]

H. G., writing in *The Observer*, was also willing to grant the play its status as a document: it "remains the delight of the antiquary." But he agreed as well that the play's pleasures were more than a trifle crude for modern taste:

> Jonson amuses himself hugely; and it is not his fault if his particular vein of clowning and knockabout—so fresh to audiences of 1614—now seems merely an echo of all the pantomimes and music halls of the intervening three centuries. If our little armour

of sophistication is too thick to be pierced by the gigantic bolts of his primitive humours [sic].[2]

Such a view led inevitably to a rejection of Roy Byford's Ursula, even though his portrayal "was more completely in the picture than anyone," since "the picture, with its tone brought up to full strength, proved almost too revolting for decency."[3]

Only Sydney W. Carroll among the prominent reviewers offered a powerful defense of Jonson's play, and he did so by invoking the names of two other great English artists:

> There is some justification for regarding his personages as eccentric and overdrawn, but the portraiture is that of a painter who loves his colours strong and vivid, whose details are Hogarthian in their minuteness, and whose characterization is as carefully extravagant as that of any study by Dickens.[4]

And though the production did not entirely meet his expectations—he found some of the players "too coarse and buffoonish . . . too lusty and overfed"—he nevertheless asserted that he "would give all the French classics ever written for an hour of *Bartholomew Fair*."[5]

The critic for *The Nation and Athenaeum* advanced a judgment that worked toward a reconciliation of the views cited above. He recognized the limitations of the mode in which Jonson chose to work. The play, he suggested, is "a masque rather than a drama, much of its psychology is mere sign-board lettering, it drags a good deal, drops into kitchen coarseness, and in style and finish is miles behind Shakespeare." Yet, given those limitations, one must admit that "Ben Jonson is just the man for the bustling Saturnalia of *Bartholomew Fair*, a trifle shallow and crude, less of a wit than a humorist, not at all a dramatist of the soul, but an attentive showman of contemporary fashion."[6] Tarn., writing in *The Spectator*, called the play "a rather dull and boisterous hodge-podge of old and valued properties."[7]

Only the reviewer for the *Daily Telegraph* seemed to find the play a great success. He thought Ben Field "beautifully unctuous as a Puritan divine with an elastic conscience" and Ernest Thesiger "almost incredibly raucous as the gay idiot of the period on a spree"; moreover, he was overwhelmed by the brilliance of Roy Byford's Ursula, "a kind of female Falstaff without breeding." For him, *Bartholomew Fair* emerged from this production as "one of the many plays which, holding us more by an appeal to our curiosity than by any direct call to our emotions, still makes us stop and wonder at the immutability of human nature."[8]

The 1950 Old Vic production, directed by George Devine, with costumes and design by Motley, entered Edinburgh with a good deal of publicity and with more than its share of the difficulties attendant on what was so obviously a "revival." Moreover, the play itself was not regarded as a classic by any of the critics, while the loyal Scots among them made it clear that they saw Jonson's play as usurping the place of a homegrown classic that had enjoyed a favored place in the Festival in previous years, Lindsay's *Ayn Satyre of the Three Estaites*. At Edinburgh, the play was staged in the Assembly Hall of the Church of Scotland, a circumstance that seemed to promise great freedom for the production but that, in reality, became the source of one of its chief weaknesses. Without the focus of a restricted stage, the fair seemed to stretch to unwieldly length, and the vast spaces of the Assembly Hall were, in the words of one reviewer, "as deserted as a garden party in a thunderstorm."[9] The fair itself is "big and noisy and it must be got into full swing"; on the Assembly Hall's platform stage the Old Vic company could have used "another 30 actors who, inventively handled, would provide the spectacle with a large, vulgar, roaring vitality."[10] Some critics inclined to blame George Devine for the production's lack of vitality and for the inability of the players to make the stage seem a place of populous holiday activity. For a writer in the *Tribune,* there was no question where the fault lay: Devine "has muffed his chances. The fair, though it is delightfully realized in Motley's backset of booths and peepshows, goes unpeopled; only on its first appearance does it contribute a perceptible flavour."[11] The *Observer* critic was even more explicit in his assessment of the director's shortcomings: in his view, the production missed "the touch of Guthrie's genius in the surge and sway of the crowds."[12] The fairest judgment seems to be that which absolved George Devine of responsibility for difficulties which had their origin in the physical conditions of the Assembly Hall, though the language of this verdict seems less than enthusiastic about the production as a whole: "It is nobody's fault that a vital requirement is lacking—the hurly-burly of the fair—and that the long exits and entrances slow the pace almost disastrously."[13]

The fair itself, both as a physical presence and as a visual statement of Jonson's ideas, was the focus of further criticism when the play opened in December 1950, at the Old Vic in Waterloo Road. Theatre critics, like most mortals, are pleased to have their ideas supported and confirmed; and for the *Times* critic the London performances redressed the weaknesses the play exhibited in Edinburgh and did so in just the ways he had foreseen.

> It seemed likely in the big Assembly Hall at Edinburgh last summer that more would be done with this piece in a smaller space: and so it worked out. The fair booths are now concentrated in the middle of the stage and made reversible; there are no long

exits and entrances to slow the action, but short twisted alleys between the booths in which crowds may surge and rascals take to flight; and in the more restricted conditions Mr. George Devine is able to produce the vital element that was lacking at the festival performance—the hurly-burly of the fair.[14]

J. C. Trewin, writing in *The Observer,* found in the Old Vic production "three times the vigour it had at Edinburgh."[15] and T. C. Kemp remarked similar improvement over the Assembly Hall presentation: "on the stage of the Old Vic the ranks had closed up and this more intimate contact of one rowdy character with his disreputable neighbour generated a much higher dramatic temperature."[16] The consensus of reviewers of the Edinburgh production was that the play required a faster pace, more of the atmosphere of the fair, and greater concentration in nearly every area—in character drawing as well as in visual focus. Most of the cuts for the Edinburgh production were apparently dictated by a puritanism that seems oddly, even violently, inappropriate for *Bartholomew Fair*. One account says that it "has been slightly purged of the broad Elizabethan language, but retains enough to give it character"; another, and a less indulgent, reviewer complains that the cuts were of a timid sort, limited for the most part to "desultory pruning of . . . the more bawdy bits."[17] Alan Dent, in his report on the London staging of the play, was thankful that the director had listened to advice and cut the play, which had run for over three hours in its festival version.[18] Thus the London staging of Jonson's giant display of Smithfield enormities was altered in ways that seemed designed to make use of critical objections to the Edinburgh version. It became more compact visually and spatially and it was trimmed to a running time that most of the critics found acceptable, though some were unhappy that time should have been saved by the additional expedient of hurrying the actors through their lines at a speed that seemed to sacrifice verbal clarity.

But even these attempts to remedy the defects of the festival production failed to bring the play the acclaim the Old Vic company hoped for. One measure of their expectations for the play appeared in the extraordinary decision of George Devine to deliver a curtain speech in defense of Ben Jonson. J. C. Trewin, who reviewed this production in several periodicals and who claimed a special personal regard for *Bartholomew Fair,* denied that it needed such a defense. In his view it was merely necessary that one recognize the play's character, and then it was possible to accept it as he did, paraphrasing the words of Dame Purecraft: "A mad play? True: but . . . 'I love you, and am glad to be mad with you in truth.' "[19] Harold Conway took another view of Devine's extraordinary plea. He saw it as a gallant defense but one that was doomed by the hopelessness of the case it argued, since "The author . . . so cluttered up his burlesque morality play with plots, sub-plots and jostling puppets that the human interest got squeezed out." Given these circumstances, the cast worked "hard and loyally . . . but . . . in a lost cause."[20]

The mixed critical reception which the Old Vic production received falls conveniently into a pattern defined by the remarks of Conway and Trewin. Negative reactions emphasized the play's failure to focus on individual characters and its inability to excite interest on a human level. At times these complaints sound like repetitions of some of the standard nineteenth-century charges against Jonson. T. C. Worsley, for example, found the play itself "the most crashing old bore," and saw interest only in Wasp, Overdo, and Busy, three characters who are given the characteristic Jonson treatment and "blown out into characters by that puff of exaggeration, which is the comic writer's particular way of infusing life."[21] For the rest, he recommended the play only to those who could imagine enjoying a whole evening of Shakespeare's low comedy. Favorable assessments of the play, on the other hand, came from those who were prepared to abandon the quest for meaning through character and to find some means of responding to Jonson's total vision. Trewin, writing in *The Observer,* argued that *Bartholomew Fair* "is less of a play than a shouting, word-inebriated pageant of the Jacobean scene."[22] Other reviewers took up the same theme and extended it in a number of critically useful directions. John Barber, finding in the play "a savage and terrifying picture of the ugliest Elizabethan low life," also argued that "the Smithfield fair is a kind of hell" in which "the plot is nothing, the characters all."[23] Perhaps Peter Fleming, who confessed that he went to this revival fearful of being forced to witness a display of insipid antiquarianism, should be allowed, as a kind of convert, to represent how these various elements of positive reaction come together in a single, fairly coherent view: "Mr. George Devine has brought to life a seedy, gaudy, violent, vulgar microcosm in which the booths and the tents, the knaves and the gulls are . . . easily established as variations on the eternal verities." Fleming goes on to make Barber's judgment explicit by describing the connection between the fair and its inhabitants. Characters and situations, he argues, are in themselves of little significance, "but when, like the ingredients of a Christmas pudding, they are all thrown into the capacious basin of the fair and stirred violently together, the turgid, ebullient amalgam is savoury and satisfying."[24]

Yet at least one reviewer who shared this view of the play found that the production had not been able to communicate it adequately. Richard Findlater agreed that "the fair itself is the hero, the energising principle," and still he found that the Old Vic players did not make an impression because the production was "too self-consciously jolly and theatrical, too much of a Harlequinade and not enough of a social documentary."[25]

This production had its admirers, notably J. C. Trewin. But the adverse reactions, focused as they are on a few specific matters, indicate what the play's failures must have been. There was a great deal of noise, yet no genuine sense of the flesh and blood reality of the fair. There was no attempt to impose any order on the play's events, and yet these were not properly balanced in presentation for them all to be attractive. The cuts for the London production brought the play down to a more manageable length, but it remained dull in spots—perhaps because the cuts involved for the most part bawdy language, a curious sort of excising given the world the play attempts to re-create. Finally, and this is quite remarkable in view of the large cast for *Bartholomew Fair,* few of the critics pause to offer special commendation to individual actors. Once one excepts those reviewers who list nearly every participant in a sort of "good time was had by all" notice, this failure to single out individual performers becomes a conspicuous fact of the accounts of this production. *What's On,* a guide to activities in London, offered this astringent appraisal: "Here and there a minor character churlishly seizes the sense and meaning of his author, and Alec Clunes (as Wasp) rebelliously regards his role as something more than an animated cartoon, but these are patently lost souls, adrift in the brawling, sprawling mob."[26] While the reviewers for the press were less openly condemnatory, their faint praise speaks volumes; and it seems probable that the acting, with only an occasional exception, failed to attain to a level of distinction.

The Bristol Old Vic production of *Bartholomew Fair,* presented in the Little Theatre on Bridge Street for four weeks beginning 30 August 1966, was not a major production either in terms of its achievement or in terms of the interest it attracted from the dramatic critics. The national press ignored it altogether, and regional papers found little to praise in a production that was, in one reviewer's resigned assessment, "not quite as hilarious as might be expected."[27] Again, as in reviews of the parent Old Vic company's 1950 presentation, there was some question about whether the production or the play itself should be seen as the source of its failure to please. John Coe found that Jonson's "quips . . . have lost the knack of making us laugh"; consequently, the players could not be faulted, since their performance of "this lusty, sprawling, bawling Jacobean play has everything but the hilarity which the lines deny it."[28] Another reviewer took up the same issue from a slightly different critical direction, but reached the same conclusion. The playwright's great success appears in his having created "a whole Vanity Fair of bawdy, overdrawn characters all vulgarly and determinedly alive"; and yet the play itself "remains only a spectacle, and one that [one] could happily trim to an hour's length at that."[29]

Perhaps the two chief features of this production were its attempt to turn to its advantage the restrictions of a very small auditorium and its being set in Bristol in 1610, rather than in the Smithfield designated by Jonson. In the first instance, Christopher Denys, the director, tried to communicate to the audience a sense of being involved in the business of the fair. Thus one reviewer describes the production as being "staged on an open platform with the gangways used for many rip-roaring entrances and plenty of chasings. The producer hardly lets you draw a breath as we enter the fair, and the din remains until the end, when some little virtue triumphs," while another reports with some enthusiasm that "the fair erupts in all its noise and colour around the audience in the tiny theatre."[30] Opinion was divided, however, on the success of all this activity and crowding. It apparently made little impression on the critic who argued that

> In the fair scenes, puppet show apart, one looked for much more bustle. Roisterers, row and a little more dirt might have repulsed the frequent tedium and added the extra smell of Jacobean low life that only came to the nostrils with the gloriously, greasily gross performance of Claire Davenport as Ursula the pig-woman.[31]

Given the paucity of reviews of this production, it is hardly possible to reconcile these conflicting views. What can be said with some assurance is that for all the vigor that went into the attempt to enliven the fair and make it a scene of enormous, surging activity, the play remained a theatrical curiosity that failed to touch the spectators. Somehow (and this impression is confirmed by pictures of the production) the intense realism of Jonson's satirical panorama was glossed over in a production that was perhaps too good-humored and jolly for its own theatrical well-being.

This last quality, a kind of exuberant happiness and self-delight, shows up in the second distinguishing feature of this production, its "Bristolization." The text reveals several instances of modifications to fit a Bristol setting, a good share of them in the puppet show where references to "the Quay," "Bridge Stairs," and "Wine Street" replace the London allusions of Jonson's play. In the same vein, Busy becomes "a Cardiff man" and "some ripe Bristol accents add to the fun and enjoyment."[32] But even these attempts at geniality were not sufficient to dissuade one critic from agreeing with Hazlitt and seeing this production as further evidence that Jonson is "the most signal example in literature of power without charm."[33] Perhpas transplanting Jonson's great fair to seventeenth-century Bristol was an attempt to add charm which succeeded only in sacrificing the energy and force of Jonson's satire. But Jonson, like Richard Wilbur's Degas, "loved the two together: / Beauty joined to energy";[34] and both qualities exist, finely balanced, in *Bartholomew Fair.* The Bristol Old Vic production, supplying an overplus of good-natured fun, seems to have upset that balance and to have made the play a smaller thing than it is.

When the Terry Hands production of *Bartholomew Fair* opened at the Aldwych on 30 October 1969, the reviews echoed one of the most overused words of the year—"relevant." Students were demanding relevance in their course work, critics called for relevant literature and relevant discussions of literature, and in every sphere of intellectual activity new ideas and methods were subjected to the most rigorous assessments of their relevance. "Relevance for what?" was a question rarely asked, since there would have been probably as many answers as there were persons who insisted on this often-asserted criterion. It was nearly inevitable in such a period that a young director, committed to the idea of the drama as a vehicle for ideas, should have shaped a vision of the fair that insistently revealed its connections with (i.e., its relevance to) contemporary life. In his search for ways of stressing these connections, Hands turned to some of the techniques used by Tyrone Guthrie in his 1962 Old Vic production of *The Alchemist.* He brought actors on "dressed in a motley of all times and periods," and he introduced an assortment of props that included, among others, "aluminum steps, a shooting stick, a supermarket wheel basket, a derelict mini."[35] Anachronism was the order of the day. Timothy O'Brien's fairground setting, with its "row of plastic suckling pigs, and a booth fitted out with bicycle pedals," accommodated a combo and provided a reasonably appropriate background for Nightingale, a hippy ballad singer with a hand microphone who was "reviving" an old tune called "Greensleeves."[36]

John Barber was one of many critics who found this riot of confusion, and the considerable energy with which it was set in motion, an enormous waste of time. It reminded him of nothing so much as the fiercely misplaced energy one might find in "some determined revival of some minor Brecht." The "gimmicks," he wrote, "no doubt underline the all-time relevance of Jonson's satire. A simple, faithful production would have done so far better."[37] J. C. Trewin, "remembering wistfully" the Old Vic production of 1950, thought that both Hands and his actors "worked too hard," and he objected to the insistent "grotesquerie" of the Royal Shakespeare Company version.[38] Herbert Kretzmer, invoking a comparison that seems initially favorable enough, saw on the Aldwych stage "a gallery of leprous, lecherous, disabled bawds and grotesques that resemble an animated Breughel painting"; yet his final judgment faulted the production for "too much animation, too much din, too many startling effects."[39]

Similar objections are scattered through most of the reviews. "The actors ... given their heads ... overdo things" in a display of energy which was for Philip Hope-Wallace "so energetic and raucous" as to obliterate the play's significant details.[40] Frank Marcus, under the headline "Bartholomew Foul," wrote that the production, which "takes place in limbo" on a stage crowded with figures "looking like rejects from the Marat/Sade," offered "noise instead of volume, activity instead of movement, speed instead of rhythm, words instead of poetry."[41] Felix Barker found the evening "an orgy of meaningless horseplay"; Peter Lewis, "a sort of historical Goon show"; and Robert MacDonald, "a confusing scrimmage in which Jonson and his play are lost in a welter of gimmickry."[42] The strain of coping with Jonson's great, shapeless excursion into the confusion of Smithfield was, it seems, all too clear from this "anxiously-considered treatment" of his play in which the actors performed their roles in "a mood of dedicated desperation."[43]

On the evidence of this production, Felix Barker thought that rare Ben Jonson "should be a good deal rarer," and most of the reviewers shared his opinion.[44] Yet there were elements of the play that succeeded. Alan Howard as Bartholomew Cokes won praise for "his gentle and touching recognition of the littleness of the puppets"; and the same critic who valued Howard's performance, Harold Hobson, found comic business worthy of notice in Helen Mirren's "being kissed and fondled by all comers at the beginning of the first act" in her portrayal of Win Littlewit.[45] Irving Wardle, though he could not "remember having seen this splendid company working to less effect," was able nevertheless to enumerate some good moments:

> Lila Kaye ... as the pig-woman mountainously immobilized flat on her back; Willoughby Goddard as a rampant Puritan trampling idolatrous gingerbread underfoot, and Patience Collier as his reluctantly virtuous consort breathing her long-simmering desires into the ear of a supposed lunatic.[46]

Although Goddard's Busy became "a figure of pure fun and not the more hypnotic and sinister being that Jonson envisaged," Michael Anderson still admired this "gargantuan actor with a face as expressive as a Hogarth drawing." "An impressive conflict between gluttony and self-righteousness played itself out on his countenance as he debated whether it was lawful to visit the fair and eat pork, and ended in lip-smacking approval."[47]

Surprisingly, and contrary to the judgment of Pepys—who reported "My wife and I to 'Bartholomew Fayre,' with puppets which I had seen once before, and the play without puppets often, but though I love the play as much as ever I did, yet I do not like the puppets at all, but think it to be a lessening to it"—the puppet show was the best-received feature of this production.[48] B. A. Young wrote that "the evening never came to life until the last ten minutes when the cleverly-manipulated puppets . . . gave us some genuine fun," while Robert MacDonald thought the puppet show "the best part of the play," and Frank Marcus found the puppets "more alive and human than the characters in the play."[49] The most detailed claim for its success was that of Ronald Bryden in *The Observer*: the

> best thing in the evening is the final puppet-show, with the cast crowding the stage in the deepening shadow of orange flares, their backs to the audience, to listen to a Dionysius doll argue with Goddard's fleshy Puritan the case for the theatre as a castigating image of its time.[50]

This event transforms "the play's shapelessness" into "a microcosm . . . of the whole history of comedy as a mirror of human folly through the ages." Bryden's whole account, confessedly that of a Jonson partisan, has an appealing freshness about it, an enthusiasm that seems vibrant while remaining well informed; and while his claims for the significance of the puppet show are perhaps a bit inflated, he seems to be justified in arguing that the last act, capped by a moving theatrical stroke which joined the audience in the theatre with the characters on stage as witnesses of Leatherhead's display, caught the attention of the spectators.

Of all the reviews of this production, the most favorable was that of D. A. N. Jones in *The Listener*.[51] His sympathy with Terry Hands' conception of Jonson's play is most strikingly apparent in his praise of those aspects of the show that other reviewers found most objectionable, and in his use of language that conveys a political outlook. Hands and O'Brien, in his judgment, "have devised a good method for making recognizable the ancient types," and he declares that, "for me, none of these anachronisms jar. They speed up the understanding." The method helps us to see, for example, that "Littlewit and his wife are doting petty-bourgeois, failed trendies." Although Jones remarks the acting of Alan Howard and the success of the puppet show, the chief interest of his review lies in his agreement with the apparent aims of Terry Hands and his belief that the director has found a way of achieving them, of transforming *Bartholomew Fair* into a "relevant" comedy.

In bringing this selection of comments to a close, it seems appropriate to take note of Irving Wardle's account of the Royal Shakespeare's version of Jonson's play. In some ways a model review, it considers the play critically and historically, describes the strengths and weaknesses of this production, touches briefly on staging and individual performers, and offers a concluding assessment of the production that seems, in view of the evidence marshalled in its support, comprehensive and just. Wardle sets out to demonstrate that Terry Hands "is not wholly to blame" for the play's lack of success, and the very phrasing of his pardon indicates that the director must in fact bear a large share of the responsibility for his actors' failure to bring Jonson's Smithfield extravaganza to life. What one missed, and what the director should have provided, was "a detailed portrait of life at the fair," a view of people "really selling gingerbread and hobby horses, really stealing and soliciting, with the seriousness due to their means of livelihood." In the absence of such an impression, much of the thrust and energy of the play must be lost, thus creating the sense of frantic but randomly disposed energy noticed by so many of the reviewers. This is a more serious fault insofar as Jonson himself, in Wardle's reading of the play, mismanaged the structure of *Bartholomew Fair* in such a way as to create a similar impression of hyperactivity. The playwright stuck firmly to the humor theory in this comedy, but

> humours generate laughter only when you see one *idée fixe* clashing with another, and by presenting a panorama rather than a plot, Jonson largely eliminates the chances for conflict. As a result you see character after character spinning relentlessly in his own obsession: and the general impression is of a mounting torrent of speeches which fail even to register, much less provoke laughter.[52]

On the whole, this production of *Bartholomew Fair* failed to excite the reviewers, and many of them, not Trewin alone, looked back to the Old Vic production of nearly twenty years earlier with renewed appreciation. For the greater part of the play the actors were too obvious in their efforts. Far from practicing the art that conceals art, they allowed their striving after effects to be seen too easily. Similarly, Terry Hands, in his pursuit of relevant meanings, imposed his didactic intentions on Jonson's play at the cost of some of its complexity, although his approach brought out certain themes with undeniable theatrical force. Michael Anderson found the play becoming "increasingly dramatic as it develops into a conflict between the anarchic and amoral appetite for life represented by the giant and Saturnalian figure of Ursula, and the envious forces of the overzealous moralist and the hypercritical Puritan"; and at least one reviewer understood the production as a sort of celebration of "the permissive society," thus illustrating how self-defeating didacticism in the theatre can be.[53] The production aimed at establishing Jonson's contemporary relevance, but that aim was frustrated in part by the very energy with which it was pursued. With its varied costumes and mixture of styles, its frenzied but unfocused energy, *Bartholomew Fair* at the Aldwych gained few adherents for its author. Nevertheless its failure was a testimony to the richness and vitality of the play, which would not be constrained within the limits of even the most earnestly benign didacticism.

Volpone

The modern stage history of *Volpone* begins in 1921. In that year, on 30 January, the Phoenix Society brought Jonson's play to the stage of the Lyric Theatre, Hammersmith. Even for a group dedicated to raising old dramatic works from the ashes of the past, this must have been a major work of resurrection. *Volpone* had not been seen on the professional stage since 1785. The production was revived by the Phoenix Society again two years later, and with nearly the same cast. This time, on 29 June 1923, the performance took place at the Regent Theatre, King's Cross. After these quite successful revivals, the account of *Volpone* on the stage becomes rather confused; for in 1926 Stefan Zweig completed an adaptation of *Volpone* ("nach Ben Jonson"). This play—a considerable triumph in Europe and America, and the source of a brilliant and influential movie—often gained the stage while Jonson's magnificent original had no hearing from the theatre public. Zweig's work had an undoubted influence on the reception of Jonson's *Volpone* in this century, though it is difficult to assess its precise impact. By calling attention to the timelessness of Jonson's themes, it has fostered an interest in that side of the great Renaissance playwright which reveals him as one of the major social critics in our dramatic literature. By supplying an updated and in some ways more accessible version of Jonson's dramatic fable, it has sometimes, like a rude child, shouldered its parent from view.

In any event, though a play called *Volpone* appeared in New York in 1928 and Paris in 1929, Ben Jonson's comedy did not reach the public stage again until 1930. Evan John directed the play at the Festival Theatre, Cambridge. In 1935, at the Birmingham Repertory Theatre, John Clifford played Volpone and Stephen Murray was Mosca. Later that year, at the Malvern Festival, Stephen Murray again played the parasite, this time to the fox of Wilfred Lawson. In 1938, London saw Jonson's *Volpone* in a public performance for the first time in over one hundred and fifty years (the Phoenix productions were private affairs). This was the first in a long series of productions, extending over more than twenty years, in which Donald Wolfit assumed the part of the wily Venetian magnifico. Revivals of the play with Wolfit in the starring role took place in 1940, 1942, 1944,

1947, 1949, and again in 1953; and Wolfit did the play for the last time in a television production for the BBC World Theatre Series in 1959.

In 1944, Ben Jonson came to Stratford-upon-Avon, where his plays have only rarely shared some of the benefits earned by his greater contemporary. This was a much abbreviated production of *Volpone,* and claims little attention on grounds of intrinsic merit; nevertheless, coming at such a time it gives remarkable testimony of the strength of the British theatre tradition. New York theatregoers, who had a chance to see Donald Wolfit in *Volpone* when he brought his company there for a short season in 1947, were presented early in the next year with an adaptation of the play by the New York City Theatre Company under the direction of Richard Barr. *Volpone* returned to Stratford-upon-Avon in 1952 with Sir Ralph Richardson as a disappointingly benign fox. Two performances in 1955— at the Bristol Old Vic and at the Theatre Royal, Stratford East—helped to make the fifties a major decade for *Volpone* in this century.

The United States did not share in this interest in the play. It was 1964 before it was seen again after the two productions of 1947. Then Sir Tyrone Guthrie staged the play at the new Guthrie Theatre in Minneapolis. The following summer it was presented at the Oregon Shakespearean Festival. Back in England, the Nottingham Playhouse presented *Volpone* in 1965 under the direction of Denis Carey; and the Oxford Playhouse made a solid hit with Jonson's satire in 1966. This highly successful production, directed by Frank Hauser, came to London in 1967, though with some loss of its earlier reputation. Sir Tyrone Guthrie, directing the National Theatre company at the Old Vic in 1968, offered London audiences another look at his treatment of Jonson after the controversial production of *The Alchemist* six years earlier. The Birmingham Repertory Company, thirty-four years after their first public performance of *Volpone,* returned to the play in 1969. The next year, the Great Lakes Shakespeare Festival company staged the play. In 1971, the Stratford Festival Players of Canada, directed by David William, followed *The Alchemist* of two years before with another inventive and consistently exciting treatment of *Volpone*. Finally, in 1972, the Bristol Old Vic, honoring Jonson with a quatercentenary production of his great satirical fable, presented a *Volpone* directed by John David that earned high marks for intelligence and for a faithful charting of the play's exploration of the varieties of human greed.

The Phoenix Society, a group of professional actors, from time to time presented revivals of specimens of early English drama, usually for no more than a single performance or perhaps two. In 1921, the year in which they brought *Volpone* back to the London stage, they also gave a performance of *The Witch of Edmonton* with Sybil Thorndike as Mother Sawyer and Edith Evans as Anne Ratcliffe. It was this production that moved Tarn., the reviewer in *The Spectator,* to lament the conditions under which this dedicated group brought long-forgotten plays to life. After praising their handling of the Dekker/Ford/Rowley play, he concluded: "But alas! . . . the Phoenix performances are spread like the snowflake on the stream—one moment here, then gone forever."[1] Yet despite the evanescence of the Phoenix *Volpone,* presented on 30 January and again on 1 February 1921, at the Lyric Theatre, T. S. Eliot called it "the most important theatrical event of the year in London."[2] "The play was superbly carried out," continued Eliot, "and the performance gave evidence of Jonson's consummate skill in stage technique, proceeding without a moment of tedium from end to end." In this Eliot had at least the partial agreement of the *Spectator* critic, who said of the play: "It is, within its convention, a masterpiece of construction. It is a sustained piece of satire, a triumph of technique of which no other Elizabethan was the least capable." Here, however, their views diverged somewhat, for Tarn. claimed that it was only Jonson's magnificent command of the technique of dramatic structure that earned *Volpone* its place as a classic; and "for this we now forgive a certain shallowness which damned it with the last generation."[3]

In his letter to *The Dial,* Eliot described the abuse which the Phoenix Society had suffered from certain of the London daily papers, especially the *Daily News* and *The Star*: "The bloodiness of Elizabethan tragedy, and the practice of the Society in presenting the complete text of the plays, were the points of attack." For his own part, Eliot wrote, "I am more and more convinced that the Phoenix is wholly justified in its refusal to admit any expurgation whatever. The sense of relief, in hearing the indecencies of Elizabethan and Restoration drama, leaves one a better and a stronger man." Such restorative powers did not, however, constitute the chief importance of this revival of *Volpone.* Eliot's claim that it was the year's most significant theatrical event was put forward on other grounds: "The performance of *Volpone* had a significance for us which no contemporary performance of Shakespeare has had; it brought the English drama to life as no contemporary performance of Shakespeare has done." For "Shakespeare . . . strained through the nineteenth century, has been dwarfed to the dimensions of a part for Sir Johnstone Forbes-Robertson, Sir Frank Benson, or other histrionic non-entities." The Phoenix Society revival was a historical landmark, but for Eliot it was primarily meaningful because, along with the continued appeal of Shakespeare, even in diminished forms, it provided some evidence that "the appetite for poetic drama, and for peculiarly English comedy or farce, has never disappeared."[4]

This first revival of Jonson's play featured Baliol Holloway as Volpone, Ion Swinley as Mosca, and D. Lewis Mannering as Voltore. Two years later, it was chosen out of all the plays done by the Phoenix to be given at a benefit performance whose proceeds would go to the Stage Society. The only cast change involved the part of Mosca; Ion Swinley had been the victim of an accident, and Rupert Harvey took his place as Volpone's parasite. The *Spectator* account, written this time by A. P., was not overly enthusiastic. In a tepid conclusion, the reviewer allowed that "the tightness of construction and the neatness of language make *Volpone* a most enjoyable comedy."[5] But such a spiritless admission could hardly be surprising coming from a writer who earlier in his discussion claimed that *Volpone* "puts no strain on the abilities of its actors. The characters represent definite and docketed 'humours'; there is no need to get 'inside' the words; and the actor's own personality, modified by the constant exhibition of one passion, will suffice to give some life to the figures of the play." One can hardly believe that such an approach to the play was what had so impressed Eliot two years earlier, nor can one think that such a description can have been read happily by any actor who has had a part in working out the relationship between Volpone and Mosca.

The Cambridge Festival production of *Volpone* featured Roy Malcolm in the title role and Frederick Piper as his parasite. Robert Donat played Corvino in a revival directed by Evan John that "aimed at speed and gaiety."[6] Much of the play's sinister force seems to have been sacrificed in a quest for lighter-weight theatrical pleasures. The Venetian justices were reduced to figures of "roaring, almost . . . knock-about farce." Roy Malcolm played Volpone with a "light touch"; and although the play's "narrowness and limitations" were apparent, it remained possible to "admire its gaiety." This production seems not to have suggested the depths of corruption that modern readers have found in *Volpone*. The *Times* reviewer was thus able to assert that "Volpone is neither man nor fox: his passions are not human, for his avarice has no power and his lust no heat—both are mere excuses for mischief."

Volpone opened on 23 March 1935, at the Birmingham Repertory Theatre for a run of two weeks, in a season of eight plays produced by Herbert M. Prentice. Announcing Jonson's play, the program offered this reassurance to timorous playgoers:

> The original was couched in extravagant language and much reference to classical incident which made the play somewhat difficult for modern requirements, this has now been deleted and it stands as a full-blooded comedy rich in wit, humour and brilliant in construction [sic].

Aware of this rather breezy attitude toward the sanctity of Jonson's text, one is less likely to be surprised by the bizarre judgment that "Even when cut to about one half of its original length *Volpone* compares unfavourably with *The Alchemist.*"[7] Although there seems to have been general agreement that "Jonson has to be expurgated for public representation," the critics reached no consensus on whether the effort was well expended.[8] One reviewer argued that "Even Jonson's knife-edged wit and savage satire fail to commend his crudities to modern ears."[9] Another saw the harshness of *Volpone* as a needed tonic:

> The play, teeming with plots and counter-plots, with diatribes in a language rich and vigorous, lashes one to attention. Our digestions of today are unused to such ample dramatic fare, being pampered by more delicate dishes, and the theatre is to be applauded for the discernment shown by the inclusion of the piece in the spring programme.[10]

Another sort of opposition appeared in the actual presentation of the play. One reviewer saw this version as a "captivating combination of bawdy bedroom farce and morality play," while another found it to be "something between a full-blooded melodrama and a sustained problem play."[11] A likely source of this opposition may have been the contrast between John Clifford's Volpone, "a very funny fox whom one cannot help but liking," and Stephen Murray's Mosca, an "adroit study" of "an oily, silkily ingratiating schemer."[12] Clifford, particularly in the mountebank scene, gave a richly comic performance, while Murray seems to have carried the burden of suggesting the depths of evil in the play.

The Birmingham company fell short, it appears, of a full realization of the dramatic possibilities in Jonson's powerful comedy of avarice. But the local reviewers found the play itself lacking. "There is something extraordinarily wearisome in undiluted depravity," complained one, "even though presented with fine jugglery of words."[13] One of his colleagues allowed that the play possessed "a savage energy, a fertility of invention, a magnificence of language." And yet, he concluded, "for all that, it remains for me an intellectual and literary exercise."[14]

The Malvern Festival production of *Volpone,* presented on four occasions during a season that ran from 29 July to 24 August 1935, had a cast that differed from the Birmingham version in several important roles. Cecil Trouncer replaced Hugh Butt as Corvino; Eileen Beldon took the part of Lady Would-be, played earlier by Elspeth March; and Clifford Marle took over Sir Pol, a role managed by Derek Prentice in Birmingham. But the most important change appeared in the assumption by Wilfred Lawson of the title role in place of John Clifford. The significance of his contribution is documented by the report in the *Times*:

> There is a tendency in revivals which are not first rate to emphasize the farcical portions of the play, and to abate the full force of the satire by denying to Volpone

that all-pervasive intelligence which adds horror to his triumphant wickedness. . . . Mr. Wilfred Lawson saw to it that the farce was dominated by the sulphurous horror of an intelligence immensely alert in the pursuit of evil, and there was terror as well as laughter in the play. A fox in flaming make-up, he was in essence a man whose cruelty and cunning and intellect had grown with age and were ripe for mischief on the grand scale.[15]

Ivor Brown seconded this praise: "Mr. Wilfred Lawson's Volpone, a tawny bandit of the city's coverts, in full cry and call after the less human raptors, was an immense performance."[16]

The *Manchester Guardian* critic saw in Lawson's playing of the role a significant realization of Jonson's animal imagery, though the beasts he envisioned are nearer the ground than the playwright's winged creatures:

With a tawny, foxy make-up and an extraordinary equipment of animal noises, Mr. Lawson goes hunting his conies with a fierce and ravening spirit, and when at last he is cornered he adds the splendour of the stag at bay to the red cunning of Reynard.[17]

With his Birmingham experience to draw upon and an actor of real power in the role of Volpone, Herbert Prentice "had things moving with rare pace and strength."[18] This production gave Jonson's play a reading that answered to its rich complexity: it presented "the whole comic spirit of the period at its ugly, coarse, relentless, and yet brilliant best."[19]

Donald Wolfit's *Volpone* ran for thirty-one performances at the Westminster Theatre, from 25 January to 19 February 1938. Aided by a "gold-encrusted Jacobean tableau" designed by Peter Goffin and a "concourse of sounds even more obnoxious . . . than the scenes they accompany," composed by Edmund Rubbra, this production achieved a blend of realism and cruelty necessary to any stage production that would capture something of the fullness of Jonson's play. W. A. Darlington, who thought this "the best Ben Jonson revival" in his memory, praised it for having "succeeded in its avowed object of conserving the 'power, gusto, and cruelty' of the original."[20] Another critic offered the view that audiences "are never likely to see this crabbed, cruel play better done"; still another praised the balanced presentation of Jonson's complex vision: "One was never allowed to forget that this is a comedy, though a grimly cynical one."[21] Wolfit, easily the dominant figure in this fable of the sleights of the Venetian fox, was "richly and even . . . savagely humourous."[22]

Michael Macowan, the director, risked criticism by cutting the Would-be sub-plot. Ivor Brown was one who disagreed with his decision; yet the effect of the loss of the witless Sir Pol, he felt, focused this production on "a single note of superhuman anger."[23] Other reviewers missed the Would-be's too, but most of them thought that this performance had found a way of achieving the comic balance the English tourists usually provided by the spectacularly successful playing by Wolfit of the mountebank scene. Here was comic business of the most persuasive kind, and here too was a source of that balance in the entire production between the realistic and the grotesque that gives to Jonson's play its peculiar ability to seize upon a viewer's imagination:

> The sales-patter, delivered in just such tones and accents as modern cheap-jacks employ in country markets, shouting and boasting and offering elaborate reasons for a special low price, was extraordinarily real; and it is indeed the triumph of this production that while it keeps a fairy-tale note with its golden caskets and the splendours of Volpone's household, it is not primarily fantastic.[24]

This production gave particular emphasis to the animal symbolism which joins this tale of the Venetian magnifico to the world of allegory, and it stressed too the pervasive theme of violations of nature which accompanies and reinforces the allegorical design. Wolfit's "self-relish in his rufous guile" was effectively set off by the Mosca of Alan Wheatley, who was "more snake than fly" but appeared nevertheless as "a memorable and properly odious reptile."[25] Michael Macowan carried Jonson's animal symbolism into the court, calling the *avocatori* owls, "and giving them appropriate head-dresses as they sit buzzing and squeaking on their perch."[26] As a final ingredient in this blend of grotesque animalism, the production included "a nightmarish touch of evil expressed particularly in Volpone's trio of clowns and in the incidental music, with its crabbed and satanic woodwind discordances."[27]

This production of *Volpone* was successful enough to lead more than one reviewer to hope for further stage presentations of Jonson's plays, even though it was clear that he had to contend for a place, perhaps unfairly, with Shakespeare. A delightful by-product of that recognition was an essay in the *Sunday Times,* in which James Agate took up the familiar terms of Hazlitt's comparison of the two great dramatists in order to describe his own critical beliefs. Hazlitt, he recalled, compared the humors of the two men—Jonson's "confined in a leaden cistern," while Shakespeare's "bubbles, sparkles . . . like a natural spring." With a slight touch of cynicism, more engaging than rough, he rejected Hazlitt's description of Jonson as being like someone who persists in talking about a disagreeable subject: "Who wants anyone to leave a disagreeable subject if he can make it more interesting than an agreeable one?" Hazlitt's problem, Agate declared, was that he "denies Jonson gusto because he does not like the things gusto is about." The nineteenth-century writer was a sentimentalist and a wishful thinker whose view of comedy was simply not capacious enough to include Jonson; he believed that "comedy should make him think better of mankind." The modern view, as Agate expressed it, readily accommodates the astringent world of Ben Jonson's plays: "I demand of comedy only that it shall make me think."[28]

One final sidelight emerges from accounts of Wolfit's 1938 version of *Volpone*. The *Times* reviewer assessed the play in a discussion that reveals a perceptive critical sense. He wrote of Volpone as a character who, far from being a mere humor, "has . . . the light and shade of an immense intelligence," and he mentioned Wolfit's delight in "the rogue's richness of imagery and sultry splendour of thought." He saw Mosca's function in the play as the controller of its two tempos, and in this respect he thought that Alan Wheatley "proves himself a perfect metronome." Mosca's control helped to prevent Volpone from hurrying his "highly polished lines" and thus becoming a "negligibly cackling monster of iniquity." But these remarks, however sound they may be as criticism, seem less than original when one compares them with the *Times* review of the 1935 Malvern Festival production. There the critic wrote of the impossibility of an actor's establishing Volpone's intellect "if he is rushed through verse whose polish is the secret of its powers"; and he praised Stephen Murray as Mosca for "helping Mr. Lawson to accept [sic. accent?] Volpone's richness of imagery and sultry splendour of thought." Given this aid, "there was nothing of the cackling dotard about this Volpone." As literary criticism, these remarks were no doubt as valid in 1938 as they were in 1935; but as dramatic criticism they are virtually worthless. The drama critic ought to offer a response to a particular production; his own view of the play may help to shape his response, but it ought not to limit it altogether. If the theatre is to be a vital force, it must find its own ways of coping with the problems that our great dramatists pose when actors attempt to bring their works to the modern stage; and an account of these efforts and the degree to which they succeed ought to be the business of the reviewer. This is, of course, to digress; but the two *Times* reviews raise the issue of the dramatic critic's responsibility so clearly that it seemed appropriate to turn aside for a moment to engage it directly. Perhaps someone will spell out the "reviewer's job of work" some day in a well ordered and persuasive way. In the meantime, one's only defense is to read the reviewers one has learned to trust.[29]

Donald Wolfit returned to the role of Volpone several times in his theatre career, and perhaps it is just as well to ignore chronology for a moment to record the significant productions of following years in which he appeared. Wolfit himself first directed *Volpone* in a production at the Arts Theatre, Cambridge, in May 1940, at the invitation of John Maynard

Keynes. In 1942, at the St. James Theatre, Wolfit again directed a production of the play which included his wife, Rosalind Iden, in the role of Celia and which partially restored the Would-be subplot. Again, the chief strength of the production came from its balance. The *Times* reviewer said of Wolfit that "without overlooking what is comic in the part, he tries by every means in his power to create a sense of that dominating intelligence which lends an almost sulphurous horror to Volpone's fierce pursuit of evil." In view of the horrors that had been unleashed in Europe, it was no longer difficult to believe in the terrifying union of evil with a mind of great power, and "we are now open to what is sinister as well as to what is comic in Jonson's satire."[30] Two years later, at the Scala Theatre, Wolfit again directed the play. Mosca was played by an actor with the improbable name of Brown Derby. Here the critics noticed a striking gap between Wolfit and the rest of the actors; this would be a persistent complaint about the productions of his company. Here too one first notices objections to his playing of the main role; he was, as one critic put it, "a little too good-humoured."[31] The Wolfit company traveled to New York in 1947. Richard Watts, Jr. welcomed their *Volpone* enthusiastically. It was, he declared, "a richly entertaining production" of "one of the most savage and scornful of plays. . . . Its contempt for the human race and its general distaste for human conduct and motive are complete and terrible, but the hatred comes out . . . in rich, full blooded, relishful laughter at the idiotic scheming of villainy and the foolish gullibility of villains."[32] As frequently happens, one taste of Jonson excited critics to wish for more. Robert Garland suggested that "although *Volpone* is Jonson's most timeless play, *Sejanus* is his most timely. I wish some adventurous producer would bring it to life some day, with its desperate rulers, impotent dictators, agents provocateur[s], book burnings and persecutions of the liberal minded."[33] While *Sejanus* may seem an odd choice, there is a certain logic in Garland's thinking of Jonson's Roman tragedy in 1947, with memories of Hitler's Germany still very much alive and with the specter of what was to become known as McCarthyism already beginning to cast its darkness over America.

Later the same year, in April, the Wolfit company played *Volpone* at the Savoy Theatre. For the first time in this century, two of Jonson's comedies were on the London stage at the same time; for the Old Vic Company was offering its brilliant version of *The Alchemist* at the New Theatre. The Wolfit revival was seen by some reviewers as working the comic side of the play too determinedly, and it is possible that this emphasis on the humor of the play was a response to criticisms in New York of the production's excessive malignity and lack of joyousness. Curiously, this production omitted Lady Would-be, though it retained her husband.

The *Stage* reviewer of this Savoy production supplies an effective detail from one moment of the play: "When Donald Wolfit's long, descending scream at the close of the trial tells us that Volpone is human after all, we are sorry to see him go, and sorrier still that his magnificence, exuberance, and grand relish for life are extinguished for ever."[34] This was, perhaps, the typical Wolfit touch designed to insure that the star performer could underline once more his central role in the proceedings. Yet at least one reviewer noted approvingly that the last of the great actor-managers did not seem in this production to be "quite so insistent as he used to be on surrounding himself with infinitely inferior actors."[35]

There were to be two further Wolfit productions of *Volpone* in London. These took place at the King's Theatre, Hammersmith, in 1949 and in 1953. On the latter occasion, Wolfit's last presentation of *Volpone* in the public threatre, the familiar complaints were heard about the quality of his supporting players. The great actor-manager had most of his old magnificence, but the acting overall was a bit down and the props a trifle shabby. One even gets the impression that the red fur of Wolfit's robe seemed unaccountably dull in what he promised would be his last revival of Jonson's play. Derek Monsey argued that the leading player was simply not rich enough for the character he portrayed, and he thought Wolfit was at his best "during the masquerading scenes; at such moments, when showing us a person playing a part, he is always fine."[36]

Ronald Harwood writes that Wolfit's "finest comic display, and by common consent one of his most magnificent creations, was Volpone, the Fox. It was a luxurious performance. No actor then alive could portray a character's relish in his own evil better than Wolfit. . . . Volpone was the first part which Wolfit stamped as his. Actors essaying the role in future would suffer by comparison; even one of Wolfit's own daring effects would be passed on, during his lifetime, as if it were traditional stage-business: the blood-curdling howl after receiving the sentence of the court, followed by the line, 'This is called the mortifying of the Fox!' and the holding on to the final hissing sibilant."[37] Donald Wolfit played Volpone for over twenty years. While not all the critics were favorably impressed by his portrayal, no one ever forgot it. When, in 1959, the BBC presented his version of Jonson's great play on the World Theatre series, it must have given him pleasure to think that one of his finest roles would be preserved for later generations. A major theatrical document, it showed an actor whose roots and instincts were in the nineteenth century taking a classical role in a rarely performed play prepared for a popular audience.[38]

The chronological account of productions of *Volpone*, interrupted after the 1938 Wolfit production, takes up again with a version of the play produced at Stratford-upon-Avon in 1944. Given the date, it is not surprising that there are few newspaper reviews of the play. Fortunately, the promptbook remains in the Nuffield Library of the Shakespeare Centre, and it affords a glimpse of some details of the production. Robert Atkins played Volpone, but failed to convey the sort of intensity the role demands. He was totally without the cruelty of the fox, and appeared instead as "a rather unpleasant old man, who unexpectedly finds himself speaking poetry in an embarrassing uprush of passion."[39] The relationship between Volpone and John Byron's Mosca was simplified by making the parasite's antagonism to his master appear at the beginning of the play. After Mosca's return with the rout to present Volpone some entertainment, he "pours wine for Volpone, falls back upstage, watches with contempt."[40] Volpone's first clear reference to the fable on which Jonson based his play was rather surprisingly cut:

> . . . and not a Fox
> Stretched on the earth, with fine delusive sleights
> Mocking a gaping crow.

Toward the end of the play, the promptbook reveals extensive cuts. The second scene of Act Five is removed altogether; thus Sir Pol is spared the embarrassment of the tortoiseshell episode, having disappeared in IV. 1. after his line, "The case appears too liquid." Act Five, scene five is also eliminated, and a large cut in V. 6., extending from "To make a snare" to "lost myself," further reduces the complications of the last act. Thus the movement toward justice is considerably speeded up, and the tedium that sometimes attends the play's conclusion somewhat obviated. But beyond the textual changes, which have an independent interest, there was apparently very little in this production to excite attention. The *Times* critic dismissed it as a production which "strives toward . . . easy laughter,"[41] perhaps the most damaging remark one could make about any production of Jonson's powerful, bitter satire.

The 1948 City Center production of *Volpone*, featuring Jose Ferrer as the title figure and Richard Whorf as his parasite, displayed the principals as "the ring-masters of a broad and noisy stage circus." They seemed to insist on making the play continuously farcical. Their stress on its physical humor was so great that Brooks Atkinson, who employed the circus figure just quoted, complained: "If you don't laugh, Mr. Ferrer and Mr. Whorf will wham you over the head."[42] Ward Morehouse was evenhanded in his assessment, granting that Ferrer "gets considerable fun into his characterization," but noting as well that "he misses a lot of the monster's slyness and vileness."[43] Other critics were less generous.

Louis Kronenberger charged that Ferrer, Whorf, and company "have gone to really prodigious pain to purge *Volpone* of every last ounce of distinction, and they have splendidly succeeded. A spectator might be expected to emerge from this version of the play exclaiming 'O rarely Ben Jonson,' " for "instead of a scathing exposure of human malevolence and greed, the City Center has put together a vaudeville show and a minor track meet." In place of the Venetian magnifico and his wily, dangerous parasite, Ferrer and Whorf present two characters who "carry on like the practical jokers at a shoe convention."[44] Another reviewer objected to this "vulgar, horseplay version" of Jonson's play, in which "for style, [the actors] substitute a sort of low-brow fashion. For wit, they offer a series of kicks aimed lower still."[45] Rowland Field saw in the production's emphasis a considerable loss and no compensating reward: "practically all the sly satire that this antique farce owns has been drained off in this present version . . . and knockabout methods are employed to the point of exasperation."[46]

Field closed his account of the City Center *Volpone* with a left-handed tribute to Donald Wolfit's company, whose production had not been highly praised in its recent New York showing. "Come back, Mr. Wolfit," he wrote, "all—or nearly all—is forgiven."[47] This comparison received its fullest development at the hand of Richard Watts, Jr., who saw in this *Volpone* directed by Richard Barr "a belated tribute to the much-abused Donald Wolfit." Whatever their faults, he argued, Wolfit "and his company gave us a performance of *Volpone* which captured its savage, mocking and contemptuous spirit splendidly. Knowing that it was bitter as well as comic and eloquent as well as rowdy, they played it accordingly, and the result was to make clear why Jonson's insect play is one of the theatre's immortal works."[48]

Only John Carradine as Voltore found consistent favor in this production. Watts saw in his interpretation of the lawyer the "one really hilarious performance" of the entire evening.[49] Joseph Wood Krutch spent some time analyzing the sources of Carradine's success in an otherwise lamentable production: "God has given him a rangy figure perfectly suited to be made into the very image of the old caricature of the Shakespearean tragedian, and he plays his role on that theme. His antics are performed with imperturbable gravity. . . . If all the big speeches had been made to count as he makes his addresses to the judges count, then the present production would have come a great deal nearer to doing Jonson justice."[50] But there was little justice for the playwright in a version of his great comedy that treated it as a "pillow-fight farce," a version "shabbily unfaithful to Jonson's spirit."[51]

The next production of *Volpone*, again at Stratford-upon-Avon, took place in 1952. Directed by George Devine, it boasted spectacular sets by Malcolm Pride. Once more there were murmurs of discontent from critics who wanted to see more of the cruel, cynical side of Jonson; but this was nevertheless a major production, and it contained at least one performance of the very first rank. The stage of the Shakespeare Memorial Theatre displayed effects and machinery unused since the 1930s productions of Theodore Komisarjevsky, all exercised to the full in creating a sense of the magnificence both of Venice and of Volpone's apartments. Sir Ralph Richardson and Anthony Quayle headed the cast as the fox and his parasite, and they received strong support from Michael Hordern, who justified Sir Pol's place in the dramatic proceedings. Another noteworthy name was Siobhan McKenna, who played Celia.

Sir Ralph's Volpone was, perhaps not surprisingly, the focus for complaints about the production's failure to explore adequately the full range of bitterness and cynicism in the play. The 1952 season had not been a great success at the Memorial Theatre, and Sir Ralph especially had experienced a bad year, with some rough handling by the critics for his performances in both *The Tempest* and *Macbeth*. "Defeated by nature" in his attempt to convey the relatively harmless chicanery of Face, he was more seriously hampered in this essay at the magnificent Venetian beast who torments the very birds of prey.[52] One reviewer complained that this Volpone was simply not in command; set against the "tawny, self-assured animal" of Donald Wolfit, he seemed "a furtive, worried, bedraggled, and almost mangy fox."[53] Harold Conway expressed his disappointment in a Volpone who "substituted ponderous flatness for the spirit of glorious, gloating rascality"; and David Farrer argued that "the sense of exultant evil which is the essence of this play escapes him altogether. This is a very parfit gentil fox."[54] T. C. Worsley raised a similar objection and went on to note its implications: "Sir Ralph's over-gentle handling of the main part," whether seen as conforming to or dictating a version of the play that is "softened and prettified," whose chief "note is antic rather than acid," jars with its surrounding elements. Volpone's mildness "doesn't match with the rapacity all about it, nor with those terrible pets of his, and the rape seems wildly out of keeping."[55]

But while Sir Ralph failed to convince with his handling of Volpone, Anthony Quayle as Mosca gave what one critic called "the performance of his career so far."[56] One could agree with Mosca's declaration—"Your parasite is a most precious creature"—for Quayle's "leer, his hunched shoulders, his sleek approach, his effortless unction all . . . were right."[57] He was, wrote Worsley, "oily, sly, and smooth, a Zeal-of-the-Land Puritan with a touch of Uriah Heep."[58] Other reviewers noted this same strange combination in the portrayal of Mosca. Although he seemed too large, physically, for his role, Quayle somehow "prances and plots and simpers, and, as it were, *shrinks* into the part. There is an oiliness about him, an air of eternal Heepishness."[59] Still another reviewer found this treatment of Mosca as a "double-faced Puritan . . . as effective as it is subtle."[60] Even the suggestion that Quayle needed "a little more unctuousness to go with the satanic scheming" describes a conception of Mosca that seizes upon the horrible duplicity of the man, a conception that points to the ultimately self-destructive path which schemers like Volpone must follow when they rely on fellow conspirators as depraved and conscienceless as themselves.[61]

This was not a great production but a good one, and several reviewers regarded it as the best offering in a bad year at Stratford-upon-Avon. The disparity between Sir Ralph's rather mild magnifico and Anthony Quayle's forceful, complex Mosca kept the play from creating a unified impression. Apart from Quayle, only Michael Hordern as Sir Politic Would-be made a great impression, and even in this instance there were dissenters who argued that the boorish English tourist "has little to do with this satire on avarice."[62] But Sir Pol's harebrained notions about international finance and his James Bond-like conception of the world of political intrigue were seen by some writers as remarkably useful for the play's design; moreover, the Alger Hiss case, with its pumpkin-patch papers, offered a striking parallel to Pol's absurd rumor about "intelligence . . . in cabbages."

Finally, the Memorial Theatre stage attracted its share of interest: "Doing quick-change service for Volpone's gold-treasured bed chamber, the Venetian Senate and the Grand Canal (complete with gondolas), the stage ascended, dived, capered sideways, did everything, in fact, but sit up and beg."[63] Gerard Fay thought, in fact, that in the entire production, "the excellencies . . . are mainly those of the staging."[64]

In its next manifestation, the soul of *Volpone* came to inhabit the stage of the Theatre Royal, Stratford East, in March 1955. Under the direction of Joan Littlewood, a group of relatively unknown players created what one reviewer called "the most excitingly alive production that London has seen for many months."[65] Jonson's characters were dressed in costumes that established immediately their significance for a modern audience. Harry Corbett as Sir Pol came on as a "Tory back-bencher with deer-stalker hat and binoculars"; and Maxwell Shaw's Mosca was, according to Stephen Williams, "the most plausible, cigarette-sucking spiv that ever grew from dead-end kidhood."[66] This updating of Jonson revealed one method of giving cogency to the often-heard assertions of his universality—by testing that contention with particular characters, and actually creating their modern equivalents. Sir Tyrone Guthrie had tried this in his Liverpool production of *The Alchemist* and he would attempt it again with that play in 1962. Terry Hands would use a modified version of the technique in the 1969 Royal Shakespeare production of *Bartholomew Fair.*

Later in 1955, the Bristol Old Vic presented *Volpone* for three weeks beginning November 29. Directed by John Harrison, with designs by Patrick Robertson, this production featured Eric Porter as Volpone and Alan Dobie as Mosca. It also had, as Corvino, a young actor who would achieve wide fame in the cinema, and, as Celia, an aspiring stage performer who had already gained renown as a ballerina and as a performer in films: Peter O'Toole and Moira Shearer. Peter Rodford, with just a hint of patronizing irony, suggested that this production was in the main faithful to the pattern of animal imagery Jonson establishes in the play and that Mosca, Voltore, Corbaccio, and Corvino "give the proceedings a strong zoological flavour." But he objected to Eric Porter's Volpone, which "has a lion's mane and a lion's roar that can hardly be reconciled with the sly cunning of a fox."[67] A curious emphasis on the idea of Volpone as "king of the spivs," supported by the playing of Alan Dobie, "costumed like a seventeenth-century Teddy Boy," gives one the impression that the class distinctions of which Jonson seems so careful were rather blurred in this production.[68]

In his review for *Plays and Players,* Peter Rodford was more straightforward in his praise of this *Volpone,* a production that "contained some of the most brilliant team-work of recent seasons"; and the writer for *The Stage* concurred, finding in this effort "the style and finish which Bristol Old Vic audiences expect, but don't always get."[69] This production had almost no attention from the national daily press, and one is forced to rely heavily on accounts from local papers for a sense of its achievement and its distinctive features. Perhaps the most striking thing about the production was its fidelity to the pattern of animal imagery in Jonson's play. The birds of prey moved, talked, and even stood like creatures of the air; Voltore (Derek Godfrey) in the trial scene threatened at every moment to swoop down upon the innocent defendants; and Alan Dobie's Mosca, dressed in black, had both the diminutiveness and the darting motions of a fly.

In 1963, the San Francisco Actors' Workshop presented a version of *Volpone* which one reviewer called "a soulful, simmering and superbly intelligent performance of Jonson's lusty text."[70] Kenneth Rexroth found the costuming by James Hart Stearns a source of "such imaginative splendor that the whole play is shifted over into a transcendent realm where every thing is greater than life."[71] Others praised the production's momentum, its richness in decor and costuming, its audacity and hilarity.

Everything seems to have been done on a grand scale. Mara Alexander gave a "devastating performance" as Lady Would-be, while Tom Rosqui made of Sir Pol "a boob of devastating proportions."[72] Elizabeth Huddle's Celia had "the chaste look of a woman pursued by a lecherous dragon," while Robert Symonds as her pursuer engaged in "monstrous sybaritic posturing" that suggested "a latter-day King Farouk."[73] The result was a *Volpone* of tremendous size and nearly unbounded energy, a nearly Jonsonian production: "undiluted, this lusty, ageless comedy puts the various adaptations we have seen to shame."[74]

Tyrone Guthrie, in his second season at the theatre he established in Minneapolis, directed a production of *Volpone* that was hailed as "the best of the eight productions this company has mounted."[75] A strong cast, headed by Douglas Campbell as Volpone and George Grizzard as Mosca, presented a fast-moving, spectacular performance in which "Ben Jonson's comic, savage display of avarice in action . . . bursts with color, movement, and the splendor of words."[76] Guthrie's program notes seem intended to shock or at least surprise his midwestern audience. "The rewards at the end," he writes, "consist of a series of juicy, sadistic punishments." And he goes on to argue that Jonson's tough-mindedness is, after all, what the theatre is all about: "who wants to see Marguerite carried aloft by hefty chorus-ladies in white wings, or that arch-bore Amelia Sedley getting her deserts when she marries dear, deadly, faithful Dobbin?" But for all the director's professed interest in the dark and cruel aspects of *Volpone,* the production failed, at least for some reviewers, to realize them. Harold Clurman complained that "Guthrie's playfulness makes Jonson appear more good-natured than he is." This was particularly true, he argued, in the cases of the leading characters, for while Campbell "is wholly the director's willing and affable instrument," and Grizzard "brings to Mosca his gift for honeyed mockery . . . both are less vividly sinister than they might be."[77] Henry Hewes commented on the same failure, describing the production as a whole as "a farcical exercise, glorying in all the external color it can create."[78]

Other reviewers discovered more complexity in Guthrie's handling of the play and particularly in the work of Campbell and Grizzard. To Dan Sullivan, Campbell's Volpone appeared as a curious mixture of man and boy. He displayed a man's intelligence and appetites, "but his soul is that of a 7-year-old boy (he loves to play sick, play dead, play soldier)"; and "he sobs his little heart out when he doesn't get to rape [Celia]."[79] Thomas Willis identified Campbell as "a voluptuary from the start" who "manages to be funny and diabolically cruel at the same time,"[80] and yet another critic argued that he gave "a magnificent performance by any definition, vocally a prodigious feat from its mighty roars to its senile quaverings, and in action a veritable catalogue of comic-heroic capers."[81] Grizzard, a Mosca who "really does go 'bzzz, bzzz' when he's thinking," provided Campbell with a parasite who was "a wonderfully intelligent foil" in a performance described as "superlative."[82]

The high points in the production were the mountebank scene and the attempted rape of Celia. In the first of these, Guthrie created a pyrotechnical finale for one of the most active and varied scenes of the whole play. Volpone, still celebrating the virtues of his elixir, mounts a ladder to Celia's balcony only to be met there by an outraged Corvino, who sends him falling backward into the arms of the crowd below. All this happened in a matter of seconds, the stage was cleared, and Peregrine and Sir Pol remained to comment on the episode. Campbell's fall was a brilliant theatrical stroke and a remarkable exclamation point (not a period) to a scene which displayed to the full Guthrie's genius in handling crowd scenes. In his later pursuit of Corvino's wife, Campbell "dances, struts like a turkey-cock, throws open his treasure chests to woo the lady, seeks to crown her, twiddles a bare foot in delighted anticipation, serenades Celia with operatic gestures, coos, roars, and when all persuasion fails, seizes her and dumps her unceremoniously on the bed."[83]

Though Campbell was unquestionably at the center of things and Grizzard, buzzing "around the stage, broadcasting intrigue as an insect broadcasts disease," was almost equally prominent, this remained an ensemble performance.[84] The trio of suitors, clad by Tanya Moiseiwitsch "in black, with beaks for noses, great feather collars to preen and puff, clawed gloves" gave a dimension of horrifying animality to Jonson's zoo story.[85] Celia and Bonario went through the motions of ineffectual goodness like figures out of *The Prisoner of Zenda*, and only the Would-be's seemed inadequate to the contribution they were called upon to make.[86] Guthrie was in the main faithful to Jonson's text. There are few cuts indicated in the promptbook and relatively little updating, although Sir Pol does speak of intelligence communiqués in *pumpkins* rather than cabbages in II. i. If something of the full flavor of Jonson's bitterness seemed to be missing, nevertheless Guthrie made a near approach to the complexity of the play. John K. Sherman called the production "a potent mixture of scalding satire and leaping fantasy," and he found it "exuberantly and quintessentially theatrical."[87] And even Harold Clurman, who missed the abrasiveness of Jonson's satire, "yielded completely to the sweep of the director's pace and comic inventiveness."[88]

Volpone next appeared in England at the Nottingham Playhouse in a production directed by Denis Carey and designed, ten years after his work on the play at Bristol, by Patrick Robertson. Hugh Manning played Volpone and Antony Webb, Mosca; they were aided by a strong performance of Corvino from John Neville and the antics of Volpone's rout, led by Maggie Jordan as a bearded Nano. The critic for *The Daily Worker* saw that "beneath all the fun is the message that gold and greed stunt and dwarf men, make them blind to higher things in life";[89] but while the play does lead one to such a conclusion about the unnaturalness that proceeds from avarice, this particular handling of it seemed, like so many others, to disguise the harshness of the play's truths behind a mask of comic hilarity. There were times when the Nottingham production moved toward a truly Jonsonian vision. Benedict Nightingale saw them in Neville's cry to Celia—"Whore, crocodile!"—and in the moment when Volpone's "pet dwarfs ape a war dance." Indeed, Nightingale saw Neville's Corvino as a highly successful reading of the character: he "creates an effect of chill avarice with sharp clutching gestures and an awful grating caw: this is a sustained, relentless performance."[90] But these isolated achievements were inadequate to supply the tone of savagery that ought to dominate *Volpone*, and most of the reviewers shared the view of a local writer who thought that "we laughed too much and too easily."[91]

Since Volpone so clearly dominates the action of the play, it is hard not to single out the actor of the leading role if a production fails to do justice to the play's complexity and its harshness. Hugh Manning apparently missed the luxuriousness of the character, the sybaritic wallowing which is yet controlled by a daunting intelligence. Instead, he "houses the cunning in the shell of a down-at-heel ex-public schoolboy who is making out by selling used cars no one in their right senses would buy."[92] This is hardly Jonson's Venetian magnifico, and it is no wonder that Piper Anderson regretted that while the sadistic dances of the rout "gave us glimpses of a darker purpose," they did not function as they should have, "as a mirror reflecting in nightmare terms the actions of the main protagonists."[93] This production contained some nice touches, including a set which suggested a cascade of golden rings. On the whole, though, it does not seem to have come together as a sustained treatment of Jonson's play; and its defects, in their typicality, were just those most likely to conceal those aspects of the play meaningful to an audience in the 1960s.

In 1965, the Oregon Shakespearean Festival presented *Volpone* as part of the festival's twenty-fifth anniversary season. Nagle Jackson directed this production, which featured Jim Baker as Volpone and Laird Williamson as his parasite. Jonson's satiric comedy was billed as an "anniversary extra" in a season that offered four Shakespearean plays: it was given three times—31 August and 5 and 10 September.

The next year, at the Oxford Playhouse, Frank Hauser directed a production of *Volpone* which made good some of the defects of earlier attempts at the play. In a program note, he wrote of Jonson's fundamental toughness: "He has no time for sex, little for sentiment. Money is his subject, both for the power it bestows and the havoc it causes: and the single-minded glee with which he pursues his interest makes a modern audience as uneasy as sex did the Victorians." To underscore this single-mindedness, Hauser cut the role of Sir Politic; and however uneasy the Oxford audiences may have been, enough of them were sufficiently impressed to make this production a solid success and warrant bringing it to London early in the next year. Hutchinson Scott designed the set for this re-creation of seventeenth-century Venice and Elizabeth Luytens created the music. Only the year before, Hauser had directed *The Alchemist* at Oxford, and his treatment of *Volpone* quite naturally elicited some comparisons between the two productions. Derick Grigs, in locating the differences between them, described the basis of Hauser's success with this "crueler, more misanthropic play. He interpreted *The Alchemist,* with its London setting, as a gallery of English types, naturalistically played and modernized enough to seem familiar; but the Venetian background and black comedy of *Volpone* suggested to him a more stylized production, peopled with Jonsonian monsters."[94]

Having shaped the general outline of the play in this way, Hauser received some excellent performances that brought it to life on the stage. Leo McKern's Volpone was "hale and sturdy" and was "played with breathy relish"; he brought "enormous agility and great vocal skill" to the leading role.[95] With his great physical presence, McKern established his control over the business on the stage. At one point he had "a memorably funny entrance, being tipped from a stretcher so that he landed on his feet, rigid as a statue; and he is one of the few actors with the magnetism to dominate a stage lying down."[96] Leonard Rossiter's Corvino was a second major acting contribution to the play. One reviewer thought it "the most original single performance of the evening" and marvelled at the way Rossiter "turns Corvino into a simpering, abject and profoundly ridiculous creature. Few actors can have applied such comic resourcefulness to so small a part; and the result is a virtuoso performance."[97] Ian Donaldson thought Rossiter "superb in his mixture of jealousy and tortured affability"; Peter Lewis wrote that his "smirking, slow-breathing, held-in violence has never pleased me more than as the merchant who is glad to sell his wife like a stock exchange share"; and Derick Grigs admired the way in which the actor "became a tense, twitching battlefield of the greed, jealousy and hypocrisy that pull Corvino apart."[98] Against the impression of McKern's massive power and Corvino's nearly manic contortions, Alan Dobie's Mosca seemed unusually restrained. While his interpretation of the role had a certain validity, it also involved difficulties for the production as a whole. In a sensitive, thorough review in *Oxford Magazine,* Daphne Levens pointed these out: Dobie's "stylized, reticent playing effectively sets off the extravagant gulls he must seem to serve—but, in being so withdrawn, he in effect anticipates, and weakens, the impact of Mosca's treachery, when that big moment comes."[99]

If one test of a good production lies in the quality of the criticism it excites, then the Oxford Playhouse *Volpone* earns very high marks indeed. Moreover, the reviewers' comments indicate that this version worked effectively to create the sort of impact that the best of modern literary criticism has discovered in Jonson's play. One writer described it as "an impeccable production" and remarked "the ease and accuracy with which it catches both the Jonsonian tone of mordant, cerebral wit, and his characteristic atmosphere created by the outsize gesture in a tight, comic situation."[100] D. A. N. Jones, who saw Leo McKern's Volpone as "a kind of Ubu, a gleeful caricature of all the frightful deeds a sufficiently willful man can get away with in an acquisitive society," pointed out the similarities between this Jacobean masterpiece and recent English comedy of the kind represented by Joe Orton's *Loot,* especially in its mixture of the farcical with the grotesque.[101] Finally, Ian Donaldson praised the careful equilibrium of a production in which "Volpone's rout and the Daumier-like gulls and advocates of the Scrutineo give sufficient grotesquerie to allow the central combat between Volpone and Mosca to be played out in a quieter, tenser, and more realistic style."[102]

On 31 January 1967, the Oxford company brought *Volpone* to London for a run at the Garrick Theatre. Zia Mohyeddin replaced Alan Dobie as Mosca and conveyed a rather different conception of that role, but otherwise the cast remained the same. Yet the reception from the critics was not so generous as the welcome they had given to the production in Oxford. Somehow, a production that had brought out the cruelty of Jonson with such incisive brilliance had lost its cutting edge. Benedict Nightingale thought that the Garrick production "muffles cruelty and presents the deadly sins as . . . eccentricities peculiar to (variously) clowns, goons, and fuddy-duddies."[103] Although the set "provided the correct atmosphere of gilded decadence," this counted for nothing given "the tone of bantering high jinks" that dominated the evening.[104] Even the terrifying creatures of Volpone's rout seemed to one reviewer "charmingly pantomimic rather than gruesome."[105] Whatever the cause of this broader comic mood, something of the full Jonsonian texture seems to have disappeared from the Oxford *Volpone* when it arrived at the Garrick. Nevertheless, on their home ground the Oxford players had brought to the stage a *Volpone* that, like a many-faceted glass, gave back true and yet disturbing images of the play's cruelty, terror, and raw power.

Such disturbing reflections flickered only occasionally in the next production of *Volpone,* directed by Tyrone Guthrie for the National Theatre at the Old Vic. The play opened on 16 January 1968. Very little was omitted from the text of this version, which ran for over three hours, with the consequence that the play seemed an undifferentiated continuum of stage business, offering display space for each of the characters but never focusing their individual efforts. So diffuse was the impression the production created that Philip Hope-Wallace believed the plot line itself had been lost in the confusion of a superabundance of the usual Guthrie resources: "a world of merry mischief, double false noses, chorus larks and all the small inventive detail whereby he has so gratefully and successfully kept tedium at bay in many a dull classic in the past."[106] D. A. N. Jones was more precise in indicating the production's failures:

> Three elements are fused—savagery, laughter, and poetry: we don't get enough of any. The first is vitiated by babyishness, fuss and jostle of a distractingly outmoded kind, wrist-slapping, tantrums and boo-hooing; the magistrates are made into odd lampoons on Lord Goddard, not matching with Jonson's hard-eyed stare at more conventional judges. The author's visual jokes—the reading of Volpone's will, the duping of Sir Politick—are worked up; wetter kinds of slapstick are invented. As for the poetry, it is not often heard.[107]

Similar objections, urged even more vigorously, dominated Hilary Spurling's review. She saw in this version by Guthrie

> a clash, not simply between two periods—the Jacobean and what we may loosely call the modern—but between two opposite temperaments, styles and habits of mind. Where Jonson is grand, lucid, bilious and, even in his most casual image—"a common rogue . . . glad / Of a poor spoonful of dead wine with flies in it"—exhilaratingly precise, this production is myopic, amiable, and vague.[108]

Given such descriptions, it is not surprising that Colin Blakely as Volpone and Frank Wylie as Mosca were faulted for their failure to dominate the proceedings and to give the play a cutting edge. It is remarkable, though, that the two performers who caught the attention of reviewers and audiences alike were Graham Crowden as Sir Politic Would-be and Gabrielle Laye as his psittaceous wife. In keeping with the production's emphasis on animal imagery and costuming, Crowden *became* a parrot: "those sprightly hops, those throaty plops and rattles, that wildly bolting eye became the exquisitely natural expression of a being at once placid and alarmist, and persuaded of his own brilliance in the role of masterspy."[109] Henry Popkin speculated on the sources of the great success of two characters who are often denied the stage by directors unpersuaded by scholarly praise of "The Double Plot of *Volpone*":[110]

The English visitors to Venice turn out beautifully, perhaps because Mr. Guthrie is haunted by no memory of previous directors who have done much with them. Sir Politick Would-be is, for once, presented as he should be, as a parrot. He has the parrot's trick of inexact imitativeness, trying vainly to be like the sinister Venetians, inventing exotic plots and repeating strange news, while he remains quite oblivious of the real hard-shelled plotting in which Volpone and his dupes are enmired. Wearing a parrot's costume, he punctuates his vacuities with clucks and whistles. His wife, also dressed in parrot's colours, gives a wildly exaggerated imitation of a proper English lady's deportment . . . these two supporting roles are the particular gems of this production.[111]

It would be incorrect, though, to suggest that this National Theatre *Volpone* offered only the Would-be's as a source of pleasure. Those who asked for a full measure of Jonson's anger and violence were disappointed especially by the magnifico and his parasite. Thus D. A. N. Jones complained that Frank Wylie merely buzzed, unlike Alan Dobie in Frank Hauser's Oxford production, who "was a true flesh-fly, still and settled on the carrion, regurgitating every morsel so that he never missed a trick."[112] On the other hand, those who were content with the comic dimensions of the play could settle for less. Philip French agreed that Guthrie discovered no new depths in Jonson's play, but he argued that "What matters is the surface, and this is, for the most part, excellent and very funny." Thus he found the two conspirators satisfactory:

Frank Wylie's Scots-accented Mosca is like some repellent insect hatched in the Gorbals, a poison dwarf dismissed from the Cameronians with ignominy for stealing the regimental silver. This is a fine performance and one matched by Colin Blakely who is equally good whether scampering around in his nightshirt or sitting up in bed eying his venal visitors with the relish of Little Red Riding Hood's granny-surrogate.[113]

Such disagreements mark nearly every issue that this production raised. Some critics found the opening business, with Blakely washing his face in gold, too farcical; others saw it as a nice touch. Some objected to the beaks, feathered cloaks, and birdlike movements Guthrie employed to bring Jonson's imagery to life; others found it singularly effective.[114] Even the ending became a source of contending opinions. Jones complained that Volpone's epilogue was cut, eliminating his unrepentant farewell and leaving "the last words . . . with the contemptible judiciary who condemned him."[115] J. C. Trewin, on the other hand, found

The final court scene . . . a perfect blend of Guthrie and Jonson. The judges, especially their principal (played by Charles Kay) are steadily crumbling, and they regard the stern sentences upon the fox and his associates as something irrepressibly comic: a heartless end to a heartless play.[116]

This was a *Volpone*, then, noteworthy for demonstrating that both Would-be's had rich comic potential. But in restoring the English tourists to a central position, Guthrie sacrificed something of the deep corruption of the Venice in which their mimicry thrives. Some critics, even granting the rewarding comedy of the Would-be's, wondered if it justified its cost.

The Birmingham Repertory Company's revival of the next year, which opened 25 February 1969, was a "coherent and appreciative" treatment of *Volpone*, one which achieved an effective balance among the characters. David King, in the title role, contended with a Mosca (Keith Drinkel) who avoided the excessive Heepishness some actors have found in the parasite's character, and with a Voltore who, in Brian Oulton's reading, became a "dangerous" and "bitterly comic" man.[117] Pamela Howard's set, "a raised platform beneath which glistens the nobleman Volpone's hoard of gold," provided a light touch, involving as it did an "ingenious shutter system" that allowed gifts to be delivered mechanically as additions to an already dazzling heap of riches.[118]

In a rather detailed program note, director Michael Simpson stressed the play's "scale and variety" and the "manic passion" which gives *Volpone* its power. But its true greatness, he thought, derived from Jonson's understanding of the actors' psychology: Volpone and Mosca "function by playing roles. It is true, of course, that disguise and deception by disguise is a stock-in-trade of picaresque comedy but these two men hug their characterizations with a carnal passion." Simpson's view here parallels that of Alvin Kernan, who had described the importance of the theme of acting some years earlier in his introduction to the play.[119] For Simpson, the comedy was in part an acting contest between the two leading characters; in his view this became a major source of the play's power and savagery. It is not surprising, then, that the terrible energy of Volpone himself created its greatest effect just at that moment when he throws off all disguises in his hunger for Celia. At this point in the play, for one reviewer at least, the Birmingham *Volpone* brought the director's vision to life:

> Sometimes, even with a classic, one waits for a theatrical experience to live up to the programme notes. And I felt last night that this happened, a little late, in the rape of the merchant's wife (Chrissy Iddon), a scene that is done with the leering approval of Volpone's obscene attendants.... From this point on one begins to be gripped by the power and massiveness of it all.[120]

Shaped by a director with a comprehensive vision of Jonson's masterpiece and blessed with a Volpone who was both capable of the oratory and the passion of "Come, My Celia" and yet sufficiently controlled to give "a performance of the right size," this *Volpone* earned high marks for the Birmingham company.[121]

At the Great Lakes Shakespeare Festival in 1970, *Volpone* emerged as a mainly farcical exercise in which the actors gave free rein to their powers of comic invention. Norma Joseph played Celia as a heroine of melodrama, John Milligan's Volpone suggested Phil Silvers in the mountebank scene and Groucho Marx in the attempted rape of Celia, and all the actors found ways to make their roles funny on the level of broad, even slapstick, comedy. This was a production that led one critic to remark how well the title role might have suited W. C. Fields. Peter Bellamy described it accurately: "As directed by Lawrence Carra, [the play] is rowdy and risqué and salted with elements of bedroom farce, slapstick comedy and burlesque. Well it is, for if this treatise on human greed and a group of cretins were treated seriously, it would be nauseating instead of consistently funny."[122] Comic byplay, broadly conceived and hurried forward by a streamlined and rapidly paced plot, replaced the savagery of Jonson's original design.

The 1971 Stratford Festival production of *Volpone* lasted a full three and one-half hours. It included a lengthy and brilliantly mimed orgy which replaced the dialogue on metempsychosis as the rout's entertainment for Volpone, a grand and expansive display in the mountebank scene, and a full treatment of the Would-be's, who were played as brash and raucous Texas visitors to the Edwardian Venice in which this production was set. This was a *Volpone* that, for many reviewers, remained "frustratingly faithful to the sprawl" of Jonson's original design.[123] David William directed a cast headed by William Hutt as Volpone and Douglas Rain (who was returning to Stratford after an absence of several seasons) as his parasite.

It was also a production that created strong effects at every point of the action. The players used broad strokes to define their several identities in Jonson's moral menagerie. Volpone's bed shone in magnificent testimony to his voluptuousness, and music, dance, lighting—all the available sources of theatrical effects—made their contribution to a scene of overwhelming wealth and power turned rotten and perverse. The sheer energy of this production, its remarkable employment of invention in the service of dramatic power, brought varying reactions from the critics. One reviewer, who saw this as the best play of a weak season, called it a "cinematic spectacle"; another complained that the show was simply "too flashy for my taste"; and still another argued that in his quest for effects David William sent the play "in so many directions at once that at times it becomes a confusing collage of unconnected images."[124] Yet few reviewers denied the surpassing theatricality of these images. Irving Wardle described one of them: "the production gets the full blasphemous magnificence from the opening invocation, backing it up with responses from the mass and with a procession of monks who then strip off for an orgy in black leather and masks."[125]

Moments like this led a local critic to remark William's "seeming passion for exploiting all that is potentially ugly and grotesque in the play."[126] On balance, though, one of the production's chief merits was its ability to communicate that ugly and cruel side of Jonson's vision while retaining a comic dimensions as well. This doubleness of *Volpone* has defeated more than one company seeking a way to present it effectively on the stage. Harvey Chusid pointed to the sort of answer the Stratford company discovered: "*Volpone* does contain elements that are sombre, grim, and even cynical. But at the same time the play commends the virtues of wit and vitality, which Volpone and Mosca both embody and exploit."[127] Thus Julius Novick, who considered the production as a whole "uneven," thought nevertheless that "in most of the play's central scenes, Mr. William . . . captures the gross, gilded splendor of Jonson's Venetian world, and the harshness with which Jonson viewed the world, without forgetting that *Volpone* is a comedy."[128]

A certain emphasis on the youth and apparent innocence of Douglas Rain's Mosca runs through several of the reviews. The actor is described as "too boyish and submissive for the crafty Mosca," "a surprisingly young and mild Mosca," "too boyish and eager to please."[129] But I think this emphasis signifies only that the critics were taken in by a guise intended to deceive the other characters in the play, not the audience. Mosca's strategy, as Rain played it, is described well by Berners W. Jackson:

> This man, who looks so young and sunny, who is so acquiescent and biddable to Volpone's whim and demand, whose wit is so serviceable and whose undertakings seem so good-natured and selfless must be trusted.
> And yet, so sensitive and intelligent is Mr. Rain's performance that you begin to suspect from the beginning that Mosca is all for Mosca, that there is the smiler with the knife beneath the cloak. You see that, but you also see why the persons around Mosca can't see it.[130]

Rain's Mosca was constantly in attendance on his master, always pleased to be of service (or so he appeared); and this self-abnegating solicitude worked beautifully with the elegant assurance of William Hutt's Volpone, whose every gesture implied that such obeisance was nothing more than his proper due.

This aloofness marked Volpone's character from the very beginning. As he walked among the writhing bodies in the opening scene's orgy, clad in black lounging pajamas and puffing distractedly on a cigarette, he seemed like the perfect host at a stylish cocktail party, pleased but not surprised to note that his guests are getting on so well. His remark on all this frenetic sexuality—"very, very pretty!"—neatly established what one critic spoke of as his "jaded depravity." Another reviewer found in Hutt's Volpone "a combination of the Marquis de Sade, Mephistopheles, and Midas."[131] Though the appeal of alliteration may have had a part in suggesting just that trio, the comparison has real validity; for nothing was more terrible in this production than Volpone's icy contempt for his victims and the cruel intellectuality of his manipulation of them. Here I would differ with Irving Wardle, who thought Hutt's Volpone "a signally un-Venetian figure . . . deficient alike in sensual and poetic relish" and who accused the actor of being "single-mindedly intent on notching up light-weight comic points."[132] In the mountebank scene, Hutt did pull out all the stops. There his performance was unfailingly exuberant, offering a Scoto who suggested at one moment a manic Groucho Marx and at the next the unmistakable tones of a former prime minister of Canada. But surely Volpone regards his performance as Scoto as just another opportunity for manipulation, and just as surely Jonson provided the scene as a counterweight to the heavy and brutal satire of the magnifico's exploitation of the legacy hunters.

Hutt's performance, like the entire production, was filled nearly to bursting with a variety of theatrical effects. It is not surprising, then, that reviewers should have objected to "excesses of movement and decoration that cloud the genius of Jonson's language."[133] In my view, these very excesses served to define the world of *Volpone,* a world running over with wealth, with perversions, with ugliness, with greed. Jonson's language was not neglected in the Stratford production; it was supported by stagecraft and acting that brought the play to life in all its terrifying overabundance.

Jonson's quatercentenary in 1972 produced nothing like the outpouring of critical reassessments, historical surveys, and festival performances that flowed (and overflowed) throughout 1964, when the four hundredth anniversary of Shakespeare's birth was so widely celebrated. The only formal theatrical recognition of the occasion came from the Bristol Old Vic, in what was designated as the "Jonson Quatercentenary Production" of *Volpone.* Directed by John David, with sets by Alexander McPherson, this was an intelligent, credible treatment of the play. Lee Montague, who had appeared at the very beginning of his career in George Devine's *Bartholomew Fair* of 1950, and who had been Face to Leo McKern's Subtle in the Guthrie *Alchemist* of 1962, here gave a finely controlled performance as Volpone. Lewis Fiander, Truewit in the 1968

Oxford Playhouse *Silent Woman*, was his parasite. Of the other performances, John Bennett's Corvino was particularly good, making of the grasping merchant an opportunist whose calculations are instinctive rather than designed and whose cunning never rises to genuine intelligence. The production worked carefully to establish Jonson's animal imagery, with the suitors to Volpone descending from a high spiral staircase, swooping to their prey in grotesque mimicry of one of nature's cruelties.

Unfortunately, little attention was paid to this production by the major papers. Only the *Times* and the *Guardian* among the London dailies ran reviews; and the *Times* account, by Charles Lewsen, was singularly unhelpful. What trust can a reader have in a critic who writes that "messy direction of the mountebank scene places him [Lee Montague as Volpone] firmly in Petticoat Lane rather than the Renaissance love affair with Greek myth"?[134] Yet nearly all the reviews concur in praising the attention to detail that marked every aspect of this production, and most of them suggest, quite correctly, that Montague, Fiander, and Bennett carried the main burden of acting.

One significantly effective feature of the Bristol *Volpone* emerged from the opposition between Mosca and Volpone. Earlier actors of the magnifico, notably Leo McKern, had been criticized for not conveying an accurate sense of his rank. Lee Montague was a nobleman without question, a man of fine taste whose taste reflected a considerable, even as awe-inspiring, intellect. Lewis Fiander, on the other hand—continually in motion and insistently eager to prove his worth—was the tough boy from the streets who lived by guile and whose contempt for Volpone's refinement was only thinly concealed. Out of the struggle between the fox and his parasite, which was apparent from early on in the dramatic action, John David created a basis of realism that made the play, even as it drew on the most grotesque elements of Jonson's invention, horribly convincing. Thus the rout, with Castrone clutching compulsively at his pants front and with all three figures in bright circus makeup, was no mere clown group but a credible, if nightmarish, reflection of Volpone's deviation from nature.

The Alchemist

The Alchemist did not keep the stage after Garrick's last performance as Drugger on 11 April 1776. Noyes records a few performances in the following decades of *The Tobacconist*, a farce based on Jonson's play and designed to capitalize on the popularity of Drugger as a dramatic character. But throughout the nineteenth century, Jonson's great satire on human gullibility found no place in the theatre. Finally, in 1899, it was seen again. A beneficiary of William Poel's activity in restoring older English drama to the stage, it was produced by the Elizabethan Stage Society in Apothecaries' Hall. In 1902 this production was revived at the Imperial Theatre in London in July and the next month at the New Theatre, Cambridge. Cambridge was the scene of the next revival as well when the play was staged there in 1914 by the Marlowe Society. Two years later, in April 1916, the play received its first professional presentation in the twentieth century when the Birmingham Repertory Company, founded only three years before by Barry Jackson, created a production of *The Alchemist* with Felix Aylmer as Subtle. The Phoenix Society, which did well by Jonson throughout its existence, brought the play to the Regent Theatre, King's Cross, in 1923; the director was Allan Wade.

The first American production of this century took place in New York in 1931, when the Fortune Players presented *The Alchemist* at the New School. Offered for only a night or two, this was not, I believe, a professional staging of the play. One year later, at the Malvern Festival, in a season designed to illustrate four hundred years of English theatre, Jonson's comedy shared the stage with such diverse offerings as *The Play of the Weather, Ralph Roister Doister, Oroonoko, Tom Thumb, London Assurance,* and *Too True to be Good.* Ronald Adam presented *The Alchemist* in 1935 first for two weeks beginning 11 March at the Embassy Theatre and then, presumably encouraged by the response, again at the Princes Theatre from 1 April to 6 April. In 1945, the York Citizens' Theatre brought *The Alchemist* to London for a short run at the King's Theatre, Hammersmith. That same year, Tyrone Guthrie directed a production of the play by the Old Vic Company at the Liverpool Playhouse; designed by Tanya Moiseiwitsch, it would later be viewed as a sort of first study for his 1962 Old Vic production. This was the first *Alchemist* presented by the Old Vic, and it was followed in 1947, when John Burrell directed a production by that company at the New Theatre.

Since 1947, *The Alchemist* has been revived fairly often. In 1952 it was staged by the Bristol Old Vic. In 1957, the Birmingham Repertory Theatre presented the play with a promising young actor named Albert Finney in the role of Face. In the next decade Jonson's play received, finally, the sort of attention that a classic of English dramatic literature might reasonably claim. It was presented first, in 1960, by the San Francisco Actor's Workshop, and in the next year at the Oregon Shakespearean Festival. The Guthrie production of 1962 was a typical display of that director's at times outrageously inventive imagination: lively, topical, bursting with energy, it brought Jonson into the modern world with great enthusiasm and panache. The following year another modernized version appeared, this time at the Cleveland Play House. In New York, Stephen Porter directed *The Alchemist* at the Gate Theatre in 1964, and two years later Jules Irving directed it with the company at Lincoln Center. Between these two productions, in 1965, the Meadow Players at the Oxford Playhouse presented an *Alchemist,* directed by Frank Hauser, that earned praise for its fidelity to Jonson and for its success in bringing the comedy to life. George Luscombe directed the play in Toronto in 1968.

Three productions of *The Alchemist* came to the stage in 1969. The first of these was an updated version presented by the Minnesota Theatre Company in a season of plays in St. Paul. The Stratford Festival of Canada included *The Alchemist* in their 1969 repertory season; Jean Gascon directed a production that had both pace and style. The Nottingham Playhouse company achieved such success with the play in the fall of 1969 that they brought their production to the Old Vic the following February. Two other productions appeared in 1970. The first of these was staged at the Arts Theatre, Cambridge, by the Cambridge Theatre Company. The second was the Chichester Festival Production, directed by Peter Dews. In 1972, as a sort of quatercentenary offering, the Young Vic presented a rock version of Jonson's play both in London and on tour in North America.

Poel's version of *The Alchemist* earned the sort of praise one associates with well-intentioned but necessarily doomed efforts. The *Times* critic described the quaint scene:

> On a small stage before a background of tapestry the actors performed their parts, while a prompter, seated unblushingly before the footlights, gave them their lines on the rare occasions when they needed them, and knocked loudly upon the floor with a stick on the frequent occasions when some one was supposed to be knocking at the door.[1]

The reviewer in *The Athenaeum* added a similarly condescending note to his report of the performance, observing that "It is pleasant to say that the elocution was, as a rule, good—better, even, than is often heard on the regular stage."[2]

But however interesting the stage picture in the Apothecaries' Hall and however successful the Elizabethan Stage Society players in communicating Jonson's complex language, the fact remained—so the reviewers argued—that Poel was dealing here with highly recalcitrant material. Whatever his interest as a satirist or as a painter of the Jacobean scene, Jonson was no playwright and *The Alchemist* was not a great play. "A dramatist, as it were, by accident," Jonson "had no love for the theatre. His real interest was in character"; and while such an interest was appropriate in the satirist, it could only damage the efforts of the writer for the stage:

> Indeed, his dramas are often marred by the intrusion of satiric portraiture which has little or no connection with the central plot. This makes him difficult to act, and causes many of his scenes to miss their full effect on the stage.[3]

Again, the *Athenaeum* critic shared the opinion of his colleague on the *Times*. He was willing to accept the judgment of earlier writers who found *The Alchemist* praiseworthy—to agree with Steele, for example, who described the play in *The Tatler* as "an example of Ben's extensive genius and penetration into the passions and follies of mankind." But granting this much, he was yet unprepared to acknowledge that the comedy had any real merit as a theatre piece:

> While admirable as a satire and unsurpassed as a picture of manners, it is . . . deficient in almost everything that makes a great play. It has scarcely a single character that is not contemptible; it paints a world of rogues and fools without a redeeming trait; not one ray of honesty steals into its plot, not one touch of love or affection redeems or elevates piece or characters, not one line of poetry such as lights up the work of Ben's rival Dekker is to be found.[4]

One can see in these objections a demand for the sort of theatrical pleasure that Jonson's plays could never provide. He was not the playwright for those who wanted a drama of delight and optimistic illusion. But the twentieth century was to be more receptive to his harsh satire; and there is perhaps a reluctant hint of his coming theatrical good fortune in the admission, in 1899, that "his enormous cleverness is undeniable, and it is in some ways a pity that his work is not more often played, for when he is acted many of his scenes become clear and interesting which in reading are somewhat wearisome."[5]

There are few newspaper accounts of the 1916 Birmingham Repertory production of *The Alchemist,* but the promptbook for that production remains in the company's archives and provides a fairly clear indication of the main lines the young group followed in bringing Jonson's great play about cheats and cheating to the stage.[6] Two sheets of paper are stuck into the book, headed "*The Alchemist,* Property Plot." The list of properties includes such necessary items as "Knocker & Bell off L throughout Play" and others that seem more distinctive—the "Orange table & stool on Platform at Back" and the "Crocodile on upper stage." On the table, which must have held an amazing jumble of stuff, property items range from "5 glass-stoppered bottles with K_2MnDg—$K_2Fc(CN)_6$—KI—$CaSO_4$—$AgNO_3$" to a "Large pepper castor with sand," to such implements of Subtle's imposture as compasses, pencils, pestle and mortar, and various phials, containers, and fire-making equipment. Surly has a snuff box, Subtle a red petticoat, and Dapper's gingerbread is set out on a plate with a dead mouse.

Cuts on the text for this production are not extensive, and though the pattern of cuts is clear enough—bawdy language, contemporary allusions, and alchemical jargon all suffer some excisions—what remains is faithful to Jonson's design and even, with modifications, to the dominant tone of his play. The opening quarrel is still a violent affair, though Subtle's first line ("I spit at thee") is rather milder than the action Jonson assigns him, and he offers no invitation to Face to lick figs. Some obsolete puns are eliminated ("a new crewel garter / To his most worsted worship") along with references to the "chiaus," "Bedlam," and some of the particulars of religious controversy scattered throughout the play. Mammon's role is trimmed a bit, losing fifty lines or so from his first scene and, inevitably perhaps, the part in the Birmingham version falls just short of the farthest reaches of imagination with which Jonson endows his character. Thus, while he retains the vision of a room lavishly adorned with erotic pictures, he does not imagine himself strolling through, "Naked between my *succubae*," reflected in the subtle angles of specially cut mirrors; and his feast, though still incredibly rich, does not include that ultimate delicacy,

> ... the swelling unctuous paps
> Of a fat pregnant sow, newly cut off,
> Dressed with an exquisite and poignant sauce.

In a number of instances, the Birmingham company sacrificed Jonson's bawdy language to some principle of decorum. The instructions to Dol are lost altogether. In one case, when Lovewit supposes that Face "has got / Some bawdy pictures to call all this ging," the line was first cut and then restored; but the examples he lists—"the Friar and the Nun," and the others—are carefully eliminated. Yet for all these cautious modifications of Jonson's text, the promptbook of the Birmingham production suggests a treatment of his play that was faithful in the main and consistently spirited and lively.

A review in the *Birmingham Post* helps to fill in further details about this version of *The Alchemist*. Not only is it a useful account of what the Birmingham Repertory players did with the play, it delineates some of the main issues that recur in discussions of *The Alchemist* over the next fifty years or more. After describing the play as Jonson's "least pedantic, ... most plausible, ... and most actable comedy," the critic identifies the source of its superiority: "the persons appear less dehumanized than the usual 'humours' of Jonson, because the vice of avarice is the most persistent and enduring of human passions. Every age has its El Dorado, its south Sea Bubble, or its Humbert Millions; the get-rich-quick are always with us."[7]

The handling of Jonson's characters received some considered attention. Felix Aylmer apparently garbled Subtle's continual flow of pretension so badly that the audience concurred with Ananias in supposing "that it was all heathenish Greek." As Mammon, W. J. Rea spoke "his perverted poetry" with admirable intensity; but at times his attempts to persuade Surly "lapsed into a touch of the blarney." Stuart Vinden's Drugger "surpassed all expectation," and it was his performance that received the highest praise. The reviewer found it remarkable that this Drugger had nothing dark about him. Instead,

> Mr. Vinden gave him a clear and childish pink and white, but he drained his face of all intelligence until it had no more expression than a sow's head in a butcher's window. Now a spark of low cunning flickered about his eyes; now some petty dissatisfaction drooped the corners of his mouth; now and then the shades of some feeble feeling drifted over his face, darkened its vacancy, and drifted away.

Such enthusiasm for the actor of this minor role seems quite inexplicable until one recalls the observation of Noyes that "the history of *The Alchemist* was virtually the history of the rôle of Abel Drugger, about whom, I believe, more was written up to Garrick's death than about any other comic character except Falstaff."[8] Vinden's performance went some way toward answering the question reviewers never seem to tire of: What did Garrick see in this part?

Yet another question emerged from this early review: How far was Jonson's comedy to be treated as a farce; or, on the other hand, how insistently must the harshness of the play's satire be communicated to the audience? A final question, and one that was to become less serious as the century wore on, appears in the reviewer's overall assessment of this production: "*The Alchemist* still needs compression and a greater rapidity of performance, and the deletion of some coarse expressions which are reiterated without force." Yet Jonson's unfettered language, so great a problem in the nineteenth century, continued to raise difficulties—even into the 1960s—for the squeamish and for those who appointed themselves guardians of public morality; and in some areas he is still regarded as one of those "frank Elizabethans" who must be understood though not necessarily excused. Given the fact that such attitudes exist today, it is not surprising that in 1916, in Birmingham, a reviewer should have raised a mild objection to a production which included a good deal of Jonson's bawdiness. In that same year, the Bishop of Birmingham, Russell Wakefield, used the occasion of the tercentenary of Shakespeare's death to suggest to his flock that the separation between Church and Stage had been an unfortunate thing. There was nothing in Shakespeare at all blameworthy except for his picture of Joan of Arc (that, however aberrant an instance, was a stain on English literature). Yet he assured his audience that no one would be harmed by reading Shakespeare's plays.[9] Perhaps the surprising thing is that Jonson got a hearing in Birmingham at all.

The Phoenix Society brought *The Alchemist* to London once again in 1923. Baliol Holloway as Subtle earned excellent reviews, as did most of the other players. Stanley Lathbury, for instance, "with his slow, grating voice, sour expression and admirable economy of movement and gesture, was an Ananias it would be impossible to better."[10] Martin Armstrong welcomed "the greatest farce of the greatest English farce-writer" and praised it as a marvel of construction:

> *The Alchemist* is a superb entertainment whose plot displays an astonishing and uproarious invention. Crisis after crisis—each dove-tailed into its neighbour with consummate ingenuity—develops, matures, and is successfully evaded until, at the summit of elaboration, the whole edifice of quackery collapses in a glorious *debacle*.[11]

But Armstrong made clear as well the limitations of his description and of his praise of Jonson. The play is merely a farce and not a true comedy, which has as its aim "to criticize society or the individual, or to illuminate a group of personalities by the light of their mutual interaction." For Armstrong, Ben Jonson's plays cannot take on such serious aims, largely because his characters lack complexity, because they remain one-dimensional:

> Although they are vividly differentiated, the individuality of each is superficial. It is that of a brightly coloured puppet rather than of a fully realized human character. Their life resides not in themselves but in the actions, and it is action and "situation" which . . . are Jonson's chief concern.

Not everyone agreed with Armstrong in a judgment that seemed to ignore the powerful didactic and satiric impulse that motivated Jonson's work. But whether he was viewed as a master of farce or as a brilliant practitioner of satiric realism, it was clear that the playwright who had been altogether neglected by the nineteenth-century theatre was the creator of a kind of "comedy which is . . . beginning to come into its own again."[12] There could be no dispute about the gain this brought to the modern stage:

> Ben Jonson's laughter is bracing, natural thunder; with little thought behind it; though intellect guides it is directed at the midriff first, only afterwards at the head, but it never lacks the majesty of courage or a flowing fecundity of invention.

The reviewer for the *Sunday Times* found that "the jovial, robust, honest humour at the back of *The Alchemist* suits exactly the sceptical spirit of the age." Yet his praise of the Phoenix Society's production underscored the conflict between the play's critical focus and its demand for a rapid, farcical performance style. In this case, he thought that the players' excess speed "was an error on the right side"; and he complimented "the whole of the company" for playing "their parts vigorously and with the right note of boisterous rudeness."[13]

The fourth Malvern Festival, held from 1 August to 20 August 1932, presented *The Alchemist* in a context of wealth and genteel leisure. At this distance one gets the impression of a dedicated, idealistic enterprise set in motion by people who had sufficient resources to realize at least some of their dreams. Malvern, superbly situated in the Cotswolds and marvelously prepared to cater for Festival visitors, provided a sort of intellectual and social haven for followers of the theatre. In conjunction with the plays, a course of lectures was given at "The Malvern Picture House" from Monday to Saturday each week of the Festival. On Tuesdays F. S. Boas spoke on "Ben Jonson and *The Alchemist*" and Allardyce Nicoll delivered an account of "Jonson's Contemporaries in Drama in the Early Seventeenth Century."

Essentially, the company for the festival was the Birmingham Repertory players. For this production, H. K. Ayliff was listed as producer and Barry Jackson as director. The cast included some of the actors from the 1916 production taking their old roles. New actors of note included Cedric Hardwicke, who delivered the prologue and took the role of Drugger; Ralph Richardson, beginning an association with Jonson that would extend over more than twenty-five years, who played Face; and Eileen Beldon, who played Dol Common.

W. A. Darlington was especially enthusiastic about the playing of Cedric Hardwicke, who demonstrated "how much a really fine actor can do with a tiny part." It was not just that the player had discovered new business that defined the character in a striking way:

> Rather it was that he had got himself a new stage personality of which the dominant expression was a pervasive credulous smile, but which every movement and gesture—the questing forefinger, the recurrent stammer—was made to interpret.[14]

The trio of conspirators—Beldon, Richardson, and W. J. Rea as Subtle—were cited for their ability to "infuse into their acting an enormous gusto";

Eileen Beldon's Dol was particularly successful in communicating "a very engaging vitality."[15] Vernon Kelso's Mammon was handicapped by cuts on the text which deprived him of his more outrageous excesses, but the actor nevertheless managed to present a figure who made a solid contribution to the Festival company's effort. That effort, in the eyes of one critic, created a thoroughly modern Jonson, a playwright whose "neo-classical realistic satire" displayed "real-life characters, types . . . but not puppets" and whose theory of humours, in an age which gave credence to physiological explanations of human character and behavior, was "the crown of topicality."[16]

Three years after the Malvern production, Ronald Adam offered London theatregoers a chance to see *The Alchemist* in a version that, according to one reviewer, "deserves to be known in theatrical history as the Swiss Cottage production."[17] Adam, a theatrical manager of remarkable independence, had presented in the same season a play by Dostoievsky and "Webster's caviare *Duchess of Malfi*," fare that even a National Theatre would find hard to match.[18] First at the Embassy Theatre and then at the Princes, the play featured Hugh Miller as Subtle and Iris Hoey as Dol. The shift to the Princes involved some cast changes in other roles. At the Embassy, Barrie O'Neill played Face; Leslie French, Dapper; Richard Goolden, Drugger; and Eric Eliott, Surly. For the brief second run these parts were taken by Austin Trevor, John Deverell, Wallace Evennett, and Bruce Belfrage.

Olga Katzin directed in a fashion that raised once again the problem of style for *The Alchemist* and focused it on the conflicting claims of rapid pace and emphasis on plot over against the demands of Jonson's poetry. *The Stage* reviewer praised all of the actors with evenhanded generosity in an account that highlighted the production's energy and drive. "Vigour," "gusto," "vehemence," characterized the play's strong points.[19] Another critic, who described the production as Jonson "played in farce-time," found it "as lively as any contemporary stage piece."[20] But most critics were less happy with the result. Cecil Chisholm remarked that the director "screwed the pace up to an almost farcical limit and missed the poetry."[21] Of a production described as "more spirited than superb," other reviewers complained that "nobody could guess that the characters are supposed to speak blank verse," that Hugh Miller "treats the rich Elizabethan phrases like slipshod modern dialogue," and that throughout the evening "we miss the *nuances* of the language."[22] Ivor Brown attributed the fault to Jonson's rather obscure vocabulary, which faces the director with a choice of approaches resolved here in a rapid-fire treatment that "stressed vigour at the risk of diction." Such an irreconcilable choice ought not, in his view, to have been necessary: "It was right to whip the players to a gallop, but surely more of the poetry might have emerged than actually met the ear."[23]

Fortunately, the one actor generally exempt from the charge of disregarding Jonson's verse was Bruce Winston, who as Sir Epicure Mammon had the role which depends most heavily on magnificent, image-laden poetry. Of all the performances, "his gorgeous Sir Epicure Mammon" was the one which "got nearest to Jonson's bizarre characterization and his voluptuous verse."[24] An actor who possessed "from nature, a broad canvas on which to display Jonsonian bravura," he alone "observed the metre and made verbal riches swing in rhythm."[25] In this, Winston was being true to the greatness of a "comedy, which, after all, has survived not because its invention is amusing but because its fun is enshrined in language that has a quality and richness that belong to literature."[26]

One of the achievements of this production was that it created an effective balance between fidelity to Jonson's conception and a demonstration of the contemporary applicability of his themes. While the actors offered "a fine, stirring picture of Jacobean times," they contrived to make it clear that the play's "humorous, satirical exposure of the everlasting credulity of the human race is as topical in these times as it was in 1610."[27] No lover of Jonson is likely to quarrel with such an assertion, though the reviewer's suggested analogues for alchemy—"crystal gazing, the bucket shop, and the beauty parlor"—are less persuasive of Jonson's abiding significance. Apart from Winston, few of the actors received special notice, though Alan Trotter was "as kickable a Puritan as ever made a Sabbath day hideous," and John Deverell, as Dapper, in the Princes staging of the play, provided "richly humorous proof that a man can live without brains."[28] Wallace Evennett, like Richard Goolden in the first production, made a more than passable Drugger; but he did not solve "that eternal question, what it was that Garrick did to this part to make it one of his most famous comic creations."[29]

The next two productions of *The Alchemist,* coming at the end of World War II, left few records behind them and almost no contemporary accounts. The first of these was the Guthrie production at the Liverpool Playhouse in 1945. The second was the production presented by the York Citizens' Theatre at the King's Theatre, Hammersmith, in 1945.

At Liverpool, the Old Vic Company created an *Alchemist* in modern dress with Dol got up "in cami-knickers and tin hat; Subtle, a cross between an over-fed Gandhi and the original Old Moore; and Face, a simpering something that should never have sported the Royal Artillery colours." One local reviewer thought that this "full-blooded farce . . . with an obbligato of air raid sirens" required no defense for its contemporary setting, but he thought too that "it is often embarrassing."[30] Peter Glenville as Face and Noel Willman as Subtle earned the praise of another critic for using "election and a mean" as Jonson might have urged and thus investing "with some credibility a subject that would otherwise be fantastic in its modern setting."[31] This disagreement over Guthrie's updating of the play would be joined more vigorously in 1962. The Liverpool version, in 1945, received little attention; it was not a milestone in the stage history of *The Alchemist*.

There is no doubt, however, about the appropriate label for the next production of Jonson's play: it was a major theatrical event. On January 4, 1947, the Old Vic company at the New Theatre introduced London audiences to a treatment of *The Alchemist* that went a long way toward reclaiming the play's position as a classic of the English stage. John Burrell directed and Morris Kestelman designed the set for a production successful enough to confirm Ivor Brown's opinion "that we are living in an epoch of really great acting."[32] Ralph Richardson, who had been knighted in the New Year's honors list, again took the part of Face, fifteen years after his performance at Malvern. George Relph played Subtle; Nicholas Hannen, Sir Epicure Mammon; Joyce Redman, Dol Common; Alec Guinness, Drugger; and Margaret Leighton, Dame Pliant.

While individual performers (especially Hannen and Guinness) gained considerable praise for their efforts, most of the reviews suggest that this was an ensemble production from start to finish and one that created its best moments from the resources of intelligent actors working under careful direction toward a common end. Anthony Goodman, who had found that "even in performance, at Malvern and other places where we learn to endure our satirical masterpieces, *The Alchemist* was never . . . much fun," saw this production as a "miracle."[33] Pace was a major factor; the company moved rapidly but without blurring through a text that had been carefully cut. Ivor Brown thought that John Burrell and his players had found the ideal answer to the problem of handling the "polysyllables, Latinities, and lickerish rhetoric" of Jonson's profuse linguistic inventiveness. Given the choice to cut or gabble, "the 'Old Vic' team cut a little and gabble much and the method is wholly effective."[34] Another reviewer thought it was acted at "dangerous speed"; "It trembles, and rightly so, on the very edge of burlesque, but not once does it topple."[35] Peter Fleming saw it as "a kind of harlequinade, swift but full of lasting verities, seamy and sardonic, but essentially gay."[36] One senses, in the great majority of the reviews, the impression that this *Alchemist* was, as one critic put it, "an affair of team-work, in the highest sense of that lack-lustre term."[37] Nicholas Hannen commanded special notice for the way he submerged his familiar stage manner in finding his way to the realization of Jonson's grandiloquent sensualist: "Mr. Hannen, that master of poise and circumspection, springs a great surprise with his Sir Epicure Mammon; here is grand, rich, full-blooded humour disporting itself against a tapestry of glorious speech."[38] Here at last one of Jonson's comedies, "universally approved and allowed just those virtues that excite the least pleasure," was given the sort of performance it deserved. George Relph as Subtle, and even the gulls who come to him to be duped,

> are incredibly eloquent, expressing the odiousness of human nature not only in the slang and catchwords of their time, but in language of wonderful richness and variety. Such eloquence can never have its full effect in the reading; to be really impressive it must combine with action, hurrying the listener past all obscurities and lost allusions, and serve as the expression of a sardonic vision which is clearly represented before his eyes. . . . Combined with action . . . the eloquent dialogue seems almost as much on the mark as if the charlatans and gulls anathematized here were of our own day. So produced, so played, the comedy may be said to keep much of its fallen topicality about it.[39]

In a production that justified *The Alchemist* and achieved, without special pleading of any sort, its claim to continuing theatrical significance, the Abel Drugger of Alec Guinness allowed one to see why Garrick placed such high value on the character of this little shopkeeper. For many reviewers, this part confirmed and extended the earlier success Guinness had achieved playing the fool in *King Lear*. Adding Drugger "to his ever-growing list of perfect clowns," he drew spontaneous applause from the audience with his line, "did you never see me play the Fool?"[40] Like all great performances this one was elusive. More than one reviewer went back to Hazlitt's comparison of Garrick and Kean in the same role, searching for an apt description of the means Guinness had discovered to make his performance, like theirs, a lapidary achievement in theatrical history. Alan Dent, while supposing that part of the actor's success came simply from doing his homework, finally could only admire the effect:

> Drugger is a wan wisp, a smiling wraith. I suspect Mr. Guinness read Hazlitt's account of Kean in the part. But it is one thing to read and quite another to communicate. Here, anyhow, for all to see and wonder at, is a reincarnation of the "exquisite piece of ludicrous naivety," and we may echo Hazlitt—as Mr. Guinness echoes Kean and Garrick—and say that "the mixture of simplicity and cunning in the character could not be given with a more whimsical effect."[41]

Lawrence Gowing found it "hard to believe that the Creature has ever been played better than here, in this moving combination of the eagerness, innocence and artfulness of a marmoset."[42] Ivor Brown, apparently responding to quite other aspects of Guinness' portrayal, saw his Drugger as "a limping nincompoop suggesting, with the text's authority, a wondrous blend of asininity and halitosis," while Peter Fleming saw a "curious, elfin importance" in the tobacconist, and Philip Hope-Wallace described his "strangely pathetic pasty absurdity."[43] Guinness seems, in fact, to have built a rather complex and yet perfectly consistent dramatic figure out of Jonson's sketch of the aspiring tobacco seller. Without glossing over the meanness of Drugger's ambitions, he contrived to show how unfit the poor man is for even the least challenging social climbing; in the process, he achieved "a glorious mingling of asininity and pathos."[44] James Agate, in a perceptive account of this production, catches something of the complexity of response that Drugger aroused: "Mr. Guinness endows the tobacco seller, for at least one spectator, with the pathos and pity of some tiny, captive monkey gamboling heartbreakingly to the full length of its chain. Or you may take the other view and, ready to tumble off your seat at clowning of such drollery, wonder what your neighbour finds to snivel at."[45] Touching yet personally unattractive, naive and helpless but somehow unworthy of the audience's concern, Alec Guinness as Drugger answered the old question about Garrick's preference for the role, and in the process established himself as one of the eminent actors of the postwar years.

While Guinness earned extraordinary attention, nearly all of the actors in this revival of *The Alchemist* were praised for the way in which they realized Jonson's characters: Ananias—"Mr. Copley's dim-witted fanatic takes us to the early seventeenth century and keeps us there"; Mammon—"Nicholas Hannen . . . is like some monstrous figure from a Rowlandson cartoon"; and Subtle—George Relph "contrives to look like a common multiple of all the classical dons that have ever been."[46] Some critics had reservations about Sir Ralph Richardson's performance as Face. The new knight, thought Caryl Brahms, "though energetic in his pursuit of evil, has been defeated by nature—his shining countenance is inalienably honest."[47] This same criticism would be directed against his handling of Volpone five years later. While Peter Fleming suggested that Richardson's Face was "too sure of himself" and too "insensible of the risks of exposure which he courted so readily," Hubert Griffith, one of the few reviewers to be unimpressed by this revival of Jonson's play (he continued to think of it, he said, as a dull museum piece) argued more simply and more damningly that Sir Ralph "played his part exactly as he has played all other parts recently."[48] Finally, Joyce Redman as Dol received the greatest share of negative comment. Most of the critics agreed that her style of playing was too near burlesque and thus conflicted with the restrained exuberance of the other actors. James Agate wrote that

"Miss Redman is, alas, too small for the rampageous part of the bawd" and suggested that she should, like Garrick, "decline roles beyond her inches."[49] These objections aside, one is justified in concluding from the reviews that this was an admirable revival indeed. It set a standard for future productions of *The Alchemist* and helped to assure a sometimes doubtful public that rare Ben Jonson, in a pun newspaper critics never seem to tire of, could please when he was well done.

A final note on this production seems worth recording. Almost all the critics found Morris Kestelman's set serviceable and attractive. They did not agree about the validity of John Burrell's decision to set the play in the eighteenth century. Ivor Brown thought that the play's popularity in that period offered some excuse "for what might seem an affectation," but he was not much taken by Burrell's program note explaining the switch in period.[50] Alan Dent, who saw in Mammon "a fat foretaste of the eighteenth century," thought that this character might have been the inspiration for transferring "the whole style of the revival to the eighteenth-century mood." He too was unpersuaded by the arguments put forward in the program, but forgot his objections in his pleasure at the outcome: "it has turned out a triumph. So who cares?"[51]

Although far from being a triumph, the New York City Center's production of *The Alchemist* in May of 1948 fared considerably better than the group's effort with *Volpone* earlier in the same year. This "jazzed-up version" of Jonson's satiric comedy moved one reviewer to describe it as "an Elizabethan *Hellzapoppin*," and no wonder, since Morton da Costa, who directed, announced that he saw the play as "an Elizabethan *Room Service*."[52] Thus the City Center troupe continued in the pattern established by their treatment of *Volpone*. The edge of Jonson's satire was dulled; incisive meaning was sacrificed to movement and slapstick. "The emphasis," wrote John S. Wilson, "is on action, action at almost any cost, whether it is Mr. Ferrer's frequent scamperings upstairs with his stockings drooping over his ankles, his almost equally frequent entrance through a fireplace or, when those two have been worn to a nub, Ezra Stone sliding downstairs on his stomach." Given such treatment, it was no surprise that "the old comedy emerges as an overextended vaudeville skit, long on energy . . . but short of material."[53]

A remarkable number of reviewers commented on the play's bawdiness. Robert Coleman offered this slangy admonition: "this reviewer recommends Jonson to the sophisticates. His plays should be seen by adults who know the facts of life. Shakespeare is the guy for the juves to read and see in high school."[54] Another critic reported that "a first night audience that wouldn't be seen at a burlesque show guffawed and gaped—at lines that would even bring a faint flush to the cheek of a 'Mr. Roberts' crewmate."[55] But although comments of this sort are frequent, one may suspect the presence of hyperbole in the *Variety* reviewer's suggestion that the play "may be one of the town's scandals, if the Comstocks ever get around to it," especially since he supports this possibility by noting that "the dialog is sprinkled with juicy Elizabethan epithets and frank physiological allusions."[56]

An effective feature of this production appeared in the balance between Subtle and Face. John Wilson remarked that "George Couloris makes the alchemist a turbulent and moody phony, a properly glum foil for Ferrer's quick-witted plotter."[57] Other critics also noted their complementary handling of the main characters, and it seems clear that the two sharpers dominated the play's action. Mammon, as presented by Ezra Stone, generated little energy. Richard Watts, for example, even found the character "too mild a figure for first-rate mockery."[58] This was, then, a production of *The Alchemist* that emphasized theatrical fun and business; it made no very serious or sustained effort to explore the full implications of Jonson's satire.

In 1952 the Bristol Old Vic revived *The Alchemist* for three weeks beginning 2 December. This was a lighter offering than Jonson purists might have liked. One reviewer called it, with admirable directness, "a legitimate and lusty adaptation of Jonson to the needs of the moment, full of comic invention and with each rise and fall of the curtain accompanied by horseplay."[59] "A virile, high-spirited romp, performed with great energy," this production moved at a great pace, unconcerned with the niceties of Jonson's verbal skill and even, at times, with the grounds of his plot: "the company's zeal to stroke forward the action" moves us past "the contention between the two sinners—with all its complicated language—with hardly a chance to draw our breath or realize what it is all about." Nevertheless, the play managed to create "a rapid series of swiftly established, vivid impressions—the dancing, black wisp with a chuckle like crackling paper that James Cairncross makes of Subtle; the Cockney cunning of John Neville's Face; Robert Cartland, puffed out with plum-coloured velvet and cutting an absurd caper as Sir Epicure Mammon."[60] It was, as John Coe exclaimed, "*The Alchemist*—without tears!";[61] and though this heavily cut version of Jonson's play received little critical approbation, it apparently promised well for the Bristol Christmas pantomime, *Christmas in King Street*, which opened Christmas Eve, the night after *The Alchemist* finished its run.

The next revival of *The Alchemist* took shape at the hands of the Birmingham Repertory Company. Like the Bristol production five years earlier, this was not an effort to stand comparison with the 1947 Old Vic *Alchemist*, which "went straight to the record-books."[62] In a production that "bristles with . . . ingenuities," some of them on the order of "an actor with smoke pouring from a funnel on the top of his head," there were few performances that reached the top level.⁶³ Albert Finney as Face and Kenneth MacKintosh as Subtle were "right without being overwhelmingly so"; and Arthur Pentelow as Mammon "savours the lines even though he could be more expansive." On the whole this seems to have been a solid, competent production but not a particularly brilliant or exciting one. Directed by Bernard Hepton, with settings by Paul Shelving, it was presented in "18th century Decorative" style, though again this shift in period seems to have had no great influence on the impact it achieved.⁶⁴

The Oregon Shakespearean Festival at Ashland included *The Alchemist* in its 1961 season, and the play became the first sellout in the Festival's history. All the available tickets were sold before its first performance. Edward S. Brubaker directed a production that was "performed with great spirit and sound recognition of [the play's] satiric points."⁶⁵ According to James Carter, the production exemplified repertory work at its best. With no star performers, the company was able to achieve a balance among the play's roles and thus put maximum emphasis on the complex and beautifully articulated structure of the playwright's artistic design.⁶⁶ Robert Horn cited one piece of acting that deserved special mention, the performance of Hugh Evans as Drugger:

> Whether or not this was Jonson's comment on what we have come to call Business, Abel's gentle trusting compound of inability and devoted affability, his personification of irresolute, aproned, lack-luster insubstantiality could stand as the creative artist's estimate of the money-makers. Standing in the text as little more than a messenger, he emerged as a jewel of characterization, and for once one might see why Garrick enjoyed such success in the role.⁶⁷

It is not clear, despite Carter's praise of the ensemble, that the rest of the company measured up to this achievement. One reviewer emphasized the farcical elements of this production; the actors "took pratfalls, walked into walls, did double takes, leered at bosoms, made off-color puns, and gestured and postured with roguish abandon."⁶⁸

The perennial tension in *The Alchemist* between its satiric focus and its opportunities for high-speed farce reappeared once again in the Ashland version. That tension was managed to good effect in a production that seems to have been a great success, yet Ben Jonson could attain only a limited sort of triumph in a festival dedicated to his great competitor:

> Jonson's deploying of his arch rascals and his nest of "filthy birds" was so unrelieved and his determination to arouse and shame the world into awareness of its venality so

pronounced, that no better reminder of Shakespeare's warm, humane and reassuring acceptance of life could have been offered.[69]

The familiar contrast—fierce Jonson, gentle Shakespeare—will always be with us. It seems, though, that in the 1960s it was repeated occasionally with the suggestion that while we might find greater comfort in Shakespeare's comic worlds, Jonson's gave a more nearly accurate reflection of our own experience.

With Tyrone Guthrie's 1962 updating of *The Alchemist* the question of period was very much at issue. This was an *Alchemist* in modern dress and modern language. Face appeared as a British army officer, Dol lounged around in baby-doll pajamas, and Kastril and Dame Pliant came into Lovewit's house wearing the regalia of motorcyclists. The promptbook documents extensive changes which replace obsolete allusions with new ones and give a texture of modernity to the entire proceedings.[70] The plague which drives Lovewit to the suburbs becomes a flu epidemic which has sent him hurrying off to the French Riviera. Some other examples, chosen at random, may provide a sense of the effects Guthrie wished to create:

> Instead of the reference to the "chiaus," which is often cut or garbled in production, we have "The Turk was here. At the Palladium, the Terrible Turk," an allusion to a professional wrestler.
>
> Subtle is not described as a "proud stag" with a "broad velvet head" but as a "Damn old egghead" in a "cap and gown."
>
> "Crackers in a puppet play" becomes "squibs on the 5th of November."
>
> "dead Holland, living Isaac," becomes "dead Einstein and living Haldane"
>
> When Ananias declares himself "A faithful brother," Surly asks, "What's that? A Buchmanite? Jehovah's Witness? Mormon?"
>
> Surly in disguise is no "adalantado" but "A Peruvian / And filthy rich," and he is mockingly referred to not as his "dagoship" but as "The Inca of Perusalem." At other times he is a "South American Joe" and "Speedy Gonzales"; and no doubt members of the audiences from the United States were a bit startled to hear the enraged Ananias dismiss him with the righteous cry: "Depart, American fiend!"

All these changes in costume and language, along with a setting in Gloucester Road with a works sign before it saying "Road Up," were bound to arouse the antagonism of purists who wanted their Jonson straight. Anticipating such a reaction, Sir Tyrone devoted his entire program note to a defense of his alteration. He chose modern dress, he said, "because it relates the play more closely to our own everyday experience, so that it can more easily be taken as a slice of life rather than as a slice of literature." In a play so dependent on disguise, modern dress helps the audience recognize the point of a particular deception. Jacobean dress would make it hard to know whether "Face was a Captain or a House Servant" and "whether Subtle was a Divine or a Doctor." Sir Tyrone described the textual changes as minimal, and yet he recognized that "If the performance is not funny, this [his alterations] will be denounced as sacrilegious." And finally, in a rhetorical question that clearly implies his own criterion for theatrical success, he asked: "Would it be any less sacrilegious to speak every syllable of a text, many of whose jokes are unintelligible without notes and a glossary, and still fail to be funny?" If it works, if it engages the audience, then the play may be considered a success—this view, or something like it, describes Sir Tyrone Guthrie's credo as a director.

Did this version of Jonson's play work? Not surprisingly, such a radical production gave rise to widely divergent responses. Bamber Gascoigne complained of "Guthrie's almost idiotic idea of what makes drama seem 'relevant' to a modern audience"; Alan Brien argued at some length to arrive at the indictment that Guthrie was catering to those who could only take "Dickens . . . in strip cartoons"; and Bernard Levin, declaring that Jonson's play is "far *more* timely, modern, up to date in its own dress and own language than in this wearisome bastard tongue," gave emphatic words at least to his disappointment: "If I were a younger man I would go down to the Waterloo Road and thrash Sir Tyrone Guthrie to within an inch of his life."[71] On the other hand, Guthrie's partisans were no less forceful in their support of his work. J. C. Trewin, who confessed that he had been a critic of Guthrie's tricks in the past, nevertheless called this production "a flashing success—something that has the secret of the philosopher's stone; almost every scene is gold."[72] Kenneth Tynan too saw Guthrie as the alchemist. In this production the director was faithful "to the shape and spirit of Jonson's play" and revealed once again his "genius" as one who "occupies and animates" the souls of his actors. Convinced earlier that the John Burrell *Alchemist* with Richardson and Guinness was one he would never see surpassed, Tynan had "reckoned, as the English theatre so often does, without Guthrie."[73] Finally, H. G. M., writing in *Theatre World,* declared that in this adaptation Guthrie had achieved for Jonson the "triumph of divination" called for by Eliot when he said that "to enjoy him at all, we must see him as a contemporary."[74]

When Tyrone Guthrie was asked by Peter Roberts why he chose to do Jonson's play, he replied quite simply that a comedy was required to balance a season that offered *Peer Gynt, The Merchant of Venice, Othello,* and *Measure for Measure,* and that *The Alchemist* "was really a farce" as well as being "a kind of ensemble company play with a lot of good parts."[75] Together, these descriptions indicate with some precision the sorts of effects generated by a production that was "more light-hearted than minatory."[76] There were few hints of darkness in a production in which "Leo McKern, . . . shooting off in all directions as The Alchemist himself, convinces us that he is in the game for the sheer joy of deception almost as much as for the money."[77] Moreover, certain roles were illuminated in surprising and fresh ways. Alan Brien thought that the parts of Mammon, Dol, and Ananias were all superior to the corresponding roles in the 1947 Old Vic production.[78] Charles Gray's Mammon was variously described as "a gorgeous, wheezing, likeably lascivious creation somewhere between Oscar Wilde and Margaret Rutherford," "a Wildean grotesque," and "someone out of Toulouse Lautrec" with "the wonderfully decadent air of a gross fin-de-siècle hedonist."[79] Priscilla Morgan as Dol, making "her entrance to Tchaikovsky's Flower Waltz played on a wheezy hand-held gramophone," was praised for catching "to a turn the boredom of prostitution."[80] The Ananias of David William gave unexpected strength to a character not often much attended to in productions of this play. Alan Brien, noting something of the cold and sharp religiosity of Ananias, wrote that "Mr. William has all the pathetic eccentricity of a ruined umbrella—a bone-handled face bent into a perpetual sneer above rusty black clothes on a spiky frame."[81] John Russell Taylor saw William's Ananias as "perhaps the best performance of the whole evening . . .; to see him quiver with rage is in itself a lesson in the art of comic timing."[82] Guthrie, always alert to possibilities for innovation, surprised nearly everyone by casting a woman, Catherine Lacey, as Tribulation Wholesome. Effectively set off by William's strong performance, she communicated a primness that was "exactly right: one realizes that, at heart, she expects to be Mistress of Ceremonies on Judgment Day."[83]

One's final impression from the reviews is of a typical Guthrie production with all the actors contributing a share to the proceedings and occasionally a share greater than their parts would seem to permit. Leo McKern, Lee Montague, and Priscilla Morgan managed the lead trio without overwhelming the actors who played their dupes. Drugger, who in the hands of Alec Guinness had emerged momentarily from obscurity, here in a reading by Russell Hunter cut a far humbler figure, distinguished chiefly by his total unawareness of the handicap his eating of bad cheese imposes on his attempts at social relations. In short, this *Alchemist* was a director's show rather than a display piece for brilliant individual performances. As such, it stands as an example of the main trend of midcentury theatre, a trend toward greater directorial control with all that implies about responsibility falling on the shoulders of a single man for the final shape the play assumes and the effects it creates. Sir Tyrone Guthrie's shoulders, literally and metaphorically, were broader than most; and given the brilliant eccentricity of his inventiveness they often had to be. His version of *The Alchemist* was typical in its liveliness and in the range of its imaginative effects. It was typical too in the remarkable variety of response it excited. Alan Brien, on the evidence of this production of Jonson, argued that "Sir Tyrone is our best director of poor plays which need every distraction from the poverty of the language. He should restrict himself to William Douglas Home, Wolf Mankowitz, and Beaumont and Fletcher." J. C. Trewin, viewing the same evidence, proposed a Jonson Memorial Theatre in which Sir Tyrone Guthrie would be "in charge of the whole Tribe of Ben."[84]

The Cleveland Play House *Alchemist,* presented in the spring of 1963, was noteworthy for its use of modern dress and for a text that was extensively modernized and Americanized as well. *Marry* becomes *why,* and *ere* becomes *before. Thou dost not know?* is transformed into *You don't think so?;* and Mammon's speeches, along with large sections of the alchemical jargon, suffer a great deal of pruning. Beyond jargon and those matters that would impart too Jacobean a flavor to the proceedings, the excisers also seem to have been careful to avoid lengthy speeches. Most of them—the rhapsodies of Mammon, for example—are abbreviated in some way. The promptbook and pictures of the production, taken together, given the impression that this was a very "civilized" *Alchemist,* focused on gambling and cardsharps, and not at all an accurate representation of the seedy and disreputable world that contains Jonson's authentic Dol and Subtle.

Bertram Tanswell as Face earned praise for "one of the most neatly calculated jobs of the season."[85] But although the play was faithful to the pace of Jonson's plotting, and although the efforts to assert its contemporary relevance were accepted without major complaints, one senses that this production did less than justice to the play. A certain toughness seems to have been missing, along with the cutting edge of satire that Jonson's language alone can provide.

In 1964, at New York's Gate Theatre, Stephen Porter directed a production of *The Alchemist* that featured Roy Schneider as Face, John Heffernan as Subtle, and Carole Macho as Dol Common. What struck most reviewers about this production was the sense of life it conveyed, its vitality and movement. Jonson's comedy, thought Howard Taubman, emerged as a work of contemporary value and it possessed "an unbuttoned gusto that makes even our plain-speaking plays seem timid and constrained."[86] Norman Nadel applauded the company's "hearty, strident style," that reminded him of London's Mermaid players and seemed to fill the evening "with that bawdy life which almost never reaches an American stage."[87] Fidelity to Jonson's vision was the key to this version of his play. Not only was "every moment . . . clear," but the production matched "at its best, the bluntness and wit and harsh audacity, if not the passion, of the script."[88]

Reservations about the production centered on a recurrent issue: how far did the demand for speed interfere with the play's ability to make significant satiric points? Porter was perhaps right in urging his cast "to attack the lines and the business at a break-neck pace and an almost uninflected fortissimo."[89] But such an attack seemed in error when it began to submerge Jonson's plot and its attendant meanings in a welter of knockabout and noise. The company seemed aware of the risks and tried to achieve a useful balance. In doing so, they and their director "made sure that Jonson's motley, malevolent characters [were] given the full-flavored individuality each deserves."[90] Altogether, this version of *The Alchemist* represented a fast-paced and yet coherent attempt to convey the complexity and strength of Jonson's comic design. To a great extent, it seems to have succeeded.

The Alchemist came to the stage of the Oxford Playhouse in 1965, under the direction of Frank Hauser, a confirmed Jonsonian and the only director in this century to have superintended the production of three different Jonson comedies on the public stage. The others are the *Volpone* of 1966 and *The Silent Woman* in 1968. In addition, he directed a production of *The Silent Woman* for the OUDS in 1948. The cast for this production included some names that were later to figure prominently in other contexts and some that had made solid impressions earlier. Judi Dench, who had been Juliet in Franco Zeffirelli's Old Vic *Romeo and Juliet,* here took the role of Dol, perhaps as far as she could have moved from the star-crossed heroine without taking up the part of Juliet's nurse, but indicative of the range of an actress who also has to her credit a brilliant Duchess of Malfi and a delightful Grace Harkaway in *London Assurance.* Zia Mohyeddin, a sensational newcomer in *A Passage to India,* which premiered at the Oxford Playhouse in 1960, was Surly. Simon Ward, the young Churchill of Richard Attenborough's film, took the part of Drugger; and Nicholas Pennell, the decent but often bemused husband of Fleur in the extremely successful television adaptation of the *Forsyte Saga,* was the even more hapless Dapper. To conclude this catalogue and to move into a discussion of the production itself, I should note that one of the most perceptive reviews of the play was written by a Cambridge student named Germaine Greer, who pronounced this a production "worthy to be sealed of the Tribe of Ben" for the way in which it "actually deepens our understanding of the play, in that it realizes most of its comedy and shows how brilliantly Jonson's verse is geared to the stage."[91]

Other reviewers offered rather mixed comments on this production. A writer in *Isis* thought that this *Alchemist* missed "the acid in Jonson's wine," and John Higgins argued that Frank Hauser's careful direction, avoiding "all excesses," was in error.[92] But Hauser, with a strong belief in Jonson's stageworthiness, was not likely to be led into major textual changes or into an attempt to impose a reading on the play that would underscore its contemporary applicability. Working with the play that Jonson gave us, only cutting judiciously from time to time in the belief that Jonson's chief artistic error was overwriting, Hauser stressed the play's realism. "Handled this way the play can speak for itself and—through a wonderfully able cast—it does, declaring Ben Jonson an outrageous and merciless wit and a superb theatrical craftsman."[93] The only apparent failure in this design—at least the only one remarked with any consistency—was the weakness of the opening scene. Several writers mentioned this fault, but only Ian Donaldson singled out the results that followed from it in an essentially realistic production: while Face and Subtle give "good independent performances," the "feeling of continual civil war between them is missing."[94] Here again, one sees a hint of the tension between the speed of farce and the essentials of plot and idea that seems to have troubled productions of *The Alchemist* all through this century.

It is a bit difficult to isolate any performers in this production for special notice. There are only a few reviews, and no unanimity among them on this matter. One critic found "the best things . . . on the margins" and gave special attention to Ananias (Julian Curry) and Drugger (Simon Ward), while another saw Alan MacNaughton's Subtle as "a comic tour-de-force of outstanding brilliance."[95] The nearest approach to consistency appears in the evaluations of the trio of sharpers. Again, the stress is on the realism of their work together; Face, Subtle, and Dol came to life in a treatment of Jonson's play that was never merely deferential but nevertheless reached its greatest successes by its fidelity to the author's vision and its attention to the intricately balanced mechanism of his dramatic design.

Even the margins offered little to praise in the 1966 Lincoln Center production of *The Alchemist.* Not only were the reviewers consistent in their condemnation of the repertory group's effort, they were nearly unanimous in their assessment of its weaknesses. Again and again the critics charged that Jules Irving and his players did not trust Jonson's comedy, that they worked too hard for comic effects, that they substituted noise and buffoonery for wit and point. Jonson, wrote Walter Kerr, "was interested in idiocies of *thought,* in stupidities of belief," but in the Lincoln Center rendering of his play "nearly everything . . . is unmistakably physical, external, whacked at from the outside, rather as though it were the tangible world itself that kept making man's messes for him."[96] "The heart of the comedy," complained another reviewer, "is mostly in the steam and the machinery,"[97] a point Robert Brustein elaborated at some length:

> Points which should be made through character are made through the use of expensive props; a huge steam-producing machine, with a female figurehead, is pumped for laughs whenever the action flags; the costumes, though handsome, do not look as if they had ever been worn by human beings; and none of the actors manages to make a vivid impression on his part.[98]

John Chapman found the whole production to be like its featured machine: "It puffs, snorts, burbles and gives off vapors and is pure Rube Goldberg."[99]

But for all the frenetic enlarging of the play's farcical dimension, the actors succeeded only in reducing its significant comic qualities. John Lahr wished they might have discerned this, for "what they were serving up as vintage Jonson was a tepid, insensitive imitation, substituting athletic spectacle for the rich banquet of humor and surprises that the play actually contains."[100] Thus Jonson's immense figures of greed and lusting imagination seemed diminished as well. George Voskovec gave "no sense of the rapturous vicarious pleasure Mammon takes in his daydreams."[101] "Mammon," argued Brustein, "is a Marlovian figure who wishes not to conquer the world but to swallow it; Voskovec turns him into a hungry middle-European who would be perfectly satisfied with a few scraps in a restaurant not even endorsed by Michelin."[102]

In a seriously flawed rendition of *The Alchemist,* only the appearance of Philip Bosco as Lovewit revealed something of the greatness of Jonson's achievement. Julius Novick wrote that Bosco played his "tiny part . . . with more authority and panache than anyone [else] in the cast."[103] His Lovewit allowed the audience at last to "hear the peculiar, ironic, candidly satirical hum that went on in Ben Jonson's head and drove him to writing iconoclastic comedies."[104] But while the last-act appearance of his master might save Face, it could not redeem this unsatisfactory treatment of Jonson's play. The Lincoln Center *Alchemist* featured a Subtle whose every gesture was too obvious, a too-elegant Dol, and a Mammon who seemed strikingly devoid of imagination. It was, moreover, a production that stressed zany action and ignored the incisiveness of Jonson's precisely calculated dialogue. Walter Kerr's judgment provides an adequate summary: "a busy, roughhouse, essentially visual attack on a play that seriously needs to find its tongue."[105] Robert Brustein offered a harsher verdict. This production, he thought, "gives the impression of having entombed the play."[106]

On 15 February 1968, the Toronto Workshop Productions group presented *The Alchemist* in their new quarters on Alexander Street. Although there are few reviews of this production, there is no lack of disagreement among the critics about its strengths and weaknesses. The reviewer in the *Toronto Telegram* complained that the style necessary in playing humor characters was absent and that "George Luscombe's players substitute a large measure of what Jonson's rival called inexplicable dumb show and noise."[107] But Nathan Cohen was disturbed instead by "the physical solemnity of the performance. Amusement is a commodity in stupefyingly short supply. Hilarity is totally missing. Jonson's boisterous laughter and sense of life have not been muted. They have been extinguished."[108] Such contrary views extended even to the set for the production, designed by Nancy Jowsey. Martin Stone objected to the structure she created—a platform with an open cellar, supporting some narrow stairways and a second level—on the grounds that it "restricts the free flow of action, which becomes ingrown and cramped."[109] Another critic thought that it "would win a place in any international theatre art magazine." He saw it as serving three distinct purposes, all of them related to Luscombe's vision of the play: "It is the mansion usurped by servants in bawdy old London, it is a jungle-gym for the athletic Workshop Productions' actors and it is a tower of Babel."[110]

No one, however thought the production did justice to Jonson's language. This was a noisy and physical attack on the play, an attack that illustrated the director's "preference for inventive action over expressive words."[111] Such an approach exacted its chief cost in a diminution of the play's leading characters. While Geoffrey Read as Mammon managed to retain something of the size of that overinflated hedonist, the performances of Edward Kelly and François-Régis Klanfer as the archconspirators were dissipated "in the frenzy" of the noise and activity all around them. This production remained faithful to the text, but mere fidelity seemed inadequate when the text emerged only as background noise for the physical activity of the actors. Once again, the farcical side of *The Alchemist* dominated, and at times even concealed, its satiric meaning.[112]

On 13 April 1969, the Minnesota Theatre Company brought *The Alchemist* to the Crawford Livingstone Theatre as one of the offerings of their St. Paul season. In the view of some critics, the production might more properly have been called a blood sacrifice. Director Mel Shapiro transformed Jonson's beautifully crafted comedy into a series of "crude vignettes."[113] Subtle, Face, and Dol became the grimy inhabitants of a hippie pad, and a nearly continuous barrage of rock music placed their activities rather firmly in a contemporary setting. Peter Altman complained that "John Jensen's costumes, which range from 17th to 20th century, and include a silly guru toga, some inappropriate police uniforms whose style is Chicago 68, and totally traditional Anabaptist frocks, are awful"; John H. Harvey merely extended the catalogue to include "some jerkins, hose and codpieces, a cycle jacket, costumes suggesting hippies and Indian gurus, and others vaguely suggesting Russian nobility in a heavy winter."[114] This production, then, grew out of the same impulses that gave rise to Gerald Frow's *Epicoene* and the *Bartholomew Fair* directed by Terry Hands. Like those productions, it gained little favor from reviewers who valued Jonson. Peter Altman called this production "an unfortunate farrago that obscured traditional virtues without providing much of substance in their stead."[115] Charles Stone thought that the playwright's intentions had been subverted at every turn: "not only are the three conspirators cruelly miscast, they are encouraged to be vicious rather than crafty, obscene rather than bawdy, and pathetically farcical rather than comic."[116] Critics less committed to Jonson tended to be more accepting of the show the Minnesota company provided. John K. Sherman, for instance, liked the performance, though he recognized that it was "more an escapade than a revival," and Mike Steele called it "a great, swinging romp."[117]

Michael Moriarity and Charles Keating played Face and Subtle. Lisa Richards was a comely if somewhat maculate Dol. Allen Hamilton as Mammon did not, apparently, make much of that great sensualist's poetry, perhaps because he was subjected to such constraining indignities as being made to woo Dol while sitting, centerstage, in an antiquated bathtub. Only Emery Battis, as Tribulation Wholesome, and John Ramsey, as Surly, received genuinely favorable notices. Battis played the role of the rationalizing hypocrite "as if he were one step away from the commedia dell'arte."[118] "Clad in the disguise of a Castilian idiot," Ramsey's caricature Spaniard—rose clenched in teeth, heels clicking out a flamenco rhythm—was a minor triumph in the play's second half.[119]

A quite complete set of documents relating to this performance is available in the Manuscripts Division of the University of Minnesota Libraries. The promptbook reveals a number of cuts, a good share of them clearly designed to eliminate particular allusions to the Jacobean world. Music for the production, including such songs as "The Magisterium" and "Love is a Circle," is also in the promptbook.[120] A study of these materials, together with a reading of the available reviews, suggests that Jonson's text offered something like a field for improvisation for the Minnesota company. Given similar treatment, almost any comedy might be transformed into a commentary on the contemporary scene. Jonson deserved better.

A second North American production of *The Alchemist* took place in 1969. This was the highly successful version by the Stratford Festival Company of Canada under the direction of Jean Gascon. First on tour in Canada and the American Midwest and later on the Festival's home stage at Stratford, it developed into a brilliantly compact ensemble show, rapidly paced and strongly focused on Jonson's superb plotting. William Hutt, as Sir Epicure Mammon, received a greater share of critical attention than any of his fellow actors; but one reviewer, after praising the magnificent comedy of his adoration of Dol, expressed the majority view when she said that "not for a moment is this a one man show—unless the one man be Gascon himself, for the clarity, the finesse and the total warmth of his direction."[121] The source of those qualities, Gascon would say, is Ben Jonson. In his program notes for the play, he wrote: "When, during the course of rehearsals, you search to find the reality of character and situation, you invariably find Jonson pointing his finger and saying explicitly, 'This is what I mean. Do not try to say anything else.'" Yet what the playwright says explicitly he does not always say simply, for, as Gascon goes on to argue, "Jonson is an incredible mixture of animality and intellectuality, of boldness and sharp critical sense, of open observation and pessimism. He is Rabelais and Johann Sebastian Bach in one package." Getting such a combination on stage might seem an impossible task, but this production had more than a little of that variety. Without falling into mere farce, it offered a continuous stream of stage activity, some of which Lewis Funke identified with burlesque house comedy and all of which he welcomed: "No matter how [Gascon] learned the tricks, I am glad. By using them—the sight gags, the bold bawdy gestures and the wildly inventive Rube Goldberg-like contraptions . . . he has infused Ben Jonson's *The Alchemist* with contemporaneity and wild rollicking humor."[122] William Leonard, reporting on a performance at Chicago's Studebaker Theater, found the same balance between stage action that suggested all-out farce and the ability of the players to preserve the play's meanings: "The Stratfordians play it in kick-in-the-pants style, leering and mugging, racing feverishly in and out of disguise, shouting and tumbling—yet somehow avoiding the aura of 'camp' that has tainted so much theatrical satire in recent seasons."[123] Here was a production that served Jonson's intentions admirably; *The Alchemist,* a play "more honored in the books than on the stage," was at last being given the theatrical treatment it deserved. Eliot Norton greeted it with appropriate enthusiasm: "Jean Gascon's production turns it out of the libraries and gives it back to the players, full of life and honest laughter, wise and incisive in its satirical attack on greed and as broadly funny as inventive comedians can make it." Again, Norton found in the play just that balance of rich comedy with telling realism that Gascon saw as the essential feature of Jonson's genius: "Although the comedy is broad and broadly played at the Festival Theater, it has a solid basis in bitter truth, in the greed of the willing victims. The Stratford production hangs on hard to this truth, makes its conspirators no mere clowns but cold-blooded thieves, then turns them loose in antic foolery."[124] Jonson himself might have delighted in a production which made the theatre reverberate "with the hard-edged merriment of a comedy which makes not only a farce of life, but holds up a mirror to human greed."[125]

At the center of this production's success was William Hutt's Sir Epicure Mammon. Frank Morriss saw him as "a figure of ecstatic pornography,"[126] and Walter Kerr wrote a long account of Hutt's performance, which he thought characteristic of the approach of the entire Stratford company. The keynote he found in a certain deliberateness which moves toward goals seen clearly in advance and underlined as they are achieved:

> Hutt takes pains to inventory all his hopes like the sound businessman he hopes to be. He is neither rapid nor delicate, but plain and precise about his wants. He takes his time listing these, so that no one will misunderstand. And why should he hurry when he loves his vision so? . . . He is a child counting blessings, chortling not over the blessings themselves but over the ascending and perhaps infinite number of them, an appetite that grows happier with itself as it exceeds reason and even possibility in size. Eventually he is jumping up and down with glee, pounding his feet against the floor in an ecstasy of sheer excessiveness. Hutt's management of this wild man is magnificent, and it has got that way because Hutt pays such close attention to articles and conjunctions.[127]

But in Hutt's total conception of Jonson's voluble and nearly onanistic hedonist there was a qualifying factor in all this enthusiasm, and Christopher Defoe pinpointed it exactly. Even as Mammon lovingly details his catalogue of pleasures, "one knows . . . that for all his long life he has been the victim of acid indigestion and sexual timidity."[128]

On this very point of Mammon's character, Jean Gascon offered, in an interview, an explanation of the chief departures from Jonson in this production.[129] There were extensive cuts in the play, noted in the program as "textual revisions" by Jack Ludwig. As is often the case with *The Alchemist,* major sections of jargon were trimmed away; and Mammon lost a good many lines from his banquet speech. Gascon, arguing a view which Frank Hauser of the Oxford Playhouse has also advanced, claimed that Jonson's inability to hold his intellect quite in check led to excessive reliance on language alone. But in the theatre, he went on, it was necessary to communicate directly with the audience. They want to learn about the characters, and there are times when they should be shown as well as told. Jonson, relying on his own powers exclusively, often told more than was strictly necessary. In this case, Mammon's speech can be shortened because he is defined early on in the play by his presence with Surly. Sir Epicure—grotesque, unnatural, hyperbolic, and probably finally impotent—is revealed immediately for what he is by juxtaposition with the normal and healthy masculine presence of the other character.

Occasionally, reviews of the Stratford, Canada, productions betray assumptions about "festival" theatre generally, and they fail to consider the accomplishments of the company in a wider theatrical context. The company does not, however, lower its standards in an attempt to create holiday entertainments. Some of its patrons may have a theatre IQ no higher than that of the reporter who informed his readers back in Kansas that not only did Stratford have streets with "names like Romeo and Macbeth" but that "its pilloried stage is an adaptation of the Globe."[130] Nevertheless, the Stratford Company maintains high theatrical standards, and it offers productions that give away nothing to those of the larger and more publicized drama centers of London and New York. With *The Alchemist* in 1969 and with *Volpone* in 1971 the Stratford Festival made a major contribution toward demonstrating the stageworthiness and continuing relevance of Jonson in our theatre.

In October of 1969 the Nottingham Playhouse presented *The Alchemist* in a production that earned generally favorable reviews and was brought to London, on the stage of the Old Vic, for a few performances early in the next year. John Barber thought it conveyed "the gusto and glitter, if not all the savagery," of the playwright's vision of the Jacobean world, but he valued it highly nevertheless: "if Jonson suggests depths of meanness and self-deception unexplored last night, the production throughout gives the feel, and hints the latent power, of a dramatic masterpiece."[131] Like the production at Stratford, Canada, the Nottingham *Alchemist,* directed by Stuart Burge, trusted in Jonson's dramatic technique. It did not "slavishly point to the obvious connections between Jonson's acquisitive society and our own"; instead, it underscored what Gareth Lloyd Evans perceived as Jonson's usual technique in his social comedies of allowing "lesser examples of perfidy to visit the ultimate in vice" and presented a "spectacle of birds of a feather . . . locked up in one cage and tearing one another to pieces."[132] In a set by Trevor Pitt, "so ingeniously real—inside and out—that the playhouse should pay rates on it," the Nottingham players raced through an abbreviated version of

The Alchemist which to Philip Hope-Wallace sounded "as modern and as louche and lewd as one of John Mortimer's translations of Feydeau."[133]

Again, as in the Canadian production earlier in 1969, the Nottingham treatment of *The Alchemist* seems to have focused on Sir Epicure Mammon, here played by Frank Middlemass. But while William Hutt gave Mammon some of the trappings of wealth and luxury—he was beringed and becurled, with a great deal of dandyism in his clothing and his affectations—Middlemass was a grubby figure altogether, whose dreams of splendid delicacies were the product, not of a gourmet palate, but of too regular a diet of beans on toast. Gareth Lloyd Evans called this the best thing in the entire production: "His teeth-sucking, head-lurching, leg-raising portrait of aged and hopeless lust is not only superbly comic but truly Jonsonian—he embodies the Satan in all of us"; and Evans' *Guardian* colleague compared Middlemass' recital of Mammon's anticipated riches with Leporello's "catalogue of the Don's conquests, a piece of virtuosity worth collecting."[134] Other critics, however, did not find his performance so successful. J. C. Trewin noted the monotony in this conception of Mammon as "a senile sensualist," and Irving Wardle thought that this mistaken notion led to a figure "prevented by sheer senility from rising to those matchlessly sensual lines."[135]

Apart from the concentration on Middlemass, there is little mention in the reviews of the actors in this production. (One gains an impression of a tightly knit company working to define the play's overall design.) For Irving Wardle, the decision of Stuart Burge to focus on "the sheer perfection of its technique" served Jonson's play well. But for the reviewer in the *Sunday Times,* Jonson remained an irredeemably lost figure, and Burge's production did nothing to make him more acceptable:

> If Jonson conveyed with passion or indignation his warped and cross-eyed vision of life—as Swift conveys it, or DeSade—I could greet him with something other than a gigantic yawn. But to me—and certainly on the stage of the National Theatre—he is sordid, decaying, and grubby. The characters seem to be stricken with everything from senility to the pox. You can almost smell the latrines.[136]

Two such divergent opinions are unlikely to be reconciled. One critic saw the "pantomime element" working usefully to stress Jonson's brilliant management of the intrigue; the other saw a shabby realism that offered neither wit nor passion. The most favorable reviewers stressed the way Burge brought these elements together; like Martin Esslin, they thought that the Nottingham Players had brought the play "to life, both as a rollicking farce and as a pungent and very topical satire."[137]

The Nottingham revival at the Old Vic coincided with another production of *The Alchemist,* this one at the Cambridge Arts Theatre. Several theatre critics, though presumably aware of Dogberry's warning against such a practice, took the opportunity to compare the two versions. The Cambridge Theatre Company, a newly formed group, was offering Jonson's play and David Turner's *Semi-Detached* in its initial season. Richard Cottrell directed both plays. Eric Shorter found the Cambridge version of *The Alchemist* strong where the Nottingham company's was weak, and vice versa. His chief objection to the Cambridge production was that Jan Waters as Dol and Harold Kasket as Mammon "allow the fooling to droop."[138] The chief contrast between the two productions, however, seems to have been that the Cambridge group offered a sanitized and deodorized Jonson in which Dol was "actually desirable," while the Nottingham version was insistently grubby and unpalatable.[139]

The Chichester Festival production of *The Alchemist,* the third to reach the stage in 1970, suffered what one reviewer called "Tribulation Wholesale" both in its preparation and in its reception.[140] Laurence Harvey, scheduled to play Face, fell in rehearsal and broke his leg. James Booth, his replacement, proved unable to learn the part before the opening of the show, so Peter Dews, the director, stepped in to take the role until he was ready. Allowances were made all around for the difficulties of presenting the play under such conditions, but even considering the special circumstances the reviewers were not disposed to give this treatment of Jonson high marks. Irving Wardle thought it started promisingly

> with a divided prologue for Face and Lovewit which lends a cyclical neatness to the production. Jonson shows Lovewit coming back to his misused house, Peter Dews shows him leaving it to the three tricksters who take over as soon as his back is turned: Subtle busily installing his alchemist's equipment and Dol arriving by cart to sample the bed and the privy.[141]

But despite this beginning, critical opinion was nearly unanimous about the production's faults. Peter Dews had fallen into a common error: "He has laboured to make riotously funny a playwright whose genius was to be riotously serious."[142] John Barber complained that although "Jonson wrote a satire that is horribly relevant to the times we live in," this production was simply "not interested in such savage implications."[143] Wardle called it "a vaudeville version which eliminates the element of danger"; Robert MacDonald labeled it "a non-stop farce" and suggested that Jonson might not have recognized it; and Felix Barker, who "felt like the Puritan at a wild party," argued that this cynical comedy "should not be played as farce." Barker even went to Jonson for a telling reminder to the Chichester company: " 'it is only the discourse of the unskillful to think rude things greater than polished.' "[144]

B. A. Young drew attention to the defects of the Chichester production in another way, by calling attention to the nature of Jonson's achievement:

> The gallery of rogues and simpletons that people *The Alchemist* are as real as the figures in Hogarth's drawings, or Cruikshank's, or George Morrow's—never spoilt by exaggeration, constantly lit by unexpected shafts of illumination that reveal some touchingly sympathetic detail.[145]

After the very real successes of recent stagings of *The Alchemist,* the Chichester version disappointed most in missing the complex blend of realism and comic invention at the heart of Jonson's satiric masterpiece. Transforming the play into a farce, Peter Dews and his players took the easy way with a play whose comic riches are inexhaustible. It was not the Jonsonian way.

Frank Dunlop, directing a production of *The Alchemist* that opened 8 June 1972, at the Young Vic, took an even more radical course with the play, revising and updating to such an extent that he described the version officially as an "entertainment mainly by Jonson." This was a Guthrie-like adaptation stretched to the limits of invention. Benedict Nightingale reported that

> The production retains the original's finer rhetoric . . . but it updates the contemporary references, transporting the whirligig plot to a world of Chelsea terraces, slippery PR men, Salvation Army bands (an inept substitute, surely, for Jonson's ferocious Anabaptists), phoney gurus, and obsessive gamblers, up from the suburbs, dreaming of ecstasy on the Costa Brava.[146]

Charles Lewsen complained that "In Mr. Dunlop's *Salad Days* land of inconsequential anachronism there is little sense of grand depravity." While Nightingale admitted that the Young Vic version "always puts fun before bite," he argued that "the original is somewhat lacking in moral force, compared to *Volpone,* and at least this is fun."[147] The reviewer in *Variety* approved of Dunlop's textual liberties. He found that despite the references to The Golden Egg, J. Paul Getty, and other contemporary places and persons, "The basic Jonson is very much there . . . and the result is a funny show superbly played and imaginatively staged."[148]

This production later toured in both the United States and Canada. In its emphasis on the play's farcical qualities and in the relaxed self-delight of the Young Vic players, it was more of an entertainment than a satiric comedy. Yet it asserted, in its own way, Jonson's continuing presence in the twentieth-century theatre.

In closing this account, however, it must be said that Jonson's presence has been consistent neither in its form nor in its emphases. Ranging from such plain abbreviated versions as the 1916 Birmingham Repertory *Alchemist* to such complex and spectacular designs as the *Volpone* of 1971 at Stratford, Ontario, and covering a spectrum of modes whose diversity reflects the variety of the modern stage, these productions of Jonson's comedies do not illustrate a coherent and easily interpretable pattern. Particular productions often reveal some aspect of what Jonson may mean in the theatre, however, and although there is great variance in the handling of individual plays and even single episodes a general outline of Jonson's twentieth-century significance is discernible. Not surprisingly, that outline can be treated as well in Jonson criticism in this period. Appreciation of the playwright's comic vitality has been a relatively constant factor. In addition, critics and theatre persons alike have come to value and emphasize the devastating satiric power in the plays—especially *Volpone,* but *The Alchemist* and *Bartholomew Fair* as well. Jonson's subject is often vice as well as folly; and the modern theatre has found that combination more manageable than it has been at any time since the early seventeenth century. In the chapter that follows, I want to trace the main lines of twentieth-century criticism of Jonson and suggest, in a more detailed fashion, the conditions that enabled him to return from the exile he suffered in the preceding century.

3

Jonson Redivivus

After nearly a century of neglect, Jonson's plays did not regain the stage easily.[1] In nearly every instance, from the Elizabethan Stage Society *Alchemist* in 1899 to the Phoenix Society *Bartholomew Fair* in 1921, the initial twentieth-century production of each play was essentially a private rather than a public performance. Many of the cultural and theatrical values that had hindered Jonson's acceptance in the previous century continued in force, making his plays box-office risks, especially through the twenties. Yet productions of his plays were being mounted, and increasingly they began to earn critical notice, not merely as antiquarian theatre pieces but as lively and entertaining specimens of dramatic art. A search for the sources of this Jonson revival leads one early and inevitably to explore the connections between the playwright's stage popularity, which experiences a steady growth right through the twentieth century, and his appeal as a subject for academic criticism, which illustrates an apparently corresponding development. As the preceding chapters indicate, Jonson's plays did not suffer critical neglect in the nineteenth century. In the main, though, they were regarded as seriously flawed and lacking in the qualities that might have secured them a hearing in the one court where they might have received a fair judgment, the theatre itself. Moreover, with the exception of Swinburne's little book, most of the discussions of Jonson were occasional and even, at times, amateurish, the sort of criticism that made little attempt to get at the plays from new directions or to find in them undiscovered sources of theatrical pleasure. Then, just before the beginning of this century, there began to grow up around Ben Jonson the early products of what would become a considerable scholarly industry.

The investigations of Josiah Penniman (1897) and Roscoe Addison Small (1899) into the circumstances surrounding the *Poetomachia* may be regarded as preliminary attempts to see Jonson more clearly, though neither book attempts much in the way of critical assessment.[2] Nevertheless, each of these writers helps to provide both a sense of the theatrical milieu in which Jonson wrote and greater awareness of a playwright who contended for his position as a dramatist in one of the liveliest episodes of the most exciting period in English dramatic history. Elisabeth Woodbridge, meanwhile, was attempting to define the nature of Jonsonian comedy, which she found to be rigorously intellectual and "judicial but not always moral."[3] She concludes on a note of regret, wishing that Jonson, "in determining the direction of his artistic genius, in pruning its growth, . . . had been a little less severe, less ruthless."[4] And yet in the field of comedy he chose—judicial, satiric, and (in the case of *Volpone*) ironic— he gained preeminence. Even his weaknesses as a dramatist came to his aid at times: thus his "habit of portraying a character by letting someone else talk about it" may produce "some of the best things in his dramas," for "it was possibly a little easier for him to explain in a crisp phrase exactly how a man was a fool, than for him to give the man free scope to act according to his folly."[5] Although Woodbridge shares some of the nineteenth-century reservations about Jonson (she would have preferred that he were more like Shakespeare than he is), she grants him the right to claim his own position, and in so doing she opens up new possibilities for appreciating his unique achievements.

Recognition of those achievements continued to increase over the next several years. In 1907, Maurice Castelain's massive biographical-critical study devoted 953 pages to the analysis of a dramatist who had been spoken of sixty and even a hundred years earlier as doomed to oblivion.[6] Charles Reed Baskervill published his study of Jonson's indebtedness to earlier English literature in 1911, thus modifying the standard view of Jonson as a rigid classicist and, in the words of one reviewer, contributing "materially to our knowledge of Jonson's literary methods and affiliations."[7] In the next year Mina Kerr's slight book followed Jonson in the opposite direction, tracing his influence on later English comic dramatists.[8] And during this period too Jonson's plays began to receive fresh editorial attention. Throughout the nineteenth century, Gifford's edition, with various slight alterations, continued to be the main textual source for the plays. Even the Mermaid edition by Brinsley Nicholson (1893), for which C. H. Herford wrote the introduction, merely reprinted Gifford's text. Now, however, several of the plays appeared in the Yale Studies in English series,[9] though Charles Hathaway, Jr., in monumentally mistaken anticipation, thought that there would be little point in the Yale enterprise looking to offer a complete edition of the playwright, since "probably the definitive edition of Jonson by Herford and Simpson, which I suppose we may expect in a year or two, will put an end to these special studies."[10] The Herford and Simpson partnership did, of course, finally produce a complete edition of Jonson that earned highest praise for values the playwright himself would have admired most—scholarship, attention to detail, and critical learning. By the time the final volumes appeared in 1952, many more scholars and critics had offered their readings of Ben Jonson; and since 1952, new studies have continued to appear at fairly regular intervals to alter or enhance or redirect our appreciation of the plays.

In retrospect, the early studies devoted to Jonson—the works of Small, Penniman, Woodbridge—are like the quiet and inconspicuous source of a powerful stream, a stream which now threatens to overflow its banks. No one seems seriously concerned, however, about the potential effects of such a disaster on our critical ecology. In 1966, the compiler of a checklist of Jonson scholarship and criticism, covering only the years 1947 to 1964 and including 288 numbered items, offered with no pretense to judgment the assertion that "Among English Renaissance playwrights, Ben Jonson ranks second only to Shakespeare in the number of editions and studies devoted to his work."[11]

Given such a proliferation of studies focused on Jonson, and given the fact that the more or less steady growth in such activity since 1900 has been paralleled by increasingly frequent stage productions of the plays, it seems only natural to suppose that so great a volume of criticism would have had an effect on the shape particular productions assumed as they came to the stage. At least, when I began to look at these two areas, I assumed that there would be a considerable amount of what one of our latest sources of jargon calls "interdigitation." That assumption now takes on the appearance of a rather touching but naive faith in the importance of academic criticism. In fact, I did not believe that theatre people, the men and women responsible for running and directing the traffic of the stage, paid a great deal of attention to the work of scholars and critics, though I did think that an awareness of the major lines of critical discussion was a necessity for anyone who assumed the responsibility of directing a play. But it was on a second and related issue that I felt the keenest disappointment. Surely, I thought, the twentieth-century critical revival of Jonson had brought a new awareness of his dramatic skills, had in some way justified his regaining a place on the stage after an absence of nearly a century. The truth of the matter is that only a negligible amount of the criticism devoted to Jonson in the past seventy-five years has provided a richer awareness of his achievement as a dramatist who wrote for the stage. As a historical figure, a creator of humor comedy, a satirist, an interpreter of the economic world, a master of language, a brilliant manipulator of images, a scholar, and a controversialist Jonson stands for us as a far richer and more complex figure in English literary history than he did for nineteenth-century readers. But he has never benefitted fully from the interest in staging and dramatic craftsmanship that has been directed toward Shapespeare; and as a consequence his dramaturgical skills remain relatively unexplored.[12]

Some conspicuous ironies reveal how far modern criticism has been from aiding the modern stage interest in Jonson. Perhaps the most influential twentieth-century study of Jonson's dramatic achievements is L. C. Knights' *Drama and Society in the Age of Jonson,* a book devoted in the main to arguing a thesis about the connection between social facts and artistic creation and a book which asserts that "the appreciation of Jonson starts from the appreciation of his verse."[13] The most brilliant critical study of the comedies is a thorough, beautifully written book by Jonas Barish which presents an overwhelming case for Jonson as a craftsman in language.[14] Edmund Wilson's description of Jonson as an anal erotic whose leading characteristics (orderliness, parsimony, obstinacy) are classic for the type as described by Freud, though a hostile account, has had some influence on twentieth-century productions.[15] But perhaps the greatest irony of all is the one pointed out by Richard Levin in an article describing how the comedies of Jonson have become "no laughing matter."[16] There Levin argues that most studies of *The Alchemist,* which he considers Jonson's funniest play, have "decomicalized" it out of all recognition and have made of it something "very grim indeed."[17] Simply stated, his thesis is that in attempting to illustrate what this play means, recent critics have forgotten what it is. In pursuit of their special theories about the meaning of *The Alchemist,* they have had to disregard or elaborately rationalize Jonson's conclusion. Much the same criticism could be directed at writers on others of Jonson's plays, most of whom lose sight of the need to understand how comic drama works on the stage and how it affects spectators in the theatre from moment to moment.[18]

The failure of modern criticism to document persuasively Jonson's skill as a writer for the theatre may, then, have its source in a willfully blinkered concentration on thematic matters, as Levin suggests. Yet most readers who attend to Edward B. Partridge's careful tracing of the image patterns in *Epicoene,* for example, surely recognize that he has presented not merely an analysis of imagery but a clue to the sort of emphasis the play should receive in production.[19] Similarly, when the same critic writes of *Bartholomew Fair*—"The picture of egos pushing, chafing, knocking against each other, contending for place, power or just notice, has rarely been drawn so vividly as it is in this play in which the mere names of the characters express their contentious natures"[20]—he describes, though admittedly in somewhat abstract terms, precisely the dominant impression a director would wish to create in conveying to his audience not only the sights and sounds but the driving, collective psychic energy which animates the world of Jonson's Smithfield Fair.[21] Alvin Kernan provides the same sort of understanding of *Volpone* when he asserts that "The idea of 'playing' " is the comedy's central theme and shows how, "As *Volpone* proceeds, the acting theme is strengthened by the knaves' constant use of the theater: plot, forced posture, epilogue, scene, feign, mask, zany, action, Pantalone; we begin to feel that we are watching a play within a play or—as the levels of deception multiply—a play within a play within a play."[22] Kernan does not extend this discussion to the point of describing how particular actions in the play might be controlled by this theme, but he does provide a conceptual framework that an imaginative stage director could turn to good account. Jonas Barish locates a central theme in *Epicoene* in the contrast between noise and silence:

> Noise, of course, is for Morose the primary torment. And his horror of it implies a horror of all strong sensory experience, and thus, by extension, of all human engagement. If silence in this play stands for impotence and death, then noise becomes the emblem of life, the inescapable ingredient of which normal existence is composed.[23]

In thus defining the grounds of thematic significance in the play Barish provides what theatre people call a concept and makes it possible for a director to build an interpretation with some assurance. Each of these critics does for a particular work what T. S. Eliot did for the entire Jonson canon when he wrote that "of all the dramatists of his time, Jonson is probably the one whom the present age would find the most sympathetic, if they knew him" and identified this potential attraction as "a brutality, a lack of sentiment, a polished surface, a handling of large bold designs in brilliant colors."[24]

What all this tells us, I think, is that twentieth-century criticism has given us some new and even brilliant insights into the "idea" of this or that play by Ben Jonson. After the work of Barish, Partridge, Enck, Bamborough, Dessen, Jackson, and others too numerous to mention it is no longer possible to agree with Eliot that "No critic has succeeded in making [Jonson] appear pleasurable or even interesting."[25] And yet it is also true that much of the criticism of Jonson in this period, particulary the "thematic" criticism deplored by Richard Levin, has not been able to suggest in any persuasive way "the joyous pleasures that the immediate, felt experience of comedy can give us, in all of its rich and complex particularity."[26] Why the criticism of comedy should fall down just at this point has to do in part with the way in which particular comic moments are realized on the stage. When Corbaccio, oblivious of the disappointment of the other legacy hunters, finally understands the terms of Volpone's will, his hoarse ejaculation—"Mosca the heir!"—puts the cap on a scene that has been carefully staged by Mosca and relished at every point of its development by Volpone. Our understanding of the scene takes in more than just the comedy of Corbaccio's response, of course. We see Volpone, that superlative actor, trapped by his own folly in allowing his protégé to devise a play and to take the major role. If Volpone makes one error in leaving his bed (where suitors come to him as to the bar of justice) and in adopting the mountebank's role as he pursues Celia, he makes an even greater blunder here as he abandons acting itself to become a spectator and a critic. But both our response to Corbaccio and our awareness of the scene's complexities come like a flash. We have no leisure to examine them, and it would violate the spirit of comedy if any of the characters were to function for us or aid us in uncovering the springs of these comic effects. A comic explosion similar to that struck off by Corbaccio appears at the brilliant moment in *The Alchemist* when Ananias, that single-minded zealot, plunges into a veritable storm of confusion, shouting "Peace to the household" and declaring the good news that "Casting of dollars is concluded lawful." Analysis may provide us with some clearer sense of the origins of our surprise and wonder at his appearance and its effects; but the theatre affords no time for analysis, and the action of the play hurries on to its next turn, its next wonderful event.

In the Stratford Festival production of *Volpone,* one of the great comic moments came at the conclusion of the rape scene. Bonario made a Captain Marvel-like leap from the balcony to the center of Volpone's huge, orange bed. After addressing his melodramatic warning to Volpone, he turned to Celia, assuring her, "Fear nought, you have a guard." Throughout this rather boringly heroic recital, William Hutt as Volpone stood to one side, crushed and dejected, almost unnoticed. Then, as the rescuer and his lady departed, but after a conspicuous pause, Hutt threw his arms upward and cried out, "Fall on me, roof, and bury me in ruin." That shout, which shattered the stillness of the auditorium, contained hints of rage, frustration, complaint, self-criticism, incredulity, and perhaps other feelings as well. But once that effect was achieved, the production moved quickly on—to Mosca, wounded and bleeding, repenting his error in admitting Bonario; to the entrance of Corbaccio; and to the further entrance of Voltore. Comic effects like these leave no time for discussion. In Volpone's cry we may in retrospect hear the lament of the overreacher who at last recognizes his folly and its cost, but that moment of recognition creates its meaning through action.

If we see Volpone as the comic equivalent of a certain sort of tragic hero, then his anguished but immensely funny "Fall on me, roof" answers to Macbeth's "My way of life is fallen into the sere, the yellow leaf," or to Faustus' "O, would I had never seen Wittenberg, never read book." Comedy lets us see; tragedy helps us to know. So many differences are bound up with this distinction. Tragedy demands sympathy, comedy requires objectivity; the tragic hero changes in time; the comic character is a static fact caught up in the flux of events. Tragedy's inevitability constrains us to reexamine and regret the hero's choices: we ask, even against our better judgment, "What if?" Comedy's inevitability leads us to applaud the plot: we delight in our experience of the wonderful. So much of tragedy seems subject to revision: bordering on unfairness, and therefore discussable. So much of comedy seems inevitable and right.

Thus it happens that when critics do try to render justice to the rich comicality of Jonson's plays they find themselves in the position of someone trying to explain a joke. The humor of any joke lies in its own rhythm, its satisfaction or frustration of a listener's expectations, in its telling. So with comedy. When Robert Knoll writes that Jonson's "great plays are centripetal," one has little difficulty assenting to that proposition: *Volpone, The Alchemist, Bartholomew Fair* all provide ample support for that assertion, and Knoll's way of regarding the plays has a value something like that of the critical assertions quoted earlier in this chapter. Like them, it points to a characteristic of the plays that might be exploited in a production. But when Knoll describes the need for rapid pace in staging *The Alchemist,* he offers nothing that would instruct the rankest beginner in the theatre:

> *The Alchemist* needs to be read as a play, not a narrative. We need to visualize it on the stage. Our interest is kept by Jonson's manipulation of his material even more than by the material itself. The action does not develop; it constantly accelerates, and this increasing speed fascinates. . . . There is an element of stunt in *The Alchemist,* and Jonson's stunt depends on its redundancy.[27]

John Enck, describing Bobadill's proposal to defeat an entire army with only nineteen men to assist him, comments that "The satirist's handiest device, the *reductio ad absurdum,* rarely has been employed for such subdued devastation." Here one sees still another failure of criticism of comedy, its inability or unwillingness to use language that might induce a wholehearted response. Commenting on a revision of Bobadill's proposal in the folio version, Enck remarks that the speaker's "wistfulness furthers the ludicrous pretensions." This is language so cool, so remote, that it never approaches the robust and emphatic comedy of the scene it purports to describe.[28] Sometimes too great an awareness of Jonson's harshness can lead to a misreading of a particular bit of stage business and thus blind a critic to its comic effects altogether. Thus J. B. Bamborough complains of Corvino's first visit to Volpone: "It is not really funny to overhear two men abusing a third who is on the point of death . . . and guardedly discuss murdering him, and it depends very much on the actor playing Volpone whether we find it bearable."[29] It hardly seems necessary to remark that Volpone is *not* on the point of death and that this fact is the entire theatrical basis of these early scenes with the legacy hunters.

The critics I mention here all come to the plays with an expressed awareness that their full power can be realized only on the stage. Bamborough refers time and again to the stage requirements of the plays, and he argues that the belief that Jonson does not act well is demonstrated to be false "every time one of his best-known comedies is acted."[30] Enck goes so far as to claim that "A production of *Sejanus* would be engrossing," and he moves beyond that assertion to argue that "It is a purer work than the English stage deserves."[31] But however sincere these professions of interest in the plays may be, the fact is that little of the extant criticism answers to the vitality and comic range of Jonson's best scenes. Thus Helena Watts Baum claims that *Volpone,* of all its author's works, most "needs the stage for its fullest expression."[32] Her analysis of the opening scenes substantiates that claim with remarkable thoroughness, for her comments fall as far short of the heady, improvisational quality of the opening action as can be imagined:

> Voltore arrives first, and with his knock on the door, the tempo of the act increases. Voltore's anxious greed is comic.
>
> The undercurrent of comedy in this scene is carried by the deafness of Corbaccio. Mosca's and Corvino's curses abound in verbal luxuriance and overstatement.

This is of course an extreme example, since what Baum supplies here is little more than a summary of action larded with descriptive indicators. Yet the weaknesses that appear so glaringly in her commentary appear as well in most of the criticism of Jonson written in the last seventy years or so.

From one point of view, then, it seems fair to say that academic criticism has offered little in the way of assistance to the revival of Jonson's stage fortunes in modern times. Perhaps one area can be exempted from the general charge. In his introduction to a collection of essays on Jonson, Jonas Barish describes how modern interest in form has benefitted the Renaissance playwright. Turning away from the romantic fascination with "beauties" and telling, isolated scenes that so influenced Lamb, modern criticism has found value in the unity of the total work and in its creation of a single, unified impression.[33] Eliot speaks for this value, as do Alvin Kernan, Edward Partridge, Ray Heffner, Jr., and many others.[34] But I believe that the influence of a particular critic on a production or on several productions would be hard to document.[35] Rather, it seems that forces operating in the culture at large enabled both critics and directors to see Jonson in a new way, a way that freed him from the necessity of satisfying certain nineteenth-century, romantic expectations about comedy.

Jonson's liberation was not a sudden matter. It certainly cannot be traced to a single event or located at a precise moment. Like all changes attributable to altered cultural circumstances it was the product of a whole complex of events taking place often without apparent connection over a considerable period of time. Nevertheless, most such changes get fastened in our memories and in the public consciousness to a specific event or time. "The publication of *The Wasteland*" becomes a kind of shorthand way of referring to fundamental shifts in modern thought. The Paris exhibition becomes the moment at which a new and radically different way of perceiving nature gets crystallized as a cultural fact. At the risk of comparing small things to great, I would argue that T. S. Eliot's review of the 1921 Phoenix Society production of *Volpone* represents the equivalent moment in Jonson's liberation from the restrictive canons of nineteenth-century dramatic taste. Eliot's earlier reviews of G. Gregory Smith's *Ben Jonson* argued that Jonson the writer of plays ought to be allowed his freedom. The account of the Phoenix production declared that Jonson the dramatist was now liberated and that his being free made a difference: "it brought the great English drama to life as no contemporary performance of Shakespeare has done."[36]

"The great English drama." I suppose that no one who reads those words today can fail to know what period they refer to or dispute their accuracy. Yet Eliot wrote when William Archer could speak of *The Duchess of Malfi* as "this farrago of horrors" and complain of its "funereal affectation."[37] The story of Jonson's revival on the twentieth-century stage is the story of his overcoming such hostile criticism, of his finally escaping from the romantic-Victorian accusations that his plays were diffuse, and dirty, and dull. Certainly the antiromantic reaction described by Barish contributed to an artistic climate in which a classicist like Jonson could be appreciated for values that were his own. But there is another factor involved in Jonson's return to the stage, and this second factor is a matter of theatrical rather than critical history. I refer of course to the Elizabethan revival and to the man whose vision and perseverance made it a reality to the theatre, William Poel.[38]

Poel's achievements in the English theatre are documented with persuasive clarity in the account by Robert Speaight.[39] There is no compelling need to repeat here the details of Poel's prolonged battle against the scenic excesses of nineteenth-century Shakespeare productions, nor is there any need to applaud his advocacy of a truly Elizabethan platform stage that would restore the long-forgotten intimacy between actors and audience. What I should like to stress is that Poel, in insisting that Shakespeare ought to be presented without the intrusion of spectacular effects and free from the interruptions of later editors' scene and act divisions, brought to the stage an equivalent of the antiromantic reaction that was soon to go forward in criticism. In doing so, he made other Elizabethan and Jacobean playwrights more accessible than they had been in over a century. Given a manner of presentation that highlighted star performers, poetic "beauties," and grand theatrical moments, Shakespeare's contemporaries must have remained forever in his shadow. Given a style of production based on what Poel thought of as Elizabethan principles—continuity, ensemble playing, audience contact—playwrights like Ford, Jonson, and even Chapman could get a fair hearing. Thus Edmund Gosse, in a program note for the Elizabethan Stage Society production of *The Broken Heart* (June 1898), wrote that "Individual beauties, gushes of exquisite lyrical extravagance, are not in Ford's way. The construction with him is not less solid than it is subtle, and it is the concentrated subtlety on which the solidity is built."[40] When Poel's group presented *The Alchemist* in the Apothecaries' Hall (February 1899), the reviewer for *The Morning Post* argued that Jonson, intent on the contemporary scene and the humors of those who populated it, benefitted from "having his characters bound down to their time and place, and reproduced in the manner present to his mind."[41] Little by little, Poel's ideas made their impression on the theatre scene at the beginning of the century. If Poel himself was often overlooked or neglected as years went by, that was only because later arrivals were able to settle with little difficulty on the territory in which he had known the hardships of a pioneer.

In helping to secure Jonson's acceptance on the modern stage, Poel produced only one of the major comedies, *The Alchemist*. He also produced *The Sad Shepherd* (1898), *The Poetaster* (1916), and *Sejanus* (1928). Perhaps equally important in creating a theatre climate in which Jonson's plays could flourish was Poel's consistent attention to other Renaissance dramatists, dating from his production of *The Duchess of Malfi* in 1892 for the Independent Theatre Society down to his 1932 production of Peele's *David and Bethsabe* for the Elizabethan Stage Circle and including along the way such plays as *Doctor Faustus, Arden of Feversham, The Coxcomb,* and *When You See Me, You Know Me*.[42] But the battle for the acceptance of Poel's ideas had been joined over the issue of producing Shakespeare, and it was on that issue that their viability would be established or denied. If Poel's "Elizabethan" way of producing Shakespeare proved effective, then other Renaissance dramatists who could not contend with him under nineteenth-century stage conditions might once again establish their stageworthiness. Not all of Poel's experiments worked, of course; and curiously enough his failures often came with plays which he had cut rather extensively. His successes, however, could be breathtaking. Brought up to direct Miss Horniman's company in Manchester, Poel achieved a triumph with *Measure for Measure* (1908). Basil Dean, who played Claudio in this production, wrote later that

> The impact of Poel's ideas upon the Horniman Company was like a fresh sea breeze in a rather self-satisfied atmosphere. In the end, despite some rather overaccentuated moments, he achieved a total effect of surge and sweep quite unlike anything I had heard before, the exhilaration of which remains still in my memory.[43]

Among those who saw this production at Stratford-upon-Avon when it was given there was Barry Jackson. His own experience of contemporary theatrical customs had made him sense that "something was wrong" and he was thus receptive both intellectually and emotionally to "the tremendous impact of Poel's *Measure for Measure* with its directness, its impetus and—simplicity."[44] Surely there is nothing fanciful about assuming that this impact remained with Barry Jackson when he began to establish the principles that would guide his own work as the Birmingham Repertory Company began to explore the riches of England's dramatic past. Poel had demonstrated a new way with Shakespeare, abolishing the excrescences of spectacle that had deformed his plays for the past century and creating a new intimacy between actors and audience. It was poetic justice of a kind that through Shakespeare, whose position for a century had wholly overshadowed them, his contemporaries would receive treatment of a sort that helped restore their effectiveness on the stage.

The Elizabethan revival, then, was not a phenomenon that flashed briefly and then evaporated into nothing. Poel's work, though not commercially successful, earned its share of public attention and gained the active support of people in the theatre. In the process, Poel himself seems to have become more certain of his principles. Perhaps this change can be seen in the difference between his first production of *Arden of Feversham* (1897), which was drastically cut, wooden in its speech, and slow-moving and the second (1925), which employed a nearly complete text and exhibited action "which provided continual movement and excitement, without slurring or distraction or over-brusqueness."[45] By 1925 "a wide interest had . . . been excited in the minor Elizabethans."[46]

Poel's Elizabethan Stage Society and afterwards the Elizabethan Stage Circle, the Birmingham Repertory Company, Miss Horniman's Company at the Gaiety Theatre in Manchester, the Renaissance Society, the Phoenix Society—all these groups had helped to confirm the stageworthiness of Shakespeare's contemporaries and, first among them, of Ben Jonson.

When J. Dover Wilson, in his inaugural lecture as Regius Professor of Rhetoric and English Literature at Edinburgh, praised Harley Granville-Barker for introducing in his *Prefaces to Shakespeare* "a fresh epoch in Shakespearian criticism," he traced its origins on the one hand to "the renaissance of the English theatre" and on the other to "the virtual rediscovery at the hands of William Poel, W. J. Lawrence, Sir Edmund Chambers, and many others of the character and methods of the Elizabethan stage."[47] Those are the origins of the Jonson revival as well, though Ben has never gained the tribute of anything like the Granville-Barker *Prefaces*. Yet it is important to see that the two lines pointed out by Dover Wilson are not truly distinct phenomena. The renaissance of the English theatre in the early twentieth century brought with it not merely an awareness of how enfeebled the immediate theatrical past had been but a belief in the existence of a vital theatrical legacy that had been either ignored or mishandled throughout the previous century, perhaps since the death of Garrick. The activities of the Phoenix Society and the retrospectives of the Malvern Festival bear this out. The renaissance of the English theatre, in other words, had involved from its beginnings in this century a strong concern to recover meaningful aspects of the past; and this concern can be seen today in the programs of the Birmingham Repertory Company, the Royal Shakespeare Company, the National Theatre, the Stratford Festival of Canada, and other such groups. In recent years *The Duchess of Malfi, The Revenger's Tragedy, The Dutch Courtesan,* and *A Woman Killed With Kindness* have returned to the stage. Meanwhile, the scholarly interest in the Elizabethan stage has continued and grown since the days when William Poel and W. J. Lawrence exchanged letters and E. K. Chambers pursued his way indefatigably through the available evidence. J. C. Adams, C. Walter Hodges, Richard Hosley, Glynn Wickham, and many other diligent researchers have added to our store of knowledge about the stages and the staging of Renaissance plays. Now theatres exist in which the facts they have uncovered and the methods they suggest can be put to the test of production. The theatrical renaissance spoken of by Dover Wilson meant not only new vitality and strength but an interest in the English dramatic past; scholarship, illuminating the details of that past, made it more accessible and thus more significant. Together, these factors helped to bring Ben Jonson back to the stage.

It was not an easy homecoming. Jonson's reputation preceded him, and directors felt constrained to keep him on his best behavior. *The Alche-*

mist was trimmed to a more manageable size and its roughness either disguised or cut out altogether. *Every Man in His Humour,* perhaps the gentlest of the comedies, was made even milder by being transformed into a catalogue of humors which featured the charm of historical accuracy. *Volpone,* the most violent, came later; even then, its full power appeared only intermittently. But as the century wore on, Jonson came to seem more at home on the stage. A more open response to his plays, a willingness to accept them on their own terms, came to dominate the views of critics and audiences alike. This was not just a matter of learning to live with someone who has decided to become a household fixture, a matter of ignoring the unkempt appearance and inuring oneself to the shocking personal habits. The fact is that as the twentieth century wore on, a whole set of literary attitudes and values took hold that confirmed Jonson's significance as a playwright and as a thinker, that assigned increasingly higher merit both to his message and his method.

Clichés are so called not merely because they are often reiterated but because they are true. The Elizabethan age *was* a period of national self-confidence and expansion and high spirits. The nineteenth century, similarly, was an age of self-conscious seriousness, of moral resoluteness, of straightforward and openly defined values. In contrast, this century has been characterized by literature that implies more than it says, that suggests far more than it ever asserts. Ours has been the literature of obliquity, of indirection. When the New Critics fastened on the values of paradox and irony in poetry they were not so much creating new canons of taste as fixing and formulating criteria that had already gained wide public acceptance. More important for the revival of Ben Jonson has been the fact that the twentieth century has been preeminently an age of satire. When one looks back at the romantic and Victorian worlds that rejected Jonson's plays, finding them too coarse, too particular in their focus, too lacking in sympathetic characters, one may discern a literary context that afforded no real place for satire. Of course satire existed as a literary mode from Byron to Butler, but this was not like the acerbic, sometimes nihilistic satire of Jonson. It developed, rather, from a perspective that allowed the satirist to retain a certain affection for the very objects of his attack. A major shift in sensibility had occurred during the century and a half that separated Jonson from the early romantics, a change documented persuasively and in great detail by Stuart Tave.[48] Parson Adams and Uncle Toby and other likable, bumbling, avuncular types brought to English literature almost a whole new dimension of humor; thus, by the mid-eighteenth century "Jonson fell on evil days: the harshness of his humor became a mere foil to Shakespeare's sweetness." The precise charges against Jonson Tave finds most fully set out in the work of Corbyn Morris (1744):

> Ben Johnson has *Humour* in his *Characters* drawn with the most masterly Skill and Judgment; In Accuracy, Depth, Propriety, and Truth, he has no *Superior* or *Equal* amongst *Ancients* or *Moderns*; But the Characters he exhibits are of a *satirical* and *deceitful*, or of *peevish*, or *despicable* Species; as *Volpone, Subtle, Morose*, and *Abel Drugger*; in all of which there is something very justly to be *hated* or *despised*.

The playwright's chosen method is thus the source of his greatest weakness:

> Johnson by pursuing the most useful intention of *Comedy* is in Justice oblig'd to *hunt down* and *demolish* his own Characters. Upon this Plan he must necessarily expose them to your *Hatred*, and of course can never bring out an amiable Person.[49]

To "bring out an amiable Person" became the great object of comic writers in the eighteenth century and throughout a great part of the century to follow. The mode of comedy within which such an aim could be achieved was lacking in a dimension of violence and, like its characters, never really threatening. It never moved its readers or spectators with the fear that a great moiling, turbulent scene of folly and idiocy endangered them and the world they inhabited.[50] It was no accident that the most tenacious of Jonson's plays on the nineteenth-century stage, *Every Man in His Humour*, is also, among the major comedies, his kindliest.

It was only in the twentieth century that an appreciation of satire developed once again that was answerable to the range of Jonson's achievements in that kind. It seems inevitable and just that Jonson should have found a receptive audience at Malvern, where Shaw's newest play was the Festival's annual drawing card; that *Volpone* should have returned to the stage in an era that rediscovered the powerful bitterness of *Troilus and Cressida*; and that the dusty hedonism of *Bartholomew Fair*, with its amoral grotesques, should have regained some share of theatrical favor in the same theatre in which certain of Harold Pinter's plays came to light.

Nearly all of the nineteenth-century objections to Jonson disappeared once the main developments of twentieth-century satire had taken place. It simply was not possible to object to the lack of justice in Jonson's plays once one had affirmed the comic brilliance of Evelyn Waugh's novels; nor was it possible, to take a later instance, to lament his inability to create sympathetic characters when one was prepared to praise the satiric vision of an Albee or an Ionesco. The development I am speaking of, which extends from Pound to Vonnegut and includes literary techniques and notions ranging from irony to the anti-hero, is part of the whole movement of modern literature. It is a development that has affirmed Jonson's right to a place of honor in our literature and on our stages.

Notes

Introduction

1. Robert Gale Noyes, *Ben Jonson on the English Stage: 1660–1776* (Cambridge: Harvard Univ. Press, 1935), p. 3.
2. Ibid.
3. Ronald Bryden, *The Observer,* 2 November 1969.
4. Derick Grigs, *Plays and Players,* November 1966, p. 30.
5. One can see rich evidence of the importance of this context that Shakespeare enjoys in Arthur Colby Sprague and J. C. Trewin, *Shakespeare's Plays Today: Some Customs and Conventions of the Stage* (Columbia: Univ. of South Carolina Press, 1971).
6. Marvin Rosenberg's *The Masks of Othello* (Berkeley: Univ. of California Press, 1961) and *The Masks of King Lear* (Berkeley: Univ. of California Press, 1972) offer examples of the skillful presentation of a single play's stage history. Dennis Bartholomeusz—*Macbeth and the Players* (London: Cambridge Univ. Press, 1969)—serves his subject less effectively. Other such studies may suggest themselves to the reader, including works like Arthur Colby Sprague's *Shakespearian Players and Performances* (Cambridge: Harvard Univ. Press, 1953), which takes a wider view of Shakespeare and stage traditions.
7. For an earlier survey of some of this nineteenth-century material see Freda L. Townsend, *Apologie for Bartholomew Fayre: The Art of Jonson's Comedies* (New York: Modern Language Association, 1947).
8. Emmett L. Avery et al., *The London Stage, 1660–1800,* 5 pts. in 11 vols. (Carbondale: Southern Illinois Univ. Press, 1960–68).
9. Herford and Simpson note this production, which took place at the Chelsea Arts Club. C. H. Herford and Percy and Evelyn Simpson, eds., *Ben Jonson* (Oxford: Clarendon Press, 1950), 9:252.

Chapter 1

1. John Genest, *Some Account of the English Stage from the Restoration in 1660 to 1830* (Bath: H. E. Carrington, 1832), 8:579.

2. Richard Hurd, *A Letter to Mr. Mason, on the Marks of Imitation* (Cambridge, 1757), p. 10.

3. Edward Young, *Conjectures on Original Composition, 1759* (Leeds: The Scolar Press, 1966), pp. 10, 80.

4. I quote from Christopher Stone, ed., *The Poems of William Collins* (London: Henry Frowde, 1907), p. 23. The "Dirge in Cymbeline" reveals yet another direction of Shakespeare's influence on Collins.

5. H. W. Starr and J. R. Henderson, eds., *The Complete Poems of Thomas Gray* (Oxford: Clarendon Press, 1966), p. 16. A humorous comment on Shakespeare's mistreatment at the hands of various editors appears in the verses entitled "William Shakespeare to Mrs. Anne, Regular Servant to the Revd. Mr. Precentor of York," p. 80.

6. Hyder Edward Rollins, ed., *The Letters of John Keats* (Cambridge: Harvard Univ. Press, 1958), 2:262.

7. Percy Bysshe Shelley, "A Defence of Poetry," in Roger Ingpen and Walter E. Peck, eds., *The Complete Works of Percy Bysshe Shelley* (New York: Gordian Press, 1965), 7:115.

8. William Wordsworth, *The Prelude,* ed. Ernest de Selincourt, 2nd ed. revised by Helen Darbishire (Oxford: Clarendon Press, 1959), 7:477-85.

9. André Maurois, *Byron,* trans. Hamish Miles (New York: Appleton, 1930), p. 249; G. Wilson Knight, *Byron and Shakespeare* (London: Routledge and Kegan Paul, 1966), p. 4.

10. Rollins, *The Letters of John Keats,* 1:133; 2:7; 1:243; 1:145.

11. Ibid., 1:238-39.

12. John Wood Warter, ed., *Southey's Common-Place Book,* 4 vols. (London: Longman, Brown, Green, and Longmans, 1850).

13. I quote from Markham L. Peacock, Jr., *The Critical Opinions of William Wordsworth* (Baltimore: Johns Hopkins Press, 1950), p. 50.

14. Ibid., p. 176.

15. Robert Gale Noyes, *Ben Jonson on the English Stage: 1660–1776* (Cambridge: Harvard Univ. Press, 1935), p. 30.

16. Allardyce Nicoll, *The History of Early Nineteenth Century Drama: 1800–1850* (Cambridge: Cambridge Univ. Press, 1930), 1:6.

17. Leo Hughes, *The Drama's Patrons: A Study of the Eighteenth-Century London Audience* (Austin and London: Univ. of Texas Press, 1971).

18. *The London Stage, 1660–1700,* ed. William van Lennep, with a critical introduction by Emmett L. Avery and Arthur H. Scouten, 1:cxxx. See also Noyes, *Jonson on the English Stage,* p. 3.

19. For evidence of Jonson's prominence and, especially, the favor in which he was held see Jesse F. Bradley and J. Q. Adams, eds., *The Jonson Allusion-Book* (New Haven: Yale Univ. Press, 1927) and Gerald Eades Bentley, *Shakespeare and Jonson, Their*

Reputations in the Seventeenth Century Compared, 2 vols. in one (Chicago: Univ. of Chicago Press, 1965 [originally published in 1945]). Bentley's view and the methodology on which it is based have been challenged by David L. Frost, though Frost is more concerned to establish Shakespeare's reputation among his contemporaries than to diminish Jonson's. See Frost's "Shakespeare's Reputation in the Seventeenth Century," *Shakespeare Quarterly* 15 (1965): 81-89, and his *The School of Shakespeare: The Influence of Shakespeare on Early Drama 1600–42* (Cambridge: Cambridge Univ. Press, 1968).

20. Quoted in *The London Stage*, 1:515. Brown complained further, "what a wretched pass is this wicked age come to, when Ben. Johnson and Shakespeare won't relish without these bagatelles to recommend them, and nothing but farce and grimace will go down" (1:516). Both passages are taken from Thomas Brown, *The Works of Thomas Brown*, 4th ed. (London, 1715), 1:216-18.

21. Emmett L. Avery, "Introduction" to William van Lennep, ed., *The London Stage, 1700–1729*, 2:lxxviii. Thus there was a shift away from the production of single plays to "the typical program of the 1720's involving a full-length drama, with entr'acte entertainment of song and dance, followed by an afterpiece, often a farce or pantomime or short ballad opera" (2:xvii).

22. Hughes, *The Drama's Patrons*, 97.

23. Avery, "Introduction" to van Lennep, ed., *The London Stage, 1700–1729*, 2:cxv. See cxvii for the emphasis on competition.

24. Ibid., clxxv.

25. Quoted in Noyes, *Jonson on the English Stage*, 34.

26. Arthur H. Scouten's "Introduction" to *The London Stage, 1729–1747*, 3:1, clxix.

27. F. W. Bateson, *English Comic Drama: 1700–1750* (Oxford: Clarendon Press, 1929), p. 7.

28. Charles Harold Gray, *Theatrical Criticism in London to 1795* (New York: Columbia Univ. Press, 1931), pp. 122, 156. For a discussion of the eighteenth-century understanding of "passion" as a theatrical term see George Taylor, "The Just Delineation of the Passions: Theories of Acting in the Age of Garrick," in Kenneth Richards and Peter Thomson, eds., *Essays on the Eighteenth-Century English Stage* (London: Methuen & Co., 1972), pp. 51-72.

29. This interest is documented in fascinating detail in Robert Hamilton Ball's study, *The Amazing Career of Sir Giles Overreach* (Princeton: Princeton Univ. Press, 1939).

30. E.V. Lucas, ed., *The Works of Charles and Mary Lamb* (London: Methuen, 1904), 4:xii.

31. Dykes Campbell, in an essay in *The Athenaeum* of 25 August 1894, wrote of this series of lectures: "Not only did the lecturer owe much to Lamb personally for encouragement to take up the subject, for inspiration, and for direction in his reading, but it must have been to the previous influence of the *Specimens* that he owed in large measure his very audience at the Surrey Institution." I quote from the reprint of Campbell's essay in Lucas, *Works of Charles and Mary Lamb*, 4:601.

32. This passage, taken from the close of Swinburne's essay on "Charles Lamb and George Wither," is quoted in Lucas, *Works of Charles and Mary Lamb*, 4:602.

33. Sir Edmund Gosse and Thomas James Wise, eds., *The Complete Works of Algernon Charles Swinburne*, The Bonchurch Edition (London: Heinemann, 1925), 5:116.

34. Quoted in Lucas, *Works of Charles and Mary Lamb*, 4:601.

35. Ibid., pp. 62-63.

36. Ibid., p. xi.

37. Ibid., pp. 243-44.

38. Ibid., p. 253.

39. Ibid., pp. 265, 271.

40. Ibid., p. 285.

41. It seems to me that Lamb's influence has, in fact, been generally overrated. Although there was a great upsurge of editorial and scholarly activity in the nineteenth century in the area of Renaissance drama, other causes contributed heavily to that development. Certainly if one asks which of the plays Lamb called attention to had any popular theatrical success during the hundred years after the appearance of his *Specimens*, his efforts seem less impressive. See my "Lamb, Poel, and Our Postwar Theater: Elizabethan Revivals," in Leonard Barkan, ed., *Renaissance Drama*, New Series 9 (Evanston: Northwestern Univ. Press, 1978), pp. 211-34.

42. This is the opinion of Gifford's biographer, Roy Benjamin Clark, in *William Gifford: Tory Satirist, Critic, and Editor* (New York: Columbia Univ. Press, 1930), p. 145.

43. Gifford claims that at the first sight of any evidence of Jonson's quoting Shakespeare, "the whole cry of commentators appear at once, 'with wide Cerberean mouths full loud, and ring a hideous peal.' " William Gifford, ed., *The Works of Ben Jonson* (London: R. H. Evans, 1816), 2:175.

44. Ibid., 1:cxvi; 6:123-24.

45. Ibid., 1:xix-xx.

46. Ibid., A^r-A^v.

47. Ibid., 3:438, 440.

48. Ibid., 7:311; 7:198; 1:ccxxv.

49. Ibid., 3:328, 332; 5:310.

50. *The British Critic*, New Series 10 (July–December 1818), 188.

51. Ibid., p. 190.

52. Ibid.

53. Quoted in Hallam Tennyson, *Alfred Lord Tennyson, A Memoir* (New York: Macmillan, 1897), 2:73.

54. T. M. Raysor, ed., *Coleridge's Miscellaneous Criticism* (Cambridge: Harvard Univ. Press, 1930), p. 47.

55. William Hazlitt, *Lectures on the English Comic Writers* (London: Taylor and Hessey, 1819), pp. 71-74.

56. Leigh Hunt, *Leigh Hunt's Dramatic Criticism: 1808-1831,* eds. Lawrence Huston Houtchens and Carolyn Washburn Houtchens (New York: Columbia Univ. Press, 1949), p. 122.

57. *The British Critic,* New Series 10 (July-December 1818), 197.

58. John Addington Symonds, *Ben Jonson* (London: Longmans, Green, 1886), p. 194.

59. Algernon Charles Swinburne, *A Study of Ben Jonson* (London: Chatto & Windus, 1889), p. 2.

60. Gifford, *The Works of Ben Jonson,* 1:ccxvii.

61. Raysor, *Coleridge's Miscellaneous Criticism,* p. 46.

62. He remarks that "the harmony of Jonson's rhyme indeed is most conspicuous—written as it was in an age when as yet Pope was not." *The Yale Literary Magazine* 8 (1843), 203-4, 207.

63. George Daniels, "Introduction" to *Lacy's Acting Editions of Plays* (London: Lacy, 1850), 91:7. Barry Cornwall (Bryan Waller Procter) found that in *Every Man in His Humour,* "amongst a good deal of sound sensible writing, and with little to object to, there is nothing to stimulate curiosity or excite any rapturous admiration. There is a deficiency of passion, and not much delicacy of character: and there is no heroism or strong feeling of any sort." See Barry Cornwall, *The Works of Ben Jonson with a Memoir of His Life and Writings* (London: Edward Moxon, 1838), p. xiv.

64. John Addington Symonds, ed., *The Dramatic Works of Ben Jonson (Selected) with an Essay Biographical and Critical by John Addington Symonds* (London: Walter Scott, 1886), p. xvii.

65. Raysor, *Coleridge's Miscellaneous Criticism,* p. 55.

66. Symonds, *Ben Jonson,* p. 87.

67. Coleridge found that only in *The Sad Shepherd* among Jonson's plays "is there any character in whom you are morally interested." Raysor, *Coleridge's Miscellaneous Criticism,* p. 49.

68. Swinburne, *A Study of Ben Jonson,* p. 29.

69. I quote from John Forster, *The Life and Letters of Charles Dickens* (1872), as cited in C. H. Herford and Percy and Evelyn Simpson, eds., *Ben Jonson* (Oxford: Clarendon Press, 1950), 2:181.

70. Raysor, *Coleridge's Miscellaneous Criticism,* p. 50.

71. Cornwall, *Works of Ben Jonson,* p. xxvii.

72. Charles Dibdin, *A Complete History of the Stage* (London: Printed for the Author, 1800), p. 296.

73. "Ben Jonson's Works," *Retrospective Review* (London: Charles and Henry Baldwyn, 1820), pp. 184, 183.

Notes for Chapter 2

74. This discussion is part of the sixth offering in a series: Shirley Brooks, "Tales from the Old Dramatists," *Gentleman's Magazine* 227 (November 1869), 713.
75. Gifford, *The Works of Ben Jonson*, 1:9-10.
76. Ibid., pp. clxxxvii-iii.
77. Sir Walter Scott, *Essays on Chivalry, Romance, and the Drama* (Edinburgh: Robert Cadell, 1847), pp. 338-39, 340. First published in the supplement to the *Encyclopedia Brittanica*, 1819.
78. H. Macaulay Fitzgibbon, ed., *Famous Elizabethan Plays, Expurgated and Adapted for Modern Readers* (London: W. H. Allen, 1890), p. iii.
79. Scott, *Essays*, p. 339.
80. Dibdin, *History of the Stage*, p. 296.
81. Swinburne, *A Study of Ben Jonson*, p. 27.
82. Symonds, *Ben Jonson*, p. 59.
83. Raysor, *Coleridge's Miscellaneous Criticism*, p. 49.

Chapter 2

Eastward Ho

1. *The Stage*, 18 June 1953.
2. *Daily Telegraph*, 11 June 1953.
3. *Daily Mail*, 11 June 1953.
4. Gerard Fay, *The Spectator*, 19 June 1953, p. 784.
5. *Punch*, 1 July 1953.
6. Ibid.
7. Ivor Brown, *The Observer*, 14 June 1953.

Epicoene

1. One indication of the relative unfamiliarity of this play is the practice of printing the cast list with initials rather than given names and using only *The Silent Woman* as the title of the play, thus presumably creating maximum hilarity when the true identity of Morose's intended is revealed.
2. There were two performances on Saturday, 13 May.
3. I had hoped to find evidence of a ripe performance from A. Corney Grain as Mute, but his efforts attracted no particular attention.
4. I quote from the season program for the Bristol Old Vic.
5. I quote from the program for this production.
6. The OUDS is mentioned favorably in C. H. Herford and Percy and Evelyn Simpson, eds., *Ben Jonson* (Oxford: Clarendon Press, 1950), 9:223. Frank Hauser told me that

Notes for Chapter 2   131

   he was quite pleased to have his work noticed in that great work of scholarship, especially since he thought that the initial reception of the OUDS *Epicoene* by Mr. Simpson was dishearteningly cool. It seems that after Mr. Simpson saw the play at Oxford in 1948, he sent the young director a note indicating little more than that the accents in the Latin scenes were conspicuously false.

7. *Illustrated London News,* 13 May 1905.

8. *Daily Telegraph,* 9 May 1905.

9. Ibid.

10. H. H., *The Observer,* 23 November 1924. I have always assumed that the ladies are well past their college days and that they should, in fact, be rather elderly grotesques. But the women in the 1968 Oxford production were quite young and even attractive.

11. *Sunday Times,* 23 November 1924.

12. H. H., *The Observer,* 23 November 1924.

13. M. F. K. Fraser, *Birmingham Evening Despatch,* 12 March 1947.

14. C. L. W., *Birmingham Mail,* 12 March 1947.

15. T. C. Kemp, *Birmingham Post,* 12 March 1947.

16. David Foot, *Bristol Evening World,* 11 November 1959.

17. Peter Rodford, *Western Daily Press,* 11 November 1959.

18. F. W. D., *Oxford Times,* 18 September 1964; Don Chapman, *Oxford Mail,* 11 September 1964.

19. Donaldson, *Guardian,* 12 September 1964.

20. Robert Gale Noyes, *Ben Jonson on the English Stage: 1660–1776* (Cambridge: Harvard Univ. Press, 1935), pp. 214-16.

21. Donaldson, *Guardian,* 12 September 1964.

22. Ian Donaldson, *Guardian,* 19 September 1968.

23. F. W. D., *Oxford Times,* 20 September 1968. In addition to *Epicoene,* Hauser directed productions of *The Alchemist* (1965) at Oxford and *Volpone* (1966, 1967) in both Oxford and London.

24. Donaldson, *Guardian,* 19 September 1968.

25. Irving Wardle, *The Times,* 17 September 1968.

26. *The Observer,* 22 September 1968.

27. William Poel, *The Times,* 22 February 1909. All the quotations that follow are also taken from this review.

Every Man in His Humour

1. *The Times,* 6 June 1816.

2. *The Times,* 9 June 1816.

Notes for Chapter 2

3. Dickens and his group performed the play first at Miss Kelly's Theatre in Dean Street, Soho, 21 September 1845, and then at the St. James's Theatre in November of the same year. In 1847, the company gave a benefit performance for Leigh Hunt in Liverpool. See the edition by Henry Wheatley in *The London Series of English Classics* (London: Longmans, Green, 1877).
4. *Birmingham Express,* 27 April 1903.
5. *The Times,* 28 April 1903.
6. *Birmingham Express,* 27 April 1903.
7. Ibid.
8. J. C. Trewin, *Benson and the Bensonians* (London: Barrie and Rockliff, 1960), p. 142.
9. *Manchester Guardian,* 30 November 1909.
10. *Manchester City News,* 4 December 1909.
11. *Manchester Evening News,* 30 November 1909.
12. *Manchester City News,* 4 December 1909.
13. *Manchester Weekly Times,* 4 December 1909.
14. G. H. M., *Manchester Guardian,* 30 November 1909.
15. *Manchester Evening News,* 30 November 1909.
16. *Manchester Evening Chronicle,* 30 November 1909.
17. *Manchester Weekly Times,* 4 December 1909.
18. *Manchester City News,* 4 December 1909.
19. Ivor Brown, *The Observer,* 7 August 1937.
20. A. D., *Manchester Guardian,* 7 August 1937.
21. *The Times,* 4 August 1937.
22. *Birmingham Mail,* 7 August 1937.
23. J. E. S., *Daily Telegraph,* 7 August 1937.
24. Milton Shulman, *Evening Standard,* 5 July 1960.
25. A. Alvarez, *The New Statesman,* 9 July 1960, p. 46.
26. Alan Brien, *The Spectator,* 15 July 1960, p. 101.
27. Julian Holland, *The Evening News,* 5 July 1960. He had strong support for his view. W. A. Darlington (*Daily Telegraph and Morning Post,* 5 July 1960) thought that only antiquarian interest could justify a revival of this "comparatively minor work," and Harold Conway (*Daily Sketch,* 5 July 1960) argued that "This Jonson bore should now be hidden away for another hundred years or so."

Bartholomew Fair

1. *The Times,* 28 June 1921. The phrases quoted in this account were of course taken from Summers' program note.

2. H. G., *The Observer*, 3 July 1921.
3. Ibid.
4. Sydney W. Carroll, *Sunday Times*, 3 July 1921.
5. Ibid.
6. H. W. M., *The Nation and Athenaeum*, 2 July 1921, p. 520.
7. Tarn., *The Spectator*, 2 July 1921, p. 15.
8. *Daily Telegraph*, 28 June 1921.
9. *Evening Standard*, 27 August 1950.
10. *The Times*, 24 August 1950.
11. *Tribune*, 1 September 1950.
12. *The Observer*, 27 August 1950.
13. *The Times*, 24 August 1950.
14. *The Times*, 19 December 1950.
15. J. C. Trewin, *The Observer*, 24 December 1950.
16. T. C. Kemp, *Birmingham Post*, 19 December 1950.
17. *Yorkshire Post*, 24 August 1950; *Evening Standard*, 25 August 1950.
18. Alan Dent, *News Chronicle*, 19 December 1950.
19. J. C. Trewin, *John O'London's Weekly*, 5 January 1951.
20. Harold Conway, *Evening Standard*, 19 December 1950.
21. T. C. Worsley, *New Statesman*, 30 December 1950.
22. J. C. Trewin, *The Observer*, 24 December 1950.
23. John Barber, *Daily Express*, 19 December 1950.
24. Peter Fleming, *The Spectator*, 29 December 1950.
25. Richard Findlater, *Tribune*, 29 December 1950.
26. *What's On*, 22 December 1950.
27. *Stage*, 8 September 1960.
28. John Coe, *Bristol Evening Post*, 31 August 1966.
29. B. J., *Bath and Wilts Evening Chronicle*, 31 August 1966.
30. *Bath Weekly Chronicle*, 3 September 1966; *South Wales Evening Argus*, 3 September 1966.
31. B. J., *Bath and Wilts Evening Chronicle*, 31 August 1966.
32. *South Wales Evening Argus*, 3 September 1966.
33. *Bath Weekly Chronicle*, 3 September 1966.

Notes for Chapter 2

34. Richard Wilbur, "Museum Piece," *The Poems of Richard Wilbur* (New York: Harcourt, Brace & World, 1963), p. 125.
35. John Barber, *The Telegraph,* 31 October 1969; Philip Hope-Wallace, *The Guardian,* 31 October 1969.
36. Irving Wardle, *The Times,* 31 October 1969.
37. John Barber, *The Telegraph,* 31 October 1969.
38. J. C. Trewin, *Birmingham Post Gazette,* 31 October 1969.
39. Herbert Kretzmer, *Daily Express,* 31 October 1969. It is, by the way, nearly *de rigueur* to mention some visual artist in the satirical mode when describing the stage pictures for *Bartholomew Fair*; Hogarth, Rowlandson, Frith and Breughel have all figured in such comparisons.
40. Philip Hope-Wallace, *The Guardian,* 31 October 1969.
41. Frank Marcus, *Sunday Telegraph,* 2 November 1969.
42. Felix Barker, *Evening News,* 31 October 1969; Peter Lewis, *Daily Mail,* 31 October 1969; Robert MacDonald, *Scotsman,* 1 November 1969.
43. J. C. Trewin, *Illustrated London News,* 15 November 1969; Harold Hobson, *Sunday Times,* 2 November 1969.
44. Barker, *Evening News,* 31 October 1969.
45. Harold Hobson, *Sunday Times,* 2 November 1969.
46. Irving Wardle, *The Times,* 31 October 1969.
47. Michael Anderson, *Plays and Players* 17 (1970): 48.
48. The entry is for 12 November 1661, *The Diary of Samuel Pepys,* ed. Henry B. Wheatley, 9 vols. (London: George Bell, 1893; reprinted New York: AMS Press, 1968), 2:135.
49. B. A. Young, *Financial Times,* 31 October 1969; MacDonald, *Scotsman,* 1 November 1969; Marcus, *Sunday Telegraph,* 2 November 1969.
50. Ronald Bryden, *The Observer,* 2 November 1969.
51. D. A. N. Jones, *The Listener,* 6 November 1969, p. 648. This defense of Hands' approach restates Guthrie's justification for his alterations to *The Alchemist* in the program note for the 1962 Old Vic production.
52. Wardle, *The Times,* 31 October 1969.
53. Anderson, *Plays and Players,* p. 48.

Volpone

1. Tarn., *The Spectator,* 5 February 1921, p. 170.
2. T. S. Eliot in his "London Letter" for May 1921, in *The Dial* 70 (June 1921): 686.
3. Tarn., *The Spectator,* 5 February 1921, p. 170.
4. Eliot, *The Dial* (June 1921), p. 687. Eliot was not alone in asserting the importance

of this production. The *Observer* critic argued that the Elizabethans could show English drama the way "to become vital and human," and he saw in *Volpone* "a quality of robustness . . . that must be brought back to our dramatic literature if it is to continue." St. J. E., *The Observer,* 6 February 1921.

Eliot's comment takes on added interest in the light of his analysis of Marlowe's *Jew of Malta,* where he defines that play as a farce, but goes on to clarify his meaning of that term:

> I say farce, but with the enfeebled humour of our times the word is a misnomer; it is the farce of the old English humour, the terribly serious, even savage comic humour, the humour which spent its last breath in the decadent genius of Dickens. It has nothing in common with J. M. Barrie, Captain Bairnsfeather, or *Punch.* It is the humour of that very serious (but very different) play, *Volpone.*

T. S. Eliot, "Christopher Marlowe," in *Selected Essays,* new edition (New York: Harcourt, Brace and Company, 1950), p. 105. The essay on Marlowe first appeared in 1919 and was reprinted in the first edition of *Selected Essays* in 1932.

5. A. P., *The Spectator,* 7 July 1923.
6. All the quotations regarding this production are taken from *The Times,* 28 April 1930.
7. *Birmingham Mail,* 25 March 1935.
8. R. C. R., *Birmingham Post,* 25 March 1935.
9. A. C. M., *Birmingham News,* 30 March 1935.
10. *Birmingham Weekly Post,* 29 March 1935.
11. *Birmingham Gazette,* 25 March 1935; M. W., *Birmingham Evening Despatch,* n.d.
12. M. W., *Birmingham Evening Despatch,* n.d.; *Birmingham Gazette,* 25 March 1935; *Birmingham Mail,* 25 March 1935.
13. A. C. M., *Birmingham News,* 30 March 1935.
14. R. C. R., *Birmingham Post,* 25 March 1935.
15. *The Times,* 31 July 1935.
16. Ivor Brown, *The Observer,* 4 August 1935.
17. *The Manchester Guardian,* 2 August 1935.
18. Brown, *The Observer,* 4 August 1935.
19. *The Manchester Guardian,* 2 August 1935.
20. W. A. Darlington, *Daily Telegraph and Morning Post,* 26 January 1938.
21. J. G. B., *Evening News,* 26 January 1938; Philip Page, *The Sphere,* 5 February 1938.
22. *The Stage,* 27 January 1938. R. B. Parker has published a most interesting account of Wolfit's handling of the play. See his "Wolfit's Fox: An Interpretation of *Volpone,*" *University of Toronto Quarterly* 55 (Spring 1976): 200-20.
23. Brown, *The Observer,* 30 January 1938.
24. D. W., *Punch,* 2 February 1938.

136 Notes for Chapter 2

25. Brown, *The Observer*, 30 January 1938.
26. D. W., *Punch*, 2 February 1938.
27. Philip Page, *The Sphere*, 5 February 1938.
28. James Agate, *The Sunday Times*, 30 January 1938.
29. The remarks quoted here are taken from *The Times*, 31 July 1935; and 26 January 1938. Readers of *The Times* of 4 March 1942 were told that Wolfit, "in the wonderful scene with Corvino's wife . . . catches all the rich imagery, all the sultry splendour, of Volpone's thought." All these observations are reiterated by A. V. Cookman, their apparent originator, in "Shakespeare's Contemporaries on the Modern English Stage," *Shakespeare Jahrbuch* 94 (1958): 29-41.
30. *The Times*, 4 March 1942.
31. *The Times*, 23 March 1944.
32. Richard Watts, Jr., *New York Post*, 25 February 1947.
33. Robert Garland, *Journal American*, 25 February 1947.
34. *The Stage*, 17 April 1947. Though the effect may have miscarried here, since it seems that Wolfit conceived of this scream as being a revelation of Volpone's animal nature. I owe this observation to R. B. Parker, who spoke with Lady Wolfit about many particulars of the Wolfit approach to *Volpone* as part of his preparation for the Revels edition of the play.
35. *News Chronicle*, 11 April 1947; see also Ronald Harwood, who spends some time trying to explain away this recurrent canard: "The truth . . . was that Wolfit feared no actor alive or dead, and did not undercut *deliberately*. He simply saw no necessity to organize the company any other way and for two reasons: the first was that Wolfit was acclaimed as a great actor despite the poor standards of his supporting players, and the second was a virtue, not a fault, of this particular actor-manager: loyalty." Ronald Harwood, *Sir Donald Wolfit, C. B. E., His Life and Work in the Unfashionable Theatre* (New York: St. Martin's Press, 1971), pp. 176-77.
36. Derek Monsey, *The Spectator*, 23 October 1953, p. 451.
37. Harwood, *Donald Wolfit*, pp. 155-56.
38. I believe now that his is too optimistic a view of this event. Parker, who was able to see a videotape of this performance, presents a quite different account. I had been told that the videotape had been destroyed. See Parker, "Wolfit's Fox," *UTQ* 55: 201.
39. *Birmingham Post*, 6 June 1944.
40. I am quoting from the promptbook, preserved in the Shakespeare Centre Library in Stratford-upon-Avon.
41. *The Times*, 6 June 1944.
42. Brooks Atkinson, *New York Times*, 9 January 1948.
43. Ward Morehouse, *New York Sun*, 9 January 1948.
44. Louis Kronenberger, *PM*, 11 January 1948.

Notes for Chapter 2   137

45. *Christian Science Monitor*, 17 January 1948.
46. Rowland Field, *Newark Evening News*, 9 January 1948.
47. Ibid.
48. Richard Watts, Jr., *New York Post*, 9 January 1948.
49. Ibid.
50. Joseph Wood Krutch, *The Nation*, 24 January 1948.
51. Kronenberger, *PM*, 11 January 1948.
52. Caryl Brahms, *Evening Standard*, 15 January 1947.
53. C. L. W., *Birmingham Mail*, 16 July 1952.
54. Harold Conway, *Evening Standard*, 16 July 1952; David Farrer, *Evening Standard*, 18 July 1952.
55. T. C. Worsley, *The New Statesman*, 26 July 1952.
56. W. A. Darlington, *Daily Telegraph*, 16 July 1952.
57. C. L. W., *Birmingham Mail*, 16 July 1952.
58. Worsley, *The New Statesman*, 26 July 1952.
59. *Coventry Evening Telegraph*, 16 July 1952.
60. *The Times*, 16 July 1952.
61. Conway, *Evening Standard*, 16 July 1952.
62. *Scotsman*, 17 July 1952; see also Worsley in *The New Statesman*, 26 July 1952, who thought that George Devine showed too great a respect for Jonson's text and that he directed in too detailed a fashion.
63. Conway, *Evening Standard*, 16 July 1952.
64. Gerard Fay, *The Spectator*, 18 July 1952, p. 96.
65. *The Stage*, 10 March 1955.
66. Ibid.; Stephen Williams, *Evening News*, 4 March 1955.
67. Peter Rodford, *The Western Daily Press*, 30 November 1955.
68. John Coe, *Bristol Evening Post*, 19 November 1955, quoting John Moody, director of the Bristol Old Vic; and *Bristol Evening Post*, 30 November 1955.
69. Peter Rodford, *Plays and Players*, January 1956; *The Stage*, 1 December 1955.
70. Stanley Eichelbaum, *San Francisco Examiner*, 26 February 1963.
71. Kenneth Rexroth, *San Francisco Examiner*, 3 March 1963.
72. Nancy Scott, *People's World*, 16 March 1963; Paine Knickerbocker, *San Francisco Chronicle*, 26 February 1963.
73. Scott, *People's World*, 16 March 1963; Paul Speegle, *San Francisco News Call Bulletin*, 25 February 1963.

138 Notes for Chapter 2

74. Theresa Loeb Cone, *Oakland Tribune*, 25 February 1963.
75. Thomas Willis, *Chicago Tribune*, 8 September 1964.
76. Richard Christiansen, *Chicago Daily News*, 18 July 1964.
77. Harold Clurman, *The Nation*, 10 August 1964.
78. Henry Hewes, *Saturday Review*, 22 August 1964, p. 20.
79. Dan Sullivan, *Minneapolis Tribune*, 30 June 1964.
80. Thomas Willis, *Chicago Tribune*, 8 September 1964.
81. John K. Sherman, *Minneapolis Star*, 30 June 1964.
82. Willis, *Chicago Tribune*, 8 September 1964; Robert Rees, *Variety* (Minneapolis), 2 July 1964.
83. John H. Harvey, *St. Paul Pioneer Press*, 5 July 1964.
84. Sullivan, *Minneapolis Tribune*, 30 June 1964.
85. Willis, *Chicago Tribune*, 8 September 1964.
86. Sullivan, *Minneapolis Tribune*, 30 June 1964.
87. Sherman, *Minneapolis Star*, 30 June 1964.
88. Clurman, *The Nation*, 10 August 1964.
89. *The Daily Worker*, 9 April 1965.
90. Benedict Nightingale, *The Guardian*, 8 April 1965.
91. Piper Anderson, *The Nottingham Observer*, May 1965.
92. Nightingale, *The Guardian*, 8 April 1965.
93. Anderson, *The Nottingham Observer*, May 1965.
94. Derick Grigs, *Plays and Players*, November 1966, p. 30.
95. *The Times*, 21 September 1966.
96. Grigs, *Plays and Players*, November 1966, p. 30.
97. *The Times*, 21 September 1966.
98. Ian Donaldson, *The Guardian*, 21 September 1966; Peter Lewis, *Daily Mail*, 21 September 1966; and Grigs, *Plays and Players*, November 1966.
99. Daphne Levens, *Oxford Magazine*, Michaelmas 1966.
100. *The Times*, 21 September 1966.
101. D. A. N. Jones, *The New Statesman*, 7 October 1966.
102. Donaldson, *The Guardian*, 21 September 1966.
103. Nightingale, *Plays and Players*, March 1967.
104. *Evening Standard*, 1 February 1967.
105. *The Times*, 3 March 1967.

Notes for Chapter 2   139

106. Philip Hope-Wallace, *The Guardian,* 17 January 1968.
107. D.A.N. Jones, *The Listener,* 25 January 1968, p. 125.
108. Hilary Spurling, *The Spectator,* 26 January 1968, p. 107.
109. Ibid.
110. I refer, of course, to the well-known article by Jonas Barish, "The Double Plot of *Volpone,*" *Modern Philology* 51 (1953): 83-92.
111. Henry Popkin, *The Times,* 17 January 1968.
112. Jones, *The Listener,* 25 January 1968. Eric Shorter, who found this *Volpone* "a modern play in many ways . . . harsh in its humour, unconcerned with psychology and convinced that every man has his price," noted nevertheless that "all one misses is the huge feeling of evil which was so obvious in a production like Wolfit's at the Savoy some years back" (*The Telegraph,* 17 January 1968).
113. Philip French, *The New Statesman,* 26 January 1968, p. 120.
114. Martin Esslin thought that the costuming provided a useful emphasis on the fable at the play's center. See his account in *Plays and Players* 15 (March 1968), p. 15.
115. Jones, *The Listener,* 25 January 1968.
116. J. C. Trewin, *Illustrated London News,* 27 January 1968, p. 28.
117. Trewin, *Birmingham Post,* 26 February 1969.
118. W. H. W., *Birmingham Evening Mail,* 26 February 1969; *Birmingham Mercury,* n.d.
119. "*Volpone,*" in Alvin Kernan, ed., *The Yale Ben Jonson* (New Haven: Yale Univ. Press, 1962), pp. 7-11.
120. W. H. W., *Birmingham Evening Mail,* 26 February 1969.
121. Trewin, *Birmingham Post,* 26 February 1969.
122. Peter Bellamy, *The Plain Dealer,* 15 August 1970. See also Tony Mastroianni in *The Cleveland Press,* 13 August 1970.
123. Urjo Kareda, *Toronto Daily Star,* 28 July 1971.
124. Fred Sagel, *Guelph Mercury,* 28 July 1971; Don Braid, *Kitchener-Waterloo Record,* 28 July 1971; Jim Clements, *Calgary Herald,* 29 July 1971.
125. Irving Wardle, *The Times,* 10 August 1971.
126. Victor Stanton, *Stratford Beacon-Herald,* 28 July 1971.
127. Harvey Chusid, *Vancouver Sun,* 28 July 1971.
128. Julius Novick, *The Village Voice,* 26 August 1971.
129. Marion I. Duke, *Listowel Banner,* 19 August 1971; Zelda Heller, *Montreal Star,* 5 August 1971; Doug Bale, *London Evening Free Press,* 28 July 1971.
130. Berners W. Jackson, *Hamilton Spectator,* 31 July 1971.
131. Kareda, *Toronto Daily Star,* 28 July 1971; Ramona B. Bowden, *The Post-Standard* (Syracuse, N. Y.), 16 August 1971.

Notes for Chapter 2

132. Wardle, *The Times*, 10 August 1971.
133. Chusid, *Vancouver Sun*, 28 July 1971.
134. Charles Lewsen, *The Times*, 3 March 1972.

The Alchemist

1. *The Times*, 25 February 1899.
2. *The Athenaeum*, 4 March 1899. The comment in *The Referee* for 26 February 1899 is similar: "They may be praised in a body. The long speeches, with all their learned hocus-pocus, were extremely well-delivered, though the absence of anything like a conflict of passions or development of character offers occasion for little more than an exhibition of understanding and skill in declamation."
3. *The Times*, 25 Feburary 1899.
4. *The Athenaeum*, 4 March 1899.
5. *The Times*, 25 February 1899.
6. The observations that follow are based on my study of the promptbook.
7. *Birmingham Post*, 10 April 1916. All the comments that follow are taken from this account.
8. Robert Gale Noyes, *Ben Jonson on the English Stage: 1660–1776* (Cambridge: Harvard Univ. Press, 1935), p. 103.
9. Reported in the *Birmingham Gazette*, 26 June 1916.
10. Desmond McCarthy, *The New Statesman*, 24 March 1923, p. 722.
11. Martin Armstrong, *The Spectator*, 24 March 1923, p. 513.
12. McCarthy, *The New Statesman*, 24 March 1923, p. 723.
13. *Sunday Times*, 23 March 1923.
14. W. A. Darlington, *Daily Telegraph*, 3 August 1932.
15. Ibid.; *The Times*, 3 August 1932.
16. *The Times*, 3 August 1932.
17. *The Stage*, 4 April 1935.
18. Such was the opinion of Cecil Chisholm in *The Sunday Referee*, 17 March 1935.
19. *The Stage*, 14 March 1935.
20. *The Evening News*, 12 March 1935.
21. Chisholm, *The Sunday Referee*, 17 March 1935.
22. H. H., *The Observer*, 17 March 1935; *Sunday Times*, 7 April 1935; M. Willson Disher, *The Daily Mail*, 2 April 1935; *The Sketch*, 17 April 1935.
23. Ivor Brown, *The Observer*, 7 April 1935.
24. Chisholm, *The Sunday Referee*, 17 March 1935.

25. H. H., *The Observer*, 17 March 1935; Brown, *The Observer*, 7 April 1935. It will be apparent that I am, in this account, conflating descriptions of the two different runs of this production. The reviewer in *The Times*, 12 March 1935, took exception to the view shared by *The Observer* critics; for him, Bruce Winston never "reached the heights to which Jonson occasionally raised Sir Epicure Mammon, or really managed the artful gradation between absurdity and genuine splendour. But of the character himself he executed a lavish and amusing caricature."
26. *The Sketch*, 17 April 1935.
27. *The Stage*, 4 April 1935.
28. Ibid.
29. Darlington, *The Daily Telegraph*, 2 April 1935.
30. R. A. C., *Liverpool Echo*, 17 April 1945.
31. *Liverpool Echo*, 1 May 1945.
32. Ivor Brown, "Ben Trovato," *The Observer*, 19 January 1947.
33. Anthony Goodman, *The Tatler and Bystander*, 29 January 1947.
34. Brown, *The Observer*, 19 January 1947.
35. *Manchester Guardian*, 23 January 1947.
36. Peter Fleming, *The Spectator*, 24 January 1947, p. 108.
37. *The Times*, 5 January 1947.
38. James Agate, *Sunday Times*, 19 January 1947.
39. *The Times*, 5 January 1947.
40. *Sound*, March 1947; *Cavalcade*, 25 January 1947.
41. Alan Dent, *News Chronicle*, 17 January 1947.
42. Lawrence Gowing, *The Sketch*, 5 January 1947. In the program for this production, each of the characters was given a label—e.g., Mammon (a Dreamer), Dapper (an Ass), Kastril (a wealthy Bumpkin). The label "Creature" seemed perfectly suited to the reading Guinness gave the character of Drugger.
43. Brown, *The Observer*, 19 January 1947; Fleming, *The Spectator*, 24 January 1947, p. 108; Philip Hope-Wallace, *Time and Tide*, 25 January 1947.
44. Goodman, *The Tatler and Bystander*, 29 January 1947.
45. Agate, *Sunday Times*, 19 January 1947.
46. Ibid.; *The Scotsman*, 16 January 1947; *Punch*, 22 January 1947.
47. Caryl Brahms, *Evening Standard*, 15 January 1947.
48. Fleming, *The Spectator*, 25 January 1947, p. 108; Hubert Griffith, *Sunday Graphic*, 19 January 1947.
49. Agate, *Sunday Times*, 19 January 1947.
50. Brown, *The Observer*, 19 January 1947.

Notes for Chapter 2

51. Dent, *News Chronicle,* 17 January 1947.
52. R. R., *New York World-Telegram,* 7 May 1948; Alan Branigan, *Newark Evening News,* 7 May 1948.
53. John S. Wilson, *PM,* 9 May 1948. Wilson quotes Richard Watts, Jr., *New York Post,* 7 May 1948, who remarked "a tendency on the part of the actors to be just a trifle too antic." This is a recurrent objection to modern stage productions of the play.
54. Robert Coleman, *Daily Mirror,* 8 May 1948.
55. R. R., *New York World-Telegram,* 7 May 1948.
56. Bron, *Variety,* 12 May 1948. But then times have changed. The *New York Times* of 21 January 1948 reported that the National Legion of Decency had given a "C" or "Condemned" rating to the Jouvet film version of *Volpone*: "According to the Roman Catholic reviewing group, the satire was condemned because, 'despite pretense of moral purposes, this film portrays vice attractively and ridicules virtue. It contains blasphemous references to religious practices and indecent and suggestive scenes.' "
57. John S. Wilson, *PM,* 7 May 1948.
58. Richard Watts, Jr., *New York Post,* 7 May 1948.
59. *The Stage,* 4 December 1952.
60. Dennis Bushell, *Bristol Evening World,* 12 December 1952.
61. John Coe, *Bristol Evening Post,* 12 December 1962.
62. *Birmingham Post,* 23 October 1957.
63. W. H. W., *Birmingham Mail,* 23 October 1952.
64. Both of the quotations are taken from the review in the *Birmingham Post,* 23 October 1957.
65. Robert D. Horn, "Shakespeare and Ben Jonson—Ashland, 1961," *Shakespeare Quarterly* 12 (1961): 415.
66. James Cunningham Carter, "*The Alchemist* through the Ages" (M. A. thesis, University of British Columbia, 1972).
67. Horn, "Shakespeare and Jonson," p. 416.
68. Carter, "*The Alchemist* through the Ages," p. 67, quoting the review in the *Medford Mail Tribune,* 22 August 1961.
69. Horn, "Shakespeare and Jonson," p. 415.
70. Through the courtesy of Molly Sole, I was able to study the promptbook at the offices of the Old Vic.
71. Bamber Gascoigne, *The Spectator,* 7 December 1962, p. 895; Alan Brien, *Harper's Bazaar,* April 1963; Bernard Levin, *Daily Mail,* 29 November 1962.
72. J. C. Trewin, *Birmingham Post,* 29 November 1962.
73. Kenneth Tynan, *The Observer,* 2 December 1962.
74. H. G. M., *Theatre World,* January 1963, p. 9.

Notes for Chapter 2   143

75. "Guthrie at the Vic," an interview with Peter Roberts, *Plays and Players*, January 1963, p. 22.
76. *The Times*, 29 November 1962.
77. John Russell Taylor, "Jacobean Behan," *Plays and Players*, January 1963, p. 47.
78. Brien, *Sunday Telegraph*, 2 December 1962.
79. D. H., *Bristol Evening Post*, 29 November 1962; Tom Stoppard, *Scene*, 6 December 1962; Gascoigne, *The Spectator*, 7 December 1962, p. 895.
80. John Rosselli, *The Guardian*, 29 November 1962; Gascoigne, *The Spectator*, 7 December 1962.
81. Brien, *Sunday Telegraph*, 2 December 1962.
82. Taylor, "Jacobean Behan," p. 47.
83. Trewin, *Birmingham Post*, 5 December 1962.
84. Brien, *Sunday Telegraph*, 2 December 1962; Trewin, *Birmingham Post*, 5 December 1962.
85. Stan Anderson, *Cleveland Press*, 25 April 1963.
86. Howard Taubman, *New York Times*, 15 September 1964.
87. Norman Nadel, *New York World-Telegram and Sun*, 15 September 1964.
88. Edith Oliver, *New Yorker*, 26 September 1964.
89. Taubman, *New York Times*, 15 September 1964.
90. Nadel, *New York World-Telegram and Sun*, 15 September 1964.
91. Germaine Greer, in an unidentified press cutting from a Cambridge undergraduate magazine in the files of the Oxford Playhouse.
92. *Isis*, 23 January 1965; John Higgins, *Financial Times*, 20 January 1965.
93. Don Chapman, *Oxford Mail*, 25 January 1965.
94. Ian Donaldson, *The Guardian*, 20 January 1965.
95. Ibid.; *The Stage*, 21 January 1965.
96. Walter Kerr, *New York Times*, 14 October 1966.
97. Richard P. Cooke, *Wall Street Journal*, 17 October 1966.
98. Robert Brustein, *The New Republic*, 29 October 1966.
99. John Chapman, *Daily News*, 15 October 1966.
100. John Lahr, *Manhattan East*, 3 November 1966.
101. Vineta Colby, *Park East*, 20 October 1966.
102. Brustein, *The New Republic*, 29 October 1966.
103. Julius Novick, *The Village Voice*, 20 October 1966.
104. Kerr, *New York Times*, 14 October 1966. Henry Hewes described the effect Bosco's

Notes for Chapter 2

presence created: "Now at last there is a force on stage to be reckoned with. Now Jeremy's attempts to extricate himself from danger are really funny because they are the inventions of a man in trouble, rather than of a man trying to be funny." *Saturday Review,* 29 October 1966, p. 49.

105. Kerr, *New York Times,* 14 October 1966.
106. Brustein, *The New Republic,* 29 October 1966.
107. *Toronto Telegram,* 16 February 1968.
108. Nathan Cohen, *Toronto Star,* 16 February 1968.
109. Martin Stone, *Canadian Tribune,* 4 March 1968.
110. H. W., *Toronto Globe and Mail,* 16 February 1968.
111. Ibid.
112. Ibid.
113. Charles Stone, *Minnesota Daily,* 18 April 1969.
114. Peter Altman, *Minneapolis Star,* 29 April 1969; *St. Paul Dispatch,* 14 April 1969.
115. Altman, *Minneapolis Star,* 29 April 1969.
116. Stone, *Minnesota Daily,* 18 April 1969.
117. John K. Sherman, *Minneapolis Star,* 14 April 1969; Mike Steele, *Minneapolis Tribune,* 14 April 1969.
118. Stone, *Minnesota Daily,* 18 April 1969.
119. Thomas Gifford, *Twin Citian,* June 1969.
120. Music for the production was composed by David Karr.
121. Zelda Heller, *Montreal Star,* 9 April 1969.
122. Lewis Funke, *New York Times,* 12 June 1969.
123. William Leonard, *Chicago Tribune,* 5 March 1969.
124. Eliot Norton, *Boston Record American,* 11 June 1969.
125. Frank Morriss, *Winnipeg Tribune,* 11 June 1969.
126. Ibid.
127. Kerr, *New York Times,* 22 June 1969.
128. Christopher Defoe, *Vancouver Sun,* 8 July 1969.
129. Jean Gascon and I talked for about an hour on 12 May 1971.
130. S. A., *Hutchinson Kansas News,* 19 June 1969.
131. John Barber, *Daily Telegraph,* 2 October 1969.
132. Gareth Lloyd Evans, *Weekly Guardian,* 11 October 1969.
133. Emyrs Bryson, *Nottingham Evening Post,* 2 October 1969; Philip Hope-Wallace, *The Guardian,* 10 February 1970. Once again, I am using reviews of productions at dif-

ferent locations as though they referred to one production. There was, in fact, no significant difference between the Nottingham company's *Alchemist* at home and the play in London. Peter Barnes edited the text, cutting over 900 lines from the original. In a program note, he made some of the same points Jean Gascon made in a note for his production. Thus while Barnes calls the play "a three-dimensional Whitehall farce," he also points out that "the plague ravaging the city is moral as well as physical."

134. Evans, *Weekly Guardian*, 11 October 1969; Hope-Wallace, *The Guardian*, 10 February 1970.

135. Trewin, *Birmingham Post*, 10 February 1970; Irving Wardle, *The Times*, 11 February 1970.

136. Wardle, *The Times*, 11 February 1970; *Sunday Times*, 15 February 1970.

137. Martin Esslin, *Plays and Players*, April 1970, p. 44.

138. Eric Shorter, *Daily Telegraph*, 17 February 1970.

139. *Sunday Times*, 15 February 1970.

140. Frank Marcus, *Sunday Telegraph*, 26 July 1970.

141. Wardle, *The Times*, 23 July 1970.

142. *The Spectator*, 1 August 1970, p. 108.

143. John Barber, *Daily Telegraph*, 23 July 1970.

144. Wardle, *The Times*, 23 July 1970; Robert MacDonald, *The Scotsman*, 24 July 1970; Felix Barker, *The Evening News*, 23 July 1970.

145. B. A. Young, *Financial Times*, 23 July 1970.

146. Benedict Nightingale, *New Statesman*, 16 June 1972, p. 847.

147. Charles Lewsen, *The Times*, 9 June 1972; Nightingale, *New Statesman*, 16 June 1972, p. 847.

148. Pit., *Variety*, 28 June 1972, p. 59.

Chapter 3

1. As always, the one exception to the pattern of neglect is *Every Man in His Humour*, which was produced up to the 1830s on the professional stage and again in mid-century by Dickens and his band of amateurs.

2. Josiah H. Penniman, *The War of the Theatres* (Boston: Ginn, 1897), and Roscoe Addison Small, *The Stage-Quarrel Between Ben Jonson and the So-Called Poetasters* (Breslau: Verlag von M. & H. Marcus, 1899).

3. Elisabeth Woodbridge, *Studies in Jonson's Comedy*, first printed in *Yale Studies in English* 5 (1898). I quote from the reprinted edition (New York: Gordian Press, 1966), p. 30.

4. Ibid., p. 79.

5. Ibid., pp. 83, 32.

6. Maurice Castelain, *Ben Jonson, l'homme et l'oeuvre (1572–1637)* (Paris: Librairie Hachette, 1907).

7. Charles Reed Baskervill, "English Elements in Jonson's Early Comedy," in *University of Texas Bulletin* 178 (1911). The quotation comes from a review of Baskervill's study by W. S. Johnson in *Journal of English and Germanic Philology* 12 (1913): 337.

8. Mina Kerr, *The Influence of Ben Jonson on English Comedy, 1598–1642* (New York: Columbia Univ. Press, 1912).

9. Among other plays the Yale series included *The Devil Is an Ass*, ed. William Savage Johnson (1905); *The Staple of News*, ed. De Winter (1905); and *Epicoene*, ed. Aurelia Henry (1906).

10. Charles M. Hathaway, Jr., review of *The New Inn*, ed. George Bremner Tennant, *Modern Language Notes* 25 (1910): 153.

11. Robert C. Steensma, "Ben Jonson: A Checklist of Editions, Biography, and Criticism 1947–1964," in Samuel Schoenbaum, ed., *Opportunities in Renaissance Drama*, The Report of the Modern Language Conference (Evanston: Northwestern Univ. Press, 1966), pp. 29-46. A subsequent compilation suggests even more emphatically how much attention Jonson has received from twentieth-century critics. See Dewey Hayward Brock and James M. Welsh, comps., *Ben Jonson: A Quadricentennial Bibliography, 1947–1972*, The Scarecrow Author Bibliographies, No. 16 (Metuchen, N. J.: The Scarecrow Press, Inc., 1974).

12. There are, of course, exceptions to this statement, most of which will be mentioned later. Here I should call attention to Eugene Waith's discussion of "The Staging of *Bartholomew Fair*," *Studies in English Literature* 2 (1962): 181-195, reproduced in somewhat altered form as Appendix II in his edition of the play for the *Yale Ben Jonson* (New Haven: Yale Univ. Press, 1963). See also L. A. Beaurline's helpful description of the "presentational" effects of speech in *Volpone*: "Volpone and the Power of Gorgeous Speech," in *Studies in the Literary Imagination* 6 (April 1973): 61-75. Franz Fricker's study, *Ben Jonson's Plays in Performance and the Jacobean Theatre*, came into my hands after I had completed this chapter. Narrowly focused on details of Jonson's stage practice, it does little to answer the problems under discussion here. This volume is No. 17 in the *Theatrical Physiognomy Series*, The Cooper Monographs (Berne: Francke Verlag, 1972).

13. L. C. Knights, *Drama and Society in the Age of Jonson* (New York: Norton, 1968; originally published 1937), p. 185.

14. Jonas A. Barish, *Ben Jonson and the Language of Prose Comedy* (Cambridge: Harvard Univ. Press, 1960). I quote from the paperback reprint (New York: W. W. Norton, 1970). I would remark that Barish never allows his reader to forget that he is talking about *dramatic* language: speech designed for the purposes of the stage. He speaks, for example, of Jonson's need to find a rhetoric with "enough potency of its own to do the subtler things for which language exists in the theater—to convey gradations of feeling, to establish atmosphere, and [to] suggest complexity of motivation" (p. 9).

15. Edmund Wilson, "Morose Ben Jonson," in Jonas Barish, ed., *Ben Jonson: A Collection of Critical Essays*, (Englewood Cliffs, N. J.: Prentice-Hall, 1963), pp. 60-74.

16. Richard Levin, " 'No Laughing Matter': Some New Readings of *The Alchemist*," *Studies in the Literary Imagination* 6 (April 1973): 85-99.
17. Ibid., p. 85.
18. Levin remarks that "there is still a good deal more to be learned about how we know what perspective to apply during our experience of a play" (ibid., p. 97).
19. Edward B. Partridge, *The Broken Compass* (London: Chatto & Windus, 1958), pp. 161-77.
20. "Introduction" to Edward B. Partridge, ed., *Bartholomew Fair*, Regents Renaissance Drama Series (Lincoln: Univ. of Nebraska Press, 1964), p. xv.
21. One may note the resemblance to "the scene of satire" as described by Alvin Kernan in *The Cankered Muse: Satire of the English Renaissance* (New Haven: Yale Univ. Press, 1959), passim.
22. "Introduction" to Alvin Kernan, ed., *Volpone, The Yale Ben Jonson* (New Haven: Yale Univ. Press, 1962), pp. 11, 10.
23. Barish, *The Language of Prose Comedy*, p. 183.
24. T. S. Eliot, "Ben Jonson," in Barish, ed., *A Collection*, p. 23.
25. In addition to the Barish and Partridge books, cited above, see John J. Enck, *Jonson and the Comic Truth* (Madison: Univ. of Wisconsin Press, 1957); J. B. Bamborough, *Ben Jonson* (London: Hutchinson, 1970); Alan C. Dessen, *Jonson's Moral Comedy* (Evanston: Northwestern Univ. Press, 1971); and Gabriele Bernhard Jackson, *Vision and Judgment in Ben Jonson's Drama* (New Haven: Yale Univ. Press, 1968).
26. Levin, " 'No Laughing Matter'," p. 99.
27. Robert E. Knoll, *Ben Jonson's Plays: An Introduction* (Lincoln: University of Nebraska Press, 1964), p. 123. The earlier reference to "the great plays" is taken from p. 27.
28. Enck, *Jonson and the Comic Truth*, p. 36.
29. Bamborough, *Ben Jonson*, p. 85.
30. Ibid., p. 148.
31. Enck, *Jonson and the Comic Truth*, pp. 108-9.
32. Helena Watts Baum, *The Satiric and the Didactic in Ben Jonson's Comedy* (Chapel Hill: Univ. of North Carolina Press, 1947), 177.
33. "Introduction" to Barish, ed., *A Collection*, p. 177.
34. Ray Heffner, Jr., "Unifying Symbols in the Comedy of Ben Jonson," in Barish, ed., *A Collection*, pp. 133-46.
35. In conversation, however, both Frank Hauser and David William have suggested to me the importance of Wilson's "Morose Ben Jonson" for their views of the plays (Barish, ed., *A Collection*, pp. 60-74).
36. T. S. Eliot, "London Letter," *The Dial* 70 (June 1921): 687. Eliot's reviews of Smith's *Ben Jonson* appeared in the (London) *Times Literary Supplement* and *The Athenaeum* and were later combined and published in *Selected Essays 1917–1932*.

37. Quoted by Eliot in "London Letter," p. 686.
38. Earl Wasserman, in "The Scholarly Origin of the Elizabethan Revival," *English Literary History* 4 (1937): 213-43, writes of this phenomenon as a fact of the nineteenth century which had its roots in the eighteenth. But the "transference of the method employed in editing classical texts to the editing of the English classics" (p. 215), while important, hardly constitutes a revival, as the case of Jonson shows.
39. Robert Speaight, *William Poel and the Elizabethan Revival* (London: Heinemann, 1954).
40. Ibid., p. 129.
41. Ibid., p. 141 (quoted by Speaight).
42. A full list of Poel's productions appears in Speaight, *William Poel,* Appendix I, pp. 281-85.
43. Ibid., p. 96 (quoted by Speaight).
44. Ibid. (quoted by Speaight from a letter by Sir Barry Jackson).
45. Ibid., pp. 122-23. Speaight refers to *The Morning Post* review for his view of the first *Arden* and to a letter from Ernest Milton about the second.
46. Ibid., p. 122.
47. Ibid., p. 148.
48. Quoted in Stuart Tave, *The Amiable Humorist: A Study in the Comic Theory and Criticism of the Eighteenth and Early Nineteenth Centuries* (Chicago: Univ. of Chicago Press, 1960).
49. Ibid.
50. Again, see Kernan's description of "the scene of satire" in *The Cankered Muse,* pp. 7-14.

Bibliography

Works by Ben Jonson

Bartholomew Fair. Edited by Edward B. Partridge. Regents Renaissance Drama Series, No. 20. Lincoln: Univ. of Nebraska Press, 1964.
Ben Jonson. Edited by C. H. Herford and Percy Simpson and Evelyn Simpson. 11 vols. Oxford: Clarendon Press, 1950.
The Devil Is an Ass. Edited by William Savage Johnson. The Yale Ben Jonson, No. 29. New Haven: Yale Univ. Press, 1905.
The Dramatic Works of Ben Jonson (Selected) with an Essay Biographical and Critical by John Addington Symonds. Edited by John Addington Symonds. London: Walter Scott, 1886.
Epicoene. Edited by Aurelia Henry. The Yale Ben Jonson, No. 31. New Haven: Yale Univ. Press, 1906.
The Staple of News. Edited by De Winter. The Yale Ben Jonson, No. 28. New Haven: Yale Univ. Press, 1905.
Volpone. Edited by Alvin Kernan. The Yale Ben Jonson, No. 9. New Haven: Yale Univ. Press, 1962.
The Works of Ben Jonson. Edited by William Gifford. 9 vols. London: R. H. Evans, 1816.
The Works of Ben Jonson with a Memoir of His Life and Writings. Edited by Barry Cornwall (Bryan Waller Procter). London: Edward Moxon, 1838.

Other Works Consulted

Avery, Emmett L., et al., eds. *The London Stage: 1660–1800.* 5 pts. in 11 vols. Carbondale: Southern Illinois Univ. Press, 1960–1968.
Ball, Robert Hamilton. *The Amazing Career of Sir Giles Overreach.* Princeton: Princeton Univ. Press, 1939.
Bamborough, J. B. *Ben Jonson.* London: Hutchinson, 1970.
Barish, Jonas A. *Ben Jonson and the Language of Prose Comedy.* Cambridge: Harvard Univ. Press, 1960. Reprinted in a paperback edition, New York: W. W. Norton, 1970.
―――, ed. *Ben Jonson: A Collection of Critical Essays.* Englewood Cliffs, N. J.: Prentice-Hall, 1963.
Barkan, Leonard, ed. *Renaissance Drama.* New Series 9. Evanston: Northwestern Univ. Press, 1978.
Bartholomeusz, Dennis. *Macbeth and the Players.* London: Cambridge Univ. Press, 1969.
Bateson, F. W. *English Comic Drama: 1700–1750.* Oxford: Clarendon Press, 1929.

Baum, Helena Watts. *The Satiric and the Didactic in Ben Jonson's Comedy.* Chapel Hill: Univ. of North Carolina Press, 1947.
Bentley, Gerald Eades. *Shakespeare and Jonson, Their Reputations in the Seventeenth Century Compared.* 2 vols. in one. Chicago: Univ. of Chicago Press, 1965.
Bradley, Jesse F., and J. Q. Adams, eds. *The Jonson Allusion-Book.* New Haven: Yale Univ. Press, 1927.
Brock, Dewey Hayward, and James M. Welsh, comps. *Ben Jonson: A Quadricentennial Bibliography, 1947–1972.* The Scarecrow Author Bibliographies, No. 16. Metuchen, N. J.: The Scarecrow Press, Inc., 1974.
Brown, Thomas. *The Works of Thomas Brown.* 4th Edition. London, 1715.
Castelain, Maurice. *Ben Jonson, l'homme et l'oeuvre (1572–1637).* Paris: Librairie Hachette, 1907.
Clark, Roy Benjamin. *William Gifford: Tory Satirist, Critic, and Editor.* New York: Columbia Univ. Press, 1930.
Coleridge, Samuel Taylor. *Coleridge's Miscellaneous Criticism.* Edited by T. M. Raysor. Cambridge: Harvard Univ. Press, 1930.
Collins, William. *The Poems of William Collins.* Edited by Christopher Stone. London: Henry Frowde, 1907.
Dessen, Alan C. *Jonson's Moral Comedy.* Evanston: Northwestern Univ. Press, 1971.
Dibdin, Charles. *A Complete History of the Stage.* London: Printed for the Author, 1800.
Eliot, T. S. *Selected Essays.* New Edition. New York: Harcourt, Brace and Company, 1950.
Enck, John J. *Jonson and the Comic Truth.* Madison: Univ. of Wisconsin Press, 1957.
Fitzgibbon, H. Macaulay, ed. *Famous Elizabethan Plays, Expurgated and Adapted for Modern Readers.* London: W. H. Allen, 1890.
Fricker, Franz. *Ben Jonson's Plays in Performance and the Jacobean Theatre.* Theatrical Physiognomy Series, The Cooper Monographs, No. 17. Berne: Francke Verlag, 1972.
Frost, David L. *The School of Shakespeare: The Influence of Shakespeare on Early Drama 1600–42.* Cambridge: Cambridge Univ. Press, 1968.
Genest, John. *Some Account of the English Stage from the Restoration in 1660 to 1830.* 10 vols. Bath: H. E. Carrington, 1832.
Gray, Charles Harold. *Theatrical Criticism in London to 1795.* New York: Columbia Univ. Press, 1931.
Gray, Thomas. *The Complete Poems of Thomas Gray.* Edited by H. W. Starr and J. R. Henderson. Oxford: Clarendon Press, 1966.
Harwood, Ronald. *Sir Donald Wolfit, C. B. E., His Life and Work in the Unfashionable Theatre.* New York: St. Martin's Press, 1971.
Hazlitt, William. *Lectures on the English Comic Writers.* London: Taylor and Hessey, 1819.
Hughes, Leo. *The Drama's Patrons: A Study of the Eighteenth-Century London Audience.* Austin and London: Univ. of Texas Press, 1971.
Hunt, Leigh. *Leigh Hunt's Dramatic Criticism: 1808–1831.* Edited by Lawrence Huston Houtchens and Carolyn Washburn Houtchens. New York: Columbia Univ. Press, 1949.
Hurd, Richard. *A Letter to Mr. Mason, on the Marks of Imitation.* Cambridge, 1757.
Jackson, Gabriele Bernhard. *Vision and Judgment in Ben Jonson's Drama.* New Haven: Yale Univ. Press, 1968.
Keats, John. *The Letters of John Keats.* Edited by Hyder Edward Rollins. 2 vols. Cambridge: Harvard Univ. Press, 1958.
Kernan, Alvin. *The Cankered Muse: Satire of the English Renaissance.* New Haven: Yale Univ. Press, 1959.
Kerr, Mina. *The Influence of Ben Jonson on English Comedy, 1598–1642.* New York: Columbia Univ. Press, 1912.

Knight, G. Wilson. *Byron and Shakespeare.* London: Routledge and Kegan Paul, 1966.
Knights, L. C. *Drama and Society in the Age of Jonson.* New York: Norton, 1968.
Knoll, Robert E. *Ben Jonson's Plays: An Introduction.* Lincoln: Univ. of Nebraska Press, 1964.
Lacy, Thomas Hailes. *Lacy's Acting Editions of Plays.* 100 vols. London: Lacy, 1850.
Lamb, Charles and Mary Lamb. *The Works of Charles and Mary Lamb.* Edited by E. V. Lucas. 7 vols. London: Methuen, 1904.
Maurois, André. *Byron.* Translated by Hamish Miles. New York: Appleton, 1930.
Nicoll, Allardyce. *A History of Early Nineteenth Century Drama: 1800–1850.* 2 vols. Cambridge: Cambridge Univ. Press, 1930.
Noyes, Robert Gale. *Ben Jonson on the English Stage: 1660–1776.* Cambridge: Harvard Univ. Press. 1935.
Partridge, Edward B. *The Broken Compass.* London: Chatto & Windus, 1958.
Peacock, Markham L., Jr. *The Critical Opinions of William Wordsworth.* Baltimore: Johns Hopkins Press, 1950.
Penniman, Josiah H. *The War of the Theatres.* Boston: Ginn, 1897.
Pepys, Samuel. *The Diary of Samuel Pepys.* Edited by Henry B. Wheatley. 9 vols. London: George Bell, 1893. Reprinted New York: AMS Press, 1968.
Richards, Kenneth and Peter Thomson, eds. *Essays on the Eighteenth-Century English Stage.* London: Methuen & Co., 1972.
Rosenberg, Marvin. *The Masks of King Lear.* Berkeley: Univ. of California Press, 1972.
―――――. *The Masks of Othello.* Berkeley: Univ. of California Press, 1961.
Schoenbaum, Samuel, ed. *Opportunities in Renaissance Drama.* The Report of the Modern Language Conference. Evanston: Northwestern Univ. Press, 1966.
Scott, Sir Walter. *Essays on Chivalry, Romance and the Drama.* Edinburgh: Robert Cadell, 1847.
Shelley, Percy Bysshe. *The Complete Works of Percy Bysshe Shelley.* Edited by Roger Ingpen and Walter E. Peck. 10 vols. New York: Gordian Press, 1965.
Small, Roscoe Addison. *The Stage Quarrel Between Ben Jonson and the So-Called Poetasters.* Breslau: Verlag von M. & H. Marcus, 1899.
Southey, Robert. *Southey's Common-Place Book.* 4 vols. London: Longman, Brown, Green, and Longmans, 1850.
Speaight, Robert. *William Poel and the Elizabethan Revival.* London: Heinemann, 1954.
Sprague, Arthur Colby. *Shakespearian Players and Performances.* Cambridge: Harvard Univ. Press, 1953.
―――――and J. C. Trewin. *Shakespeare's Plays Today: Some Customs and Conventions of the Stage.* Columbia: Univ. of South Carolina Press, 1971.
Swinburne, Algernon Charles. *The Complete Works of Algernon Charles Swinburne.* Edited by Sir Edmund Gosse and Thomas James Wise. 20 vols. The Bonchurch Edition. London: Heinemann, 1925.
―――――. *A Study of Ben Jonson.* London: Chatto & Windus, 1889.
Symonds, John Addington. *Ben Jonson.* London: Longmans, Green, 1886.
Tave Stuart. *The Amiable Humorist: A Study in the Comic Theory and Criticism of the Eighteenth and Early Nineteenth Centuries.* Chicago: Univ. of Chicago Press, 1960.
Tennyson, Hallam. *Alfred Lord Tennyson, A Memoir.* 2 vols. New York: Macmillan, 1897.
Townsend, Freda L. *Apologie for Bartholomew Fayre: The Art of Jonson's Comedies.* New York: Modern Language Association, 1947.
Trewin, J. C. *Benson and the Bensonians.* London: Barrie and Rockliff, 1960.
Wheatley, Henry B., ed. *The London Series of English Classics.* London: Longmans, Green, 1877.

Wilbur, Richard. *The Poems of Richard Wilbur.* New York: Harcourt, Brace & World, 1963.
Woodbridge, Elisabeth. *Studies in Ben Jonson's Comedy.* New Haven: Yale University Press, 1898; Reprint ed. New York: Gordian Press, 1966.
Wordsworth, William. *The Prelude.* Edited by Ernest de Selincourt. Second Edition revised by Helen Darbishire. Oxford: Clarendon Press, 1959.
Young, Edward. *Conjectures on Original Composition, 1759.* Leeds: The Scolar Press, 1966.

Index

Adam, Ronald, 79, 86
Adams, J.C., 122
A.D.C. Theatre, Cambridge, 41
Agate, James, 58–59, 90–91
Alchemist, The, 3, 4, 15, 16, 19, 23–24, 25, 27, 28, 29, 40, 48, 53, 56, 60, 66, 70, 77, 78–109, 111, 114, 116, 117, 120, 122–23
Aldwych Theatre, 41, 48–52
Alexander, Mara, 67
Altman, Peter, 102
Anderson, Michael, 49, 51
Anderson, Piper, 69
Apothecaries' Hall, 79, 80–81, 120
Archer, William, 119
Armstrong, Martin, 84
Arnold, Matthew, 20
Arts Theatre, Cambridge, 59–60, 80, 107
Atkins, Robert, 62
Atkinson, Brooks, 62
Attenborough, Richard, 98
Aubrey, John, 18
Avery, Emmett, 10
Ayliff, H.K., 85
Aylmer, Felix, 79, 83

Baker, Jim, 69
Bamborough, J.B., 117–18
Barber, John, 45, 48, 105, 107
Barish, Jonas, 114, 115, 118, 119
Barker, Felix, 49, 107
Barr, Richard, 53, 63
Bartholomew Fair, 2, 5, 11, 15, 27, 40–52, 66, 77, 102, 109, 111, 114, 117, 124
Baskervill, Charles Reed, 112
Bateson, F.W., 12
Battis, Emery, 102
Baum, Helena Watts, 118
Bawdiness, in Jonson's plays, 24, 32, 46, 82, 84, 91–92, 98
Beaumont, Francis, 24
Beldon, Eileen, 56, 85, 86

Belfrage, Bruce, 86
Bennett, John, 78
Benson, F.R., 36–37
Bibby, Charles, 38
Birmingham Repertory Company, 30, 32, 53, 74–75, 79, 81–84, 109, 121, 122
Birmingham Repertory Theatre, 52, 55–56, 79, 92–93
Blakely, Colin, 72, 73
Boas, F.S., 85
Booth, James, 107
Bosco, Philip, 100
Brahms, Caryl, 90
Brien, Alan, 40, 95, 96, 97
Bristol Old Vic, 30, 33, 41, 46–48, 53, 66, 77, 79, 92
Brooks, Shirley, 24
Brown, Ivor, 29, 39, 57, 86, 88, 89–90, 91
Brown, Thomas, 11
Brubaker, Edward S., 93
Brustein, Robert, 100, 101
Bryden, Ronald, 2, 50
Burge, Stuart, 105, 106
Burrell, John, 79, 88, 91, 95
Butt, Hugh, 56
Byford, Roy, 42
Byron, George Gordon, Lord, 9, 21, 40
Byron, John, 62

Cairncross, James, 92
Cambridge Theatre Company, 80, 107
Campbell, Douglas, 67–68
Carey, Denis, 53, 68
Carter, James, 93
Cartland, Robert, 92
Carr, Philip, 30
Carra, Lawrence, 75
Carridine, John, 63
Carroll, Sydney W., 42
Case Is Altered, The, 15
Castelain, Maurice, 112

Index

Catiline, 15
Cattley, Cyril, 30
Chalmers, Alexander, 18
Chambers, Sir Edmund, 122
Chapman, George, 28
Chapman, John, 100
Characters, Jonson's: devoid of power, 19–21; failure to create interesting ones, 21–23; lack of depth in, 22; lack of involvement in, 23; lack of sympathy in, 23
Chichester Festival Production, 80, 107–8
Chisholm, Cecil, 86
Chusid, Harvey, 76
City Center production, 62–63
City of London Festival Players, 41
Clark, Alfred, 31
Cleveland Play House, 80, 97
Clifford, John, 52, 56
Clunes, Alec, 46
Clurman, Harold, 67, 68
Coe, John, 46, 92
Cohen, Nathan, 101
Coleman, Robert, 91
Coleridge, Samuel Tayler, 13, 20, 21–22, 23, 25
Collins, William, 8
Colman, George, the Elder, 33
Comedy, Jonson's, criticism of, 115–18
Conway, Harold, 44–45, 64
Corbett, Harry, 65
Cornwall, Barry, 23
Costa, Morton da, 91
Cottrell, Richard, 107
Couloris, George, 92
Covent Garden, 36
Crawford Livingstone Theatre, 101
Crowden, Graham, 72
Curry, Julian, 99

Dante Alighieri, 8
Darlington, W.A., 57, 85
David, John, 53, 77, 78
Dean, Basil, 121
Dench, Judith, 98
Dent, Alan, 44, 89, 91
Denys, Christopher, 47
Derby, Brown, 60
Deverell, John, 86, 87
Devine, George, 42, 43, 44, 64, 77
Dews, Peter, 80, 107, 108
Dibdin, Charles, 23–24, 25
Dickens, Charles, 23, 35, 36
Dobie, Alan, 66, 70–71, 73
Donaldson, Ian, 33–34, 70, 71, 99
Donat, Robert, 55

Drama: Jonson's view of, 17; Lamb's view of, 17
Drinkel, Keith, 74
Drummond, William, 17, 18
Dryden, John, 10, 11, 21, 30–31
Dublin University Players, 41
Dunlop, Frank, 108

Eastward Ho, 28–30
Edinburgh Festival, 40
Eliot, T.S., 37, 54, 55, 115, 118–19
Eliott, Eric, 86
Elizabethan Stage Circle, 5, 120, 122
Elizabethan Stage Society, 79, 80–81, 111, 120, 122
Embassy Theatre, 79, 86–87
Enck, John, 117
Epicoene, 15, 18, 24, 30–35, 102, 114, 115
Esslin, Martin, 106
Evans, Dame Edith, 53
Evans, Gareth Lloyd, 105, 106
Evans, Hugh, 93
Evennett, Wallace, 86, 87
Every Man in His Humour, 22, 23, 24, 35–40, 123, 124

Farrer, David, 64
Fay, Gerard, 29, 65
Ferrer, Jose, 62–63
Festival of Britain, 40
Festival Theatre, Cambridge, 52, 55
Fiander, Lewis, 34, 77–78
Field, Ben, 42
Field, Rowland, 63
Findlater, Richard, 45
Finney, Albert, 79, 93
Fitzgibbon, H. Macaulay, 24
Fleming, Peter, 45, 88, 90
Fletcher, John, 24
Ford, John, 14, 15
Fortune Players, 79
Fraser, M.F.K., 32
French, Leslie, 86
French, Philip, 73
Frow, Gerald, 30, 33, 34, 102
Funke, Lewis, 103

Gaiety Theatre, Manchester, 36, 37–38, 122
Garland, Richard, 60
Garrick, David, 10, 11, 78, 83, 87, 89, 91, 122
Garrick Theatre, London, 71
Gascoigne, Bamber, 95
Gascon, Jean, 80, 103–4
Gate Theatre, New York, 41, 80, 97–98

Index   155

Genest, John, 7
Gifford, William, 7, 13, 17–19, 21, 24, 112
Gill, Alexander, 18
Glenville, Peter, 88
Goddard, Willoughby, 49
Godfrey, Derek, 66
Goodman, Anthony, 88
Goolden, Richard, 86, 87
Gosse, Edmund, 120
Gowing, Lawrence, 89
Granville-Baker, Harley, 122
Gray, Charles, 96
Gray, Charles Harold, 13
Gray, Thomas, 8
Great Lakes Shakespeare Festival Company, 53, 75
Great Queen Street Theatre, 30
Greer, Germaine, 98–99
Griffith, Hubert, 90
Grigs, Derick, 2, 70
Grizzard, George, 67–68
Guinness, Sir Alec, 88, 89–90, 95, 96
Guthrie, Sir Tyrone, 27, 48, 53, 65–66, 67–68, 72, 73, 74, 77, 79, 87, 88, 94–97
Guthrie Theatre, Minneapolis, 53, 67–68

Hale, John, 30, 33
Hamilton, Allen, 102
Hands, Terry, 27, 48, 50, 51, 66, 102
Hannen, Nicholas, 88–89, 90
Hardwicke, Cedric, 30, 31, 85
Harrison, John, 66
Harvey, John H., 102
Harvey, Laurence, 107
Harvey, Rupert, 55
Harwood, Ronald, 61
Hathaway, Charles, Jr., 112
Hauser, Frank, 2, 30, 34, 53, 69–70, 73, 80, 98, 99, 104
Hazlitt, William, 13, 36, 37, 40, 47, 58–59, 89
Heffernan, John, 97
Heffner, Ray, 30, 119
Hepton, Bernard, 93
Herford, C.H., 112
Hewes, Henry, 67
Higgins, John, 99
Hobson, Harold, 49
Hodges, C. Walter, 122
Hoey, Iris, 86
Holland, Julian, 40
Holloway, Baliol, 54, 84
Hope-Wallace, Philip, 49, 72, 90, 106
Hordern, Michael, 64, 65
Horn, Robert, 93

Horniman's Company, Miss, 36, 37–38, 121, 122
Hosley, Richard, 122
Howard, Alan, 49, 50
Howard, Pamela, 74
Howard, Sir Robert, 11
Hudle, Elizabeth, 67
Hughes, Leo, 10, 11
Hunt, Leigh, 21
Hunter, Russell, 96
Hurd, Bishop, 7
Hutt, William, 75, 76–77, 103, 104, 106, 116

Iden, Rosalind, 60
Imperial Theatre, London, 79
Independent Theatre Society, 120
Irving, Jules, 80, 99

Jackson, Barry, 79, 85, 121
Jackson, Berners W., 76
Jackson, Nagle, 69
Jensen, John, 102
John, Evan, 52, 55
Jones, D.A.N., 50, 71, 72, 73
Jones, Penny, 33
Jones, Steven, 18
Jonson, Ben: nineteenth-century view of, 7–25; rejection of, 4; stage craftsmanship of, 36; twentieth-century view of, 27–109; see also Bawdiness, Characters, Comedy, Drama, London theater, Pedantry, Shakespeare, titles of plays
Jordan, Maggie, 69
Joseph, Norma, 75
Jowsey, Nancy, 101

Kasket, Harold, 107
Katzin, Olga, 86
Kean, Edmund, 35, 36, 89
Keating, Charles, 102
Keats, John, 8, 9, 20
Kelly, Edward, 101
Kelso, Vernon, 86
Kemp, T.C., 32–33, 44
Kenton, Godfrey, 39
Kernan, Alvin, 74, 115, 119
Kerr, Mina, 112
Kerr, Walter, 99–100, 104
Kestelman, Morris, 88, 91
Keynes, John Maynard, 59–60
King, David, 74
King's Theatre, Hammersmith, 61, 79, 87
Klanfer, François-Régis, 101
Knight, G. Wilson, 9

156 Index

Knights, L.C., 114
Knoll, Robert, 117
Komisarjevsky, Theodore, 64
Kretzma, Herbert, 48–49
Kronenberger, Louis, 63
Krutch, Joseph Wood, 63

Lacey, Catherine, 96
Lahr, John, 100
Lamb, Charles, 13, 14, 15, 16; view of drama, 17
Lathbury, Stanley, 84
Lawson, Wilfred, 52, 56–57
Lawrence, W.J., 122
Laye, Gabrielle, 72
Leighton, Margaret, 88
Leonard, William, 103
Levens, Daphne, 71
Levin, Bernard, 95
Levin, Richard, 114, 115
Lewis, Peter, 49, 70
Lewsen, Charles, 77, 108
Lincoln Center, 80, 99–101
Lincoln's Inn Fields, 11
Little Theatre on Bridge Street, 46
Littlewood, Joan, 36, 40, 65
Liverpool Playhouse, 79, 87–88
London Festival Players, City of, 41
London theater, Jonson's place in, 10
Lowell, James Russell, 14, 15
Ludwig, Jack, 104
Luscombe, George, 80, 101
Luyten, Elizabeth, 70
Lyric Theatre, Hammersmith, 52, 54

MacDonald, Robert, 49, 50, 107
Macho, Carole, 97
Mackay, Fulton, 29
MacKintosh, Kenneth, 93
MacNaughton, Alan, 99
Macowan, Michael, 57, 58
Magnetic Lady, 18
Malcolm, Roy, 55
Malone, Edmund, 18
Malvern Festival Theatre, 52, 56–57, 59, 79, 85–86, 122, 124
Mannering, D. Lewis, 54
Manning, Hugh, 68, 69
March, Elspeth, 56
Marcus, Frank, 49, 50
Margate Stage Company, 30, 33, 34
Marle, Clifford, 56
Marlowe, Christopher, 22
Marlowe Society at Cambridge University, 5, 34, 79
Marston, John, 14, 28

Massey, Raymond, 30
Massinger, Philip, 17
Maurois, André, 9
McKenna, Siobhan, 64
McKern, Leo, 70, 71, 77, 78, 96
McPherson, Alexander, 77
Meadow Players, 80
Mermaid Repertory Company, 30, 31
Mermaid Theatre, 28
Middlemass, Frank, 106
Miles, Bernard, 28, 29
Miller, Hugh, 86
Milligan, John, 75
Milton, John, 8, 20, 21
Minnesota Theatre Company, 80, 101–3
Mirren, Helen, 49
Mohyeddin, Zia, 71, 98
Moiseiwitsch, Tanya, 68
Monsey, Derek, 61
Montague, Lee, 77, 78, 96
Morehouse, Ward, 62
Morgan, Priscilla, 96
Moriarity, Michael, 102
Morris, Corbyn, 123–24
Morriss, Frank, 104
Murphy, Arthur, 13
Murray, Stephan, 52, 56, 59

Nadel, Norman, 97–98
National Theatre Company, 53, 72–74, 122
National Youth Theatre, 41
Neville, John, 69, 92
New Inn, The, 5, 15
New Oxford Theatre, 40
New School, 79
New Theatre, 60, 79, 88
New York City Center, 91–92
New York City Theatre Company, 53
Nicholson, Brensley, 112
Nicoll, Allardyce, 10, 85
Nightingale, Benedict, 69, 71, 108
Norton, Eliot, 103–4
Nottingham Playhouse, 53, 68–69, 80, 105–6
Novick, Julius, 76, 100
Noyes, Robert Gale, 1, 4, 10, 11, 78, 83

O'Brien, Timothy, 48, 50
Old Vic Company, 5, 40, 42–46, 48, 51, 60, 72, 79, 87–91, 96, 98
Old Vic Theatre, 40, 43, 53, 80, 105
O'Neill, Barrie, 86
Oregon Shakespearean Festival, 53, 69, 79, 93–94
Orton, Joe, 71
O'Toole, Peter, 66

Oulton, Brian, 74
Oxford Playhouse, 2, 30, 34, 53, 69–71, 78, 80, 98
Oxford University Dramatic Society, 30
Oxford University Experimental Theatre, 41

Papkin, Henry, 72–73
Partridge, Edward B., 114, 119
Payne, B. Iden, 36, 37, 39
Pedantry, Jonson's, 25
Pennell, Nicholas, 98
Penniman, Josiah, 111, 113
Pentelow, Arthur, 93
Pepys, Samuel, 30, 49–50
Percy, Esmé, 38
Phoenix Society, 5, 30, 31, 40, 41–42, 52, 53–55, 79, 84–85, 111, 119, 122
Pinter, Harold, 124
Piper, Frederick, 55
Pitt, Trevor, 105
Poel, William, 5, 34–35, 79, 80, 119–22
Poetaster, The, 5, 15, 16, 120
Porter, Eric, 66
Porter, Stephen, 80, 97, 98
Prentice, Derek, 56
Prentice, Herbert, 55, 57
Pride, Malcolm, 64
Princes Theatre, 79, 86–87

Quayle, Anthony, 64–65

Rain, Douglas, 75, 76
Ramsey, John, 102
Rea, W.J., 83, 85
Read, Geoffrey, 101
Redman, Joyce, 88, 90–91
Regent's Theatre, King's Cross, 30, 52, 79
Relph, George, 88, 89, 90
Renaissance Society, 122
Rexroth, Kenneth, 66
Richards, Lisa, 102
Richardson, Sir Ralph, 53, 64–65, 85, 88, 90, 95
Roberts, Peter, 95
Robertson, Patrick, 30, 66, 68
Rodford, Peter, 66
Rosmer, Milton, 30
Rossiter, Leonard, 70
Rosqui, Tom, 67
Royal Court Theatre, 41
Royal Shakespeare Company, 2, 27, 41, 48–52, 66, 122
Royal Theatre, Drury Lane, 35
Rubbra, Edmund, 57

Sad Shepherd, The, 15, 120
St. James Theatre, 60
San Francisco Actor's Workshop, 66–67, 79
Savoy Theatre, 60–61
Scala Theatre, 60
Schneider, Roy, 97
Scott, Hutchinson, 70
Scott, Sir Walter, 24, 25
Scouten, Arthur, 10
Sejanus, 5, 15, 25, 120
Shadwell, Thomas, 11
Shakespeare Memorial Theatre, 39, 64
Shakespeare, William, 3, 17, 18, 20, 24, 35, 45, 54, 58, 84, 94, 112, 113, 114, 120–21; and Jonson compared, 7–10, 20–22
Shapiro, Mel, 101
Shaw, George Bernard, 40, 124
Shaw, Maxwell, 65
Shearer, Moira, 66
Shelley, Percy Bysshe, 8, 21
Shelving, Paul, 93
Sheridan, Richard Brinsley, 10
Sherman, John K., 68, 102
Shorter, Eric, 107
Shulman, Milton, 40
Siddons, Mrs., 33
Silent Woman, The, 98
Simpson, Michael, 74
Small, Roscoe Addison, 111, 113
Smith, G. Gregory, 119
Southey, Robert, 9
Speaight, Robert, 119
Spurling, Hilary, 72
Staple of News, The, 19
Stearns, James Hart, 66
Steele, Mike, 102
Steele, Sir Richard, 81
Steevens, John, 18
Stoker, Willard, 30, 33
Stone, Charles, 102
Stone, Ezra, 92
Stone, Martin, 101
Stratford (Canada) Festival Players, 53, 75–77, 80, 103–5, 109, 116, 122
Stratford-upon-Avon, 36–37, 41, 53, 62, 63–65, 121
Studebaker Theater, Chicago, 103
Sullivan, Dan, 67
Summers, Montague, 41
Swinburne, Algernon Charles, 13–14, 21, 22, 25, 111
Swinley, Ion, 54, 55
Swinstead, Joan, 28, 29
Symonds, John Addington, 21, 22, 25

Symonds, Robert, 67

Tanswell, Bertram, 97
Taubman, Howard, 97
Tave, Stuart, 123–24
Taylor, John Russell, 96
Tennyson, Alfred, Lord, 20
Theatre Royal, Stratford East, 53, 65
Theatre Workshop Group, 36, 40
Thesiger, Ernest, 42
Thorndyke, Sybil, 53
Toronto Workshop Productions, 101
Trevor, Austin, 86
Trewin, J.C., 37, 44, 45, 46, 48, 51, 73, 95, 97, 106
Trotter, Alan, 87
Trouncer, Cecil, 56
Turner, David, 107
Tynan, Kenneth, 95

Vanburgh, Sir John, 31
Vinden, Stuart, 83
Volpone, 2, 4, 15, 19, 22, 24, 25, 27, 29, 40, 52–78, 98, 105, 109, 112, 115, 116, 118, 119, 123, 124
Voskovec, George, 100
Voss, Philip, 34

Wade, Allan, 30, 79
Wakefield, Russell, 84
Ward, Simon, 98, 99
Wardle, Irving, 34, 49, 50–51, 75–76, 77, 106, 107

Waters, Jan, 107
Watts, Richard, Jr., 60, 63, 92
Waugh, Evelyn, 124
Webb, Antony, 68
Webster, John, 14, 15
Westminster Theatre, 57–59
Wheatley, Alan, 58, 59
Whorf, Richard, 62–63
Wickham, Glynn, 122
Wilbur, Richard, 48
William, David, 53, 75, 76, 96
Williams, Stephen, 65
Williamson, Laird, 69
Willis, Thomas, 67–68
Willman, Noel, 88
Wilson, Edmund, 114
Wilson, J. Dover, 122
Wilson, John S., 91, 92
Winn, Godfrey, 31
Winston, Bruce, 87
Wylie, Frank, 72, 73
Wolfit, Donald, 36, 52–53, 57, 58, 59–61, 63, 64
Woodbridge, Elisabeth, 112, 113
Wordsworth, William, 8, 9, 13
Worsley, T.C., 45, 64
York Citizen's Theatre, 79, 87
Young, B.A., 50, 108
Young, Edward, 7
Young Vic, 80, 108

Zeffirelli, Franco, 98
Zweig, Stefan, 52

OHIO UNIVERSITY LIBRARY

Please return this book as soon as you have finished with it. In order to avoid a fine it must be returned by the latest date stamped below.

RETURN BY

DEC 2 1992

QUARTER LOAN
DEC 11 1992
APR 0 6 1989
JUN 0 6 1999

CF